Management for Professionals

More information about this series at
http://www.springer.com/series/10101

Stefanie Auge-Dickhut • Bernhard Koye •
Axel Liebetrau

Customer Value Generation in Banking

The Zurich Model of Customer-Centricity

Springer

Stefanie Auge-Dickhut
Swiss Institute for Financial Education
Zurich, Switzerland

Bernhard Koye
Swiss Institute for Financial Education
Zurich, Switzerland

Axel Liebetrau
BIG - Banking Innovation Group GmbH
Stuttgart, Germany

Originally published in German with the title Client Value Generation: Das Zürcher Modell der kundenzentrierten Bankarchitektur, ISBN 978-3-658-01523-7, by SpringerGabler in 2014

ISSN 2192-8096 ISSN 2192-810X (electronic)
Management for Professionals
ISBN 978-3-319-19937-5 ISBN 978-3-319-19938-2 (eBook)
DOI 10.1007/978-3-319-19938-2

Library of Congress Control Number: 2015946108

Springer Cham Heidelberg New York Dordrecht London

Printed on acid-free paper

Springer International Publishing AG Switzerland is part of Springer Science+Business Media (www.springer.com)

Foreword by Dr. Markus Sulzberger

A new future has begun for the financial industry, and it is striding rapidly and inexorably forward in various substantial directions. What makes the accompanying challenges especially demanding is the fact that these developments tend to occur insidiously or even unnoticed, rather than emerging as a big bang or a catastrophe. As a result, the best time frame for triggering strategic initiatives and projects is often missed. In addition, it is very tempting to wait before starting a serious discussion about the future. Time and energy are becoming ever more scarce resources. Currently, there are a number of projects being carried out in banks under the overall heading of industrialisation, which are primarily concerned with optimising the actual situation. These are necessary steps for many reasons, mostly due to sinking margins and the associated demand for increasing efficiency. But they are simply not enough to ensure a long-term future. Frequently, greater priority is placed on examining the internal situation than on global developments and the "new" customer. This customer is now supremely educated and very familiar with the instruments of the digital world. Furthermore, these industrialisation projects are so complex and costly that hardly any time remains to contemplate, reflect, and think specifically about future challenges, opportunities and risks. And finally the clamouring by stakeholders for increased efficiency is constantly growing louder. In combination with trying to manage rapidly growing regulation at a global level, which do not allow for any time delays in their realisation, most employees and managers at all levels are working to capacity, or indeed often overworked. Initiatives in the area of company development cannot be regarded simply as a sideline.

Most external developments that are relevant to the successful future of the bank are continuously rapid in nature or develop even in discontinuous spurts. The main drivers are the almost endless options to attract the "new" customer, especially members of Generations X and Y. The second main driver is technology as an enabler. Very many questions are still open, the direction is unclear and the chances and risks can be predicted only to a limited extent, let alone quantified. Dealing with such challenges has never been a pronounced competence of banks. In large global bank concerns in particular, internal innovation ideas often rebound against the hierarchical structures. It is likely that smaller and medium-sized institutes have a much better starting point here.

The wake-up call has been made long ago. Many institutes have heard it and are striving to truly place the "new" customer at the core, to adapt organisational and management structures, and to implement flexible solutions such as sourcing, where the traditional value chain is being successively broken up, or the use of temporary staff. The resulting demands on the corporate culture must be processed in detail. All of these activities lead to concrete advantages for customers, stakeholders, and the bank. This can be seen very clearly from the success stories of many new providers in the banking environment. In addition, fundamental changes are foreseeable in the area of infrastructure. Increasingly, customers are demanding a system-based bank consultation. This provides them with additional and wide-ranging freedoms such as independence from time and place, with corresponding price advantages. Resources that have been freed up for infrastructure must be used for the smart integration of the customer. Such an appreciated customer will become more easily enthused by exciting innovations.

All of this is very demanding in terms of conception and implementation, but sadly it is not even the whole truth. For many years to come, there will still be a number of customers who renounce the "24-h online society" and who will demand personal contact. This will result in the opening up of niches for new providers on the one hand, but on the other hand, banks must grow accustomed to dealing with fundamentally different customer needs. Such segment-specific demands have always existed; the difference today is that more cost-intensive technical infrastructures are necessary, and new providers can threaten traditional market shares to a much greater extent. Banks must cope with new dualities. More and more paradoxes are occurring, which demand great intuition, openness, and flexibility from all employees and managers.

Bank institutes are social constructs that are being increasingly shaped by employees with different requirement profiles in terms of work, working environments, and a new understanding of life-domain balance. The classic top-down structures, which are already being softened today, will transfer gradually from being self-organised units to self-regulating ones. Organisational economy is taking great steps towards understanding the company no longer based on classic business functions—production, advice, financing—but rather by taking a holistic view under consideration of new values and by making space for the preferences of staff. This opens up the potential that responsible employees, shaped by productive well-being, are the best partners for the increasingly demanding customer.

This requires new, further developed management and organisational approaches. Many relevant answers can be found behind terms such as agile management, agile leadership, sustainable management, and agile project-based network organisations. It is becoming even more difficult for the management of a bank to find orientation in this abundance of solution approaches and recipes for success. With such ground-breaking developments, there must also be encouragement to concentrate on a few, fundamental values (trust, openness) that shape people, both customers and employees. Two components are identified here as success factors. One concerns management, in particular self-management. This dimension, which is still underestimated in management theory and practice, provides opportunities to avoid excessive demands and workloads. This is very important in an age of great change. Another component is dealing with meaningful experiments. These can help to sound out sustainable solutions. Organisational learning must be supported and, in the event of a negative outcome of an experiment, the collective fear of failure must be removed.

This work is a stroke of luck for the financial industry and, specifically, for banks. In an exceptionally clear, transparent, comprehensive, and substantial manner, the authors have managed to outline the need for action, present the chances and risks, and summarise the essences repeatedly and memorably in wrap-ups. The authors do not assume that everything is familiar and clear. Much is yet to emerge. There are topics in which the questions are as yet unknown. One example of this is how to handle and productively use big data.

With the Zurich Model of customer-centred banking architecture, the authors have filled a large gap in the present range of academic, practical, and implementation-oriented expert contributions. Thanks to the clear structure of the book, readers can easily select the content and chapters that are most relevant to them. It is especially important that the authors have devoted much space to success-critical implementation.

I sincerely hope that the work will receive wide acceptance commensurate with its extraordinarily important topic for banks, and that readers will derive many insights, findings, much inspiration from this exciting book, as well as the realisation that the time and willingness for consideration and reflection are necessary at the beginning of every strategic initiative. Reading this book is certainly a good start.

August 2015

Dr. Markus Sulzberger
President SGO Swiss Association for
Organization and Management

Foreword by Dr. Alex Osterwalder

Business models expire like yogurt in a refrigerator. Whereas it was once possible for a manager to pursue the same business model throughout an entire career, that is certainly a rarity now.

Entire industries need to rethink their business models. This first began with digital industries such as music, news, and film. Nowadays, however, traditional industries such as the pharmaceutical and banking sectors are also affected. It is therefore not surprising that business model innovations are right at the top of the priority lists of global managers.

Yet only very few established companies have been really successful in renewing their business models to date. These days, new business models often arise by chance or from a crisis. Many managers have recognised that this cannot form the basis for a successful strategy.

Three problem areas hinder the development of new business models:

There is a lack of a unified and clear language and a shared methodology: business models and value propositions are frequently used terms, but they are interpreted differently. Without a shared understanding it is very difficult to hold good strategic discussions that will lead to results. We have a lot of success with our business model Canvas, a tool that offers a simple, unified, and visual language for the development of new business models.

Managers have often "become great" with previously successful business models: many decision makers pursued only one business model throughout their career and were successful with it. They find it difficult to keep step with the new world of rapidly expiring business models and to imagine new business models in their own industry. Decision makers must get used to developing a business model portfolio proactively before the crisis strikes and is then often too late to act. Decision makers must involve more entrepreneurial spirits and doers in their companies, in order to create something new before the company is compelled to act.

Company processes, tools, and culture often do not allow proactive business model innovations: because the topic is so new, companies often lack the processes and tools to develop new business models proactively. In addition, developing new models requires a totally different company culture than merely executing and improving existing business models (keyword "cost-cutting"). Searching for new models demands an interest in experimentation, the courage to fail, and the willingness always to start again—a culture that would even be counterproductive in the execution and improvement of existing models.

If you are holding this book in your hand, you have already taken the first step towards new and successful business models. Congratulations! The financial sector urgently needs new business models. Perhaps you will even be the one to create the "Apple of banking".

Dr. Alex Osterwalder
Co-founder Strategyzer.com
and author of Business Model Generation

Foreword by Prof. Dr. Marcel Seidel

The banking landscape is in upheaval. Therefore, a stringent adaption of business models—for a long time discussed hesitantly—is merely the admission ticket to the game of changing business models. All banks are subject to the necessities arising from regulation and the short-term measures prompted by sinking margins. This also places great pressure on the IT and innovation budgets and will change the market landscape for the long term in the next few years. Reducing the cost-income ratio to optimise the business model is therefore necessary, but not sufficient. The existing business models must be adapted. This is the focus of management in the banking sector, today and in the near future. In the medium term—and this is the bad news—this "adaption" will not be enough to remain marketable. Whoever wishes to remain successful with a business model must already set the course for a sustainable banking architecture today. Strategically, management must design their own business model in such a manner that services will be accepted from "old customers", but especially also by future generations, the "digital natives".

This can be done with an innovative recollection. Customer-centred banking architectures place the customer at the centre of all activities. Not only shareholder value but also client value will be the future benchmark. The objective is to generate a win–win situation. Only when both sides, the bank and the customer, gain advantages, will a long-term successful relationship come about.

Critics will argue that this is not really new. CRM has been around for ages. But what is new is that the customer relationships are not only managed, but rather actively designed. That is not an easy task. It means that banks have to approach customers actively. They must know the goals and desires of their customers much better than before. Equally, the employees must be enthusiastic in following the company's path. In the global internet age, competition does not pause even for a single day. New services are emerging everywhere and can be used everywhere. Excellent quality, ease of use, and the highest service quality are also becoming ever more important in banks. Service design has a good chance to become the decisive core competence of the future. Customer focus and innovative business models will be the main differentiating features in the future.

There are no clear rules for the necessary change. Due to the very complex nature of the sectors, competitors, products, services, and actors involved, pragmatic solutions are needed. Experiences from other subject areas and industries can help to throw some light on the matter.

Can you remember your first encounter with Google? Google began as a search engine and is now the market leader in online advertising—ignored for a long time, then ridiculed, now admired. What are the key lessons for banks? How can transformation be achieved? How can customers be brought along?

This book provides orientation for these questions. It illustrates that the future of the sector has already begun, and what the cornerstones of the new future logic are. Furthermore, it also enables an understanding of the drivers of change at the interface between industrialisation, innovation, and customer focus. And: it does not stop at describing the 'WHAT', but also places a decisive focus on the 'HOW': how can business models be made strategically, structurally, and culturally sustainable—from the inside? Large companies invest in so-called think tanks to answer these questions. Small and medium-sized institutes avail of various individual and laborious sources.

Precisely here is the special value of this book. It allows the reader to acquire in a compact form the equipment for understanding and successfully implementing business models. Based on a fundamental examination, pragmatic steps towards change—grounded in theory—are demonstrated.

Prof. Dr. Marcel Seidel
FOM Hochschule für Oekonomie & Management
and Co-founder of the Banking Innovation Group

Preface

How You Can Use This Book

So the banking sector is going through a process of change, something we have all accepted by now. But the prevailing attitude is the hope that everything will soon continue just as it did in previous decades and that "normality" will return. It is very tedious to have been faced for a number of years with constantly sinking margins and more critical customers—although luckily not all are so critical—and sometimes also being asked about the values of the banking sector. This is a sector that for a long time represented a dream occupation for many graduates, that contributed to laying the foundation for Europe's wealth since the beginning of industrialisation, and that at the same time overstepped the mark in the last 20 years, in the eyes of many citizens.[1] Why should you read this book? There are three reasons, whether you are an interested private person or a bank manager or employee: this book will provide you with an understanding of the underlying logic of the twenty-first century and its effects on the banking sector. Moreover, it presents the current thought traps with regard to customer behaviour and modern business tools and therefore allows you to utilise the logic of the twenty-first century successfully. And finally it answers the question of how the necessary changes can be implemented successfully in the company.

Part I: Thought Traps from the Past and Who Benefits from Them (Chaps. 1–2)

This is the part for the view from the putative future, which has already begun. You have already heard a lot about the supposedly new business models that threaten banking in the long term? Google has taken out a banking license. PayPal has done the same. Zalando is doing what Quelle could have done—oh well. Or perhaps not

[1] This includes the stream of endless bad news, such as the fine of 725 million € charged to Deutsche Bank due to Libor exchange rate manipulation or the raids on the offices of the Commerzbank in December 2013, which were first related "only" to the dubious business of an insurance provider, whose products lay in the depot of the Commerzbank (Manager Magazin 2013). UBS (NZZ 2012) and Credit Suisse (Tagesanzeiger 2013a) have also hit the headlines with billions in fines. The same also applies to other Swiss institutes such as the Basle cantonal bank (NZZ 2014) or the Zurich cantonal bank (Tagesanzeiger 2013b).

oh well, but time for "oh wow"? Do you want to check if these change prophecies are simply good marketing by consultancy firms and that nothing has really happened since the dotcom boom? Will the predictions come true and is there something to be said for the ground-breaking changes to business models? What about best practice on the basis of the new success factors? Get a structured overview of these two questions.

Part II: The Logics of the Twenty-First Century and the Tools for Business Model Transformation (Chaps. 3–7)
This is the section for the reader who is interested in relevant and perfectly tailored business instruments. Do you want to understand the fundamental logic behind the pressure to change, in which direction the business models of banks must change in the next 10 years, and what are the most effective business tools for successfully managing this change? Do you believe that classic instruments continue to do their job well? Are you convinced that you have always placed customer needs at the centre of your thoughts and actions? And yet—be honest—you notice that customers are becoming ever more critical and, following the successful industrialisation of your bank's business model, you might not have approached all of the future challenges to ensure that your bank will still be successful in 10 years? Then it is worthwhile reading this part—addressing industrialisation in such a manner that you will still have a decisive advantage over your competitors in 2 or 3 years is the value proposition of this section.

Part III: Building Specific Bridges and Making Them Accessible (Chaps. 8–9)
This is the section for the reader who is interested in true implementation. One can write all day long—but that doesn't get things implemented. Many concepts remain on the shelf—in the last 10 years, 75 % of previous change projects have failed. This book does not stop at the diagnosis, but instead shows how change from the inside can be effective—by making those affected to those involved, by liberating oneself from the idea that implementation can be dictated from above. The network age invites dialogue about arguments—and that must be learned. Companies that manage this will also win the customers of the future.

Part IV: Connecting the Dots—How the Components Fit Together (Chap. 10)
This is the section for the fast reader. It combines the findings from parts I to III on the Zurich Model of customer-centred banking architecture. Many books provide good impulses, but do not answer the question as to how they can be implemented in the here and now. This book goes a step further. The Zurich Model of customer-centred banking architecture offers an orientation framework that combines the classic concept and the challenges of modernity in one model. The Zurich Model is the analytical tool for the perfectly tailored transformation of the business model. It gives guidelines for concrete transformation work. The choice is yours—help to design the future!

Appeal for a New Type of Banking

This book can help you to understand the necessity of the evolution of business models towards a customer-centred banking architecture and to master the changes that lie ahead. On the one hand it is an appeal to see the customer as the pivot of business activities in the digital age. You will achieve true differentiation, however, only when you give the added value for the customer the same importance as the added value for the bank—that is the central hypothesis of this book. The following appeal is clichéd, one-sided, and incomplete. But it is very likely to be true when we look back in 10 years.

The age of the seller's market is long gone (Geyer 2009). In the seller's market, services were developed in a quite chamber and brought to the customer via the sales department. The processes were clearly and technocratically organised and separated into production and sales. There was no place for the customer in the "standard" value chain. The Cluetrain Manifesto (1999), a collection of 95 theses about the relationship between companies and their customers in the age of social and mobile internet, which was published as early as 1999, begins as follows:

"If you only have time for one insight today, then it should be this one. We are not seats or eyeballs or end users or consumers. We are human beings—and our reach exceeds your grasp. Deal with it.

Networked markets are starting to organise themselves faster than the companies that have traditionally supplied them. With the help of the web, markets are becoming better informed, more intelligent, and more demanding with regard to the characteristics that most organisations still lack."

Even back then—at the climax of the dotcom boom—a pragmatic view of people, markets, and new communications technologies was formulated. The industry structures in many sectors have changed since 1998. Physical music stores have disappeared from the scene; bookshops and electronics businesses are thinning out drastically as a result of the news sales channel of the internet (KPMG 2013). This book shows why the changed customer behaviour will also affect banking in the next few years.

The theses describe the influence that the new technologies will have on the relationship between service providers and customers. The Cluetrain Manifesto sketches the end of one-sided communication and one-sided sales. The markets and sales of the future will be based on network-like relationships between and among people, between companies and people, and between companies as part of a network.

This shift in power has already begun in banking today. Purely one-sided communication and one-sided sales—without any consideration of customer needs—are working less and less. The buyers' market in the social and mobile web and in the real world stand for

- Conversations between equals
- Human beings and not target groups
- Cooperation and equality
- Openness and transparency

The more Internet based the business model and the customer behaviour, the more advance the shift in power seems to be. In some cases, the historic, self-evident customer focus of every bank—retail banks such as the Raiffeisen and cooperative banks, the cantonal banks, and savings banks as the partners of agriculture and medium-sized firms; major banks as the partners of industry—has experienced an unexpected renaissance in recent years, at least in terms of communication with the outside.

The primary orientation of activities towards creating a high shareholder value has retreated into the background, somewhat, at least in terms of external communication. Instead, investments are being made in a better understanding of customers, their lifestyles, and their needs.[2] Customer Relationship Management (CRM) has developed from being purely a collection point for customer data to a company-wide and process-integrated support for the whole customer relationship process. CRM systems were supplemented by IT-based customer ratings and statements on the future potential of customers. In some cases, customer break-even analyses were also introduced, even if control is still generally conducted by means of the number of customer contacts at present. Concepts such as Customer Lifetime Value (CLV), ABC analyses, programme structure analyses, and IT-supported customer-scoring models are now also being deployed today in addition.

In banks, customer orientation was frequently reduced to the "golden path" on the way to more profitability and was simply another word for the optimisation of shareholder value and profit. Instead of the truly important question of customer orientation—what added value does a bank gives its customers—more interest was shown in the economic value of the customer for the bank. The one-sided optimisation of the "win" worked due to the fact that customers were satisfied with rising prices and portfolio yields, among other things. Real win-win advice in the sense of the honourable trader was not always expected by customers and thus often neglected by the financial services industry, with differing consequences, depending on the prevailing institute culture. From this point of view, the customer loyalty programmes familiar today are something of an uprising against the growing power of customers, who wish to conserve and continue the "good old times". The next development stage is the creation of effective win-win situations. Striving to achieve win–win—in the sense of the equal importance of the benefits of the business relationship for both customers and banks—is the central criterion of true customer focus and sustainably successful business models—that is the hypothesis of this book. That does not contradict the still valid fundamental corporate principle of achieving profit, but rather expands it by including the long-term and sustainable perspective of added value for both sides.

The authors define win–win as the result of an exchange relationship in which all involved receive a recognisable benefit, which could not be realised without this

[2] Private banking advisors at Credit Suisse, for example, use a needs-oriented advisory approach (Handelszeitung 2013).

relationship. A balance that suits both sides is aspired to between equal partners. This approach is oriented towards sustainable success and long-term cooperation, rather than short-term profit.

The challenge for banks now is to orient themselves towards effective future added value factors from the point of view of the customer in the digital age. This might sound easy, but the road is a rocky one. This book will provide you with the necessary orientation framework—as a private individual and as a designer of change.

Zurich, Switzerland — Prof. Dr. Stephanie Auge-Dickhut
Zurich, Switzerland — Prof. Dr. Bernhard Koye
Stuttgart, Germany — Axel Liebetrau
August 2015

References

Cluetrain Manifest. (1999). *Cluetrain Manifest.* Retrieved September 29, 2013, from http://www.cluetrain.com

Geyer, G. (2009). *Das Beratungs- und Verkaufsgespräch in Banken: Mehr Erfolg durch Aktiven Verkauf.* Heidelberg

Handelszeitung. (2013). *Bedürfnisanalyse: Nach Maß geschnittene Finanzpläne.* Retrieved December 3, 2013, from http://www.handels-zeitung.ch/unternehmen/beduerfnisanalyse-nach-mass-geschnittene-finanzplaene

KPMG. (2013). *Die Zukunft des Einkaufens.* Retrieved December 5, 2013, from http://www.kpmg.at/uploads/media/Studie_Die_Zukunft_des_Einkaufens_01.pdf

Manager Magazin. (2013). *Razzia: Steuerfahnder filzen Commerzbank.* Retrieved December 4, 2013, from http://www.manager-magazin.de/unternehmen/banken/razzia-bei-der-commerzbank-a-936950.html

NZZ. (2012, December 29). *UBS bezahlt 1,4 Milliarden Franken.* Retrieved February 3, 2014, from http://www.nzz.ch/aktuell/wirtschaft/wirtschaftsnachrichten/ubs-bezahlt-14-milliarden-franken-busse-1.17897647

NZZ. (2014, February 3). *Basler Kantonalbank—100 Millionen Franken für Busse zurückgestellt.* Retrieved February 3, 2014, from http://www.nzz.ch/aktuell/newsticker/basler-kantonalbank-100-millionen-franken-fuer-busse-zurueckgestellt-1.18207763

Tagesanzeiger. (2013a). *Hornung: Credit Suisse droht Milliardenbusse.* Retrieved February 3, 2014, from http://www.tagesanzeiger.ch/wirtschaft/unternehmen-und-konjunktur/Hornung-Credit-Suisse-droht-Milliardenbusse/story/27443723

Tagesanzeiger. (2013b). *ZKB fürchtet hohe Busse.* Retrieved February 3, 2014, from http://www.tagesanzeiger.ch/wirtschaft/unternehmen-und-konjunktur/ZKB-fuerchtet-hohe-Busse/story/29827359

Contents

Part I

New Rules: The Drivers of Future-Viable Banking

1 Customers: Unknown Entities!

In order to analyse the importance of the change from a seller's to a buyer's market, it is necessary to understand the guidelines of customer behaviour in the digital age. The danger here is that the experiences of the past may be perpetuated. But even where it is possible to approach the customer in an innovative manner, there is still no guarantee that future-viable solutions will emerge. Customers cannot be expected to know in advance the innovative solutions to their needs. All that people wished for prior to the invention of the automobile were faster horses; before the introduction of the PC they sought more flexible data processing, and before the advent of the iPhone the integrated use of all data. This chapter outlines the trends that influence customers (see Sect. 1.1) and the "blunders" intrinsic to the development of a modern understanding of the customer (see Sect. 1.2).

1.1 Introduction: Understanding Customers and Their Transformation

Correctly understanding future customer behaviour and customer needs is an important prerequisite for the successful strategic orientation of a bank. Frequently, customer behaviour that has already experienced fundamental change is mistaken for a temporary trend.

During the period of sales orientation in the sellers' markets, the finance industry focussed on competitor analysis. Customers were informed to a much lesser degree, and their demands were therefore also fewer, as they were unaware of their options for action. In the digital age, in contrast, informed customers are increasingly less prepared to accept this sales logic. The transformed customer behaviour results from an abundance of sociocultural trends as well as their interaction with and among each other. Some of these sociocultural trends, which have already

S. Auge-Dickhut et al., *Customer Value Generation in Banking*, Management for Professionals, DOI 10.1007/978-3-319-19938-2_1

influenced sustainably customer behaviour in banking and indeed continue to do so, will be presented below. The list serves merely as an example and is not comprehensive[1]:

Mobile Internet and Digitalisation Growing mobile interconnectedness is constantly adopting new forms and penetrates all areas of private and professional life.

Individualisation This is the progressive process from outside influence to the self-determination of the individual. With regard to economic topics, this represents the manifold possibilities for individual decisions, for example in terms of lifestyle, consumption or use of media.

Education The transition from the industrial society to the creative and knowledge society has transformed creativity and knowledge into key resources. At the same time, society's collective level of education has grown significantly.

New Forms of Work New flexible, mobile and project-oriented forms of work have softened rigid job descriptions and types of occupation.

Trend research and future studies can help us to understand the customer better by focussing on the future. By these means it is also possible to identify potential thought traps that result from the perpetuation of existing explanatory patterns.

1.2 Thought Traps

1.2.1 Thought Trap: Innovation Is Possible Without the Customer

Based on Gassmann and Sutter (2008), innovative companies grow disproportionately and are more profitable than their competitors. For Vahs and Burmester (2005), innovations contain essential driving forces for economic but also social progression. Against the background of a saturated market in the financial services sector and the more critical customer, the issue of innovation is gaining in significance, also for banks, even if the sector has already been successful so far in simply continuing the systems of the past in the area of customer care. The pressure to innovate is becoming ever greater due to the customer's desire for integrated solutions, the banks' striving for an expansion of their market share, and growing international competition—for example from direct investment banks in Germany—in combination with the pressure on margins resulting from the informed customer (Gassmann and Sutter 2008). It is astonishing that the customer

[1] It is certainly the case that many of the sociocultural trends listed can be described sensibly in another context and in a different time framework as megatrends, consumption trends, technology trends, etc. For an overview of sociocultural trends see e.g., Trend Report (2012).

is considered to be a source of innovation only in very rare cases. Banks fall into the thought trap of wanting to develop everything themselves, involving the customer in innovation development either too late or not at all. But why should they stew only in their own juices? Outsourcing the development of ideas and innovation to the intelligence and labour of the customer is an exciting option. Access to knowledge and the sources of knowledge is a potential factor of success in terms of innovative capability—not only in knowledge-intensive sectors. Many banks have recognised this fact and have begun in recent years to optimise continually their internal processes in knowledge and innovation management and in adjacent subjects. Some banks[2] already integrate external sources of knowledge such as customers, partners or suppliers. While this is not a completely new approach, it demonstrates the tendency for banks to reject isolating themselves from the outside world, as well as the new role of external sources of knowledge and innovation.

The key question when it comes to implementation is: What drives customers to get actively involved in the innovation developments of banks? There is a variety of opinions on this matter. Specialist articles and discussions with experts have produced the so-called "four Fs" of online participation, which Marsden (2009) summarised in a white paper on ideas platforms:

- Fame
- Fortune
- Fulfilment
- Fun

Only very few employees or customers derive their motivation solely from monetary incentives (Wilkesmann and Rascher 2005). Yet these are nevertheless important in order to show that the ideas and suggestions are welcome and taken seriously. Furthermore, the unchecked attractiveness of reality and casting shows also demonstrates that people strive for public fame and status. Thus some banks motivate their staff not with monetary incentives, but instead with the opportunity to contribute actively to the development of ideas and innovations, with the chance of becoming a known force in the bank and expanding their personal network.

For the most part, the willingness to participate in developing ideas and innovations is based on the opportunity for personal fulfilment. This can be expressed by helping to develop a solution, establishing contact with interesting people or unleashing one's own creativity. Without doubt the most important motivation is and remains fun and the joy of communal, playful work. Boring questions, or laborious and time-consuming participation should be avoided where possible (Eckstein und Liebetrau 2012).

---

[2] The Royal Bank of Scotland (RBS), for example, attempts to involve its customers actively in the improvement of existing products, and the development of new ones, by means of the IDEAS web platform. There customers can post their ideas for improving bank services. They get an overview of the topics being discussed the most, but also of the implementation measures taken by the RBS in 2013.

Co-creation or open innovation and joint innovation development excites customers, partners and employees and sets change in motion. The boundaries between the bank and the customer become more penetrable and blurred. Something new emerges simply from the fact that old situations are seen with new eyes (Reichwald and Piller 2009). Therefore those responsible for innovation in banks should take a closer look at the phenomenon before rashly deciding for or against it. As with every new management instrument, co-creation also has advantages and disadvantages that demand conscious consideration. Whether one calls it co-creation, user innovation or open source: in each case the new, open innovation model means a drastic change in the way a bank deals with its customers.

The following three key theories summarise the chances for the idea and innovation management of the finance industry that are provided by the integration of customers and other external sources:

1. Access to creativity, that "vital raw material"
   Banks that wish to continue operating profitably must learn to gain and use "creative capital". *"In the creative and knowledge economy the value of a company is assessed according to the degree to which it succeeds in being a magnet for creative people and provides structures in which the "creative capital" can best evolve and drive innovation."* (Liebetrau and Hirsig 2012). Irrespective of whether the creativity and the ideas come from one's own employees, from external sources, or from joint interaction: co-creation can provide sensible access to external creativity and knowledge.
2. Magnet effect for high potentials and experts
   The attractiveness of tasks or clients is being redefined. It occurs wherever creative people encounter an inspiring environment: in innovative banks with other creative thinkers in their own organisation and among external partners. Creative people attract other creative people. The tasks that are set and the available innovation culture are also decisive. Boring tasks and bank attract only one thing: boring ideas, boring staff and even more boring customers and partners.
3. No fountain of youth for non-creative banks
   Banks that are already considered not to be very creative or innovative today are not likely to get better with co-creation. The extension of an insufficient innovation culture or strategy by means of co-creation is rarely successful (Liebetrau and Hirsig 2012). In order to be able to raise the potential of co-creation, one's own strengths and competencies must first be examined. What is my innovation strategy? What does my innovation culture look like? How do I deal with ideas and know-how? What drives me/us? Only when the bank has a firm grip of its knowledge and innovation management, and can implement innovations and creativity without outside help, can it successfully outsource creative tasks to its customers. If co-creation is done well, the innovative strength necessary for survival and the image in general are increased in the long term. The bank is then open to new impulses and not only "listens" to its customers but starts a true dialogue among equals. Dealing with increasing

uncertainty in product and process design with previously unknown touchpoints,[3] short-term decision-making pressure in the speed of implementation (time-to-market orientation) and the increased flow speed of the markets and processes determine a new, open form of organisation for fresh innovations, with the early involvement of customers and other partners. The call in the finance industry to be clearer, more creative, more courageous, faster and more decisive is getting louder. The integration of the customer in the development of ideas and innovations is a clear step towards a more flexible bank. Bankers and customers can all work together on the same issues and problems. The boundaries with customers, partners—and in some cases even with the competition—are becoming more penetrable.

1.2.2 Thought Trap: Customers Are Rational and Informed

In the media and in the banking sector we constantly encounter the two terms Homo oeconomicus[4] and the informed customer.[5] If we combine both terms it is easy to get the impression of the purely rationally thinking customer who is comprehensively informed. Both terms are thought models that help to better understand the behaviour of customers and in part to predict it. However, with regard to banks, both thought models can lead to a hazardous thought trap by assuming that customers will act as expected and thus that their behaviour is predictable and calculable. This trap is based on the widespread assumption that customers behave in a rational and informed manner in financial matters. The field of Behavioural Economics studies this phenomenon and associated behavioural patterns as a part of business studies. It analyses and interprets human behaviour in business situations, and observes such situations in which people act contrary to the Homo oeconomicus. The field of Behavioural Finance is concerned with irrational behaviour on financial and capital markets. In addition, anomalies in customer behaviour that can arise from the irrational interplay between the bank and the customer, for example, are also examined, recorded and interpreted (Rapp 2000). Behavioural Economics also addresses the systematic mistakes made by customers when making decisions (Fuller 1998). The objective is not only the detection of such anomalies, but also of the systematics of the resulting actions of the customer.

Until the end of the last century the theory of efficient markets clearly dominated financial market theory. The publication of the research results of Kahneman and

---

[3] By touchpoints the authors mean points of contact between the bank (company, brand, employees or products/services) and the customer.

[4] The Homo oeconomicus is characterised by unlimited rational behaviour. For customers, their pursuit of maximum utility is characteristic, while at the company level the primacy of profit maximisation dominates (Gabler Wirtschaftslexikon 2013a).

[5] A further additional characteristic in the context of Homo oeconomicus is the assumption that seamless information is available about all alternative decisions and their consequences for the customer in the sense of complete market transparency (Gabler Wirtschaftslexikon 2013a).

Tversky (1979) and Thaler (1991) led to a discussion about the meaningfulness and practicability of this theory. Then, at the beginning of this century, it was shown that people sometimes act contrary to the theory of rational decision-making. Kahneman and Tversky (1979) showed how market participants deal systematically with uncertainties and information in practice, and which techniques people used in the face of complex problems. What is remarkable is that people ignore, in part, previously postulated laws of economics and mostly act according to objective criteria. For example, if the value of an item is to be determined, people are generally influenced by self-chosen criteria and the "rule of thumb" (heuristics[6]). People always seek certain patterns of action and safety nets (Jurczyk 2006). For instance, customers have a general aversion to losses and often place greater value on these than on any profits gained. Customers' decision patterns are often very far removed from that which one might call rational. According to the findings of Kahneman and Tversky (1979) and Thaler (1991), the rational and efficient Homo oeconomicus is rather a delusion or a thought trap that has little in common with reality.

If we transfer the findings from behaviour-oriented financial market theory to the behaviour of bank customers, we arrive at new findings, and possible thought traps can be recognised and avoided. According to Shleifer (2000), Shefrin (2002), Kahneman (2003) and Kahneman and Tversky (1973), the findings of Behavioural Economics can be divided into four main areas:

- Heuristics (rules of thumb)
- Framing effects
- Loss aversion
- Cognitive dissonance

The researchers place the person, i.e., the customer, as an individual at the core of their research.

From the perspective of behavioural theory, customers cannot fully process the available relevant factors. Due to the amount of information, but also become more is being constantly generated, it is difficult to grasp everything. Customers therefore try to simplify as much as possible the content of the information and their possible impact. In order to manage the high degree of complexity the customer is forced to regularly employ heuristics. According to Goldberg and von Nitzsch (2004, S. 42), heuristics mean *"rules or strategies for processing information that lead to a fast result, but not one that is guaranteed to be perfect, in brief: rule of thumb"*. Such rules of thumb are applied consciously or subconsciously by customers.

[6] Heuristics are approaches to solving problems for which there are no clear solutions, or only ones that appear too complex. "Rules of thumb" are used on the basis of subjective experience and passed-down behaviour, especially in problem areas that are difficult to comprehend (Gabler Wirtschaftslexikon 2013b).

Kahneman and Tversky (1972, 1973) also describe the phenomenon of framing. Simply changing the way in which options are phrased already influences the perception of the matter and can lead to completely different decisions. The framing effect can be better understood by means of an example. In health promotion campaigns the damaging long-term consequences of smoking or obesity are frequently highlighted by appealing to fear. This is known as a loss frame. With preventative measures, however, messages that are embedded in a gain frame are more successful. The positive consequences of the desired change in behaviour are emphasised (Rothman et al. 1993; Jones et al. 2003; Meyerowitz and Chaiken 1987).

Loss aversion refers to the aforementioned tendency to place greater weight on losses than on gains. For example, customers often get more annoyed about the loss of x EUR than they would delight in the gain of the same sum. Kahneman and Tversky (1979) were also responsible for discovering this irrational customer behaviour.

Furthermore, customers frequently demonstrate a distinct desire for harmony. Many decisions with two or more alternatives present customers with a conflict. They look for arguments and information that justify the decision reached. This inner conflict is known in the field of psychology as cognitive dissonance, a kind of "disturbing emotion". The core of this theory is that every individual tries to remove contradictions of perception and thought as quickly as possible, because they are considered to be unpleasant and burdensome. The phenomenon can be observed in the famous example of smokers who try, with the help of fudged arguments to trivialise the dangerous effects of smoking (Brehm and Cohen 1962).

1.2.3 Thought Trap: Understanding the Customer Is Sufficient for Securing Future Viability

The vast majority of banks operating on the market has been dealing with customers for decades, and in some cases even centuries. Equally, bank employees usually have many years of experience with direct customer contact, they are very well trained and usually have a high level of "basic friendliness" as well as a genuine interest in their customers. When recruiting new staff, social competencies such as likeability and empathy are demanded in equal measure with professional competence and assessed accordingly. In addition, not only have many banks been conducting "alibi market research" for a number of years, but they also integrate professional market research into their marketing activities. So banks understand their customers. But what is also key, alongside an understanding of the needs of the customer, is the awareness that customers often cannot translate their needs into new product or service configurations. One can survey customers, and they will respond using their own language. But it is not easy for customers to formulate what they really want, what they need, what satisfies them, what enthuses them, what it is that makes them a fan! We are all customers, and it is true of all of us. This phenomenon can be observed not only in banking, but also in many other sectors and industries. We cannot always specify what drives us, what fascinates us, or what convinces us. The phenomenon is expressed in a quotation attributed to Henry Ford: *"If I had asked people what they wanted, they would have said 'faster horses'!"* His customers at the time knew only horses as a means of transport (Ford 2013).

But even in recent times innovative products have emerged without the involvement of customers in the product development. When presenting the iPad Steve Jobs was asked what market research his company had done. Jobs replied indignantly: *"It's not the consumers' job to know what they want."* (FAZ 25.8.2011).

Today's customers know only classic banking as a business concept. Understandably, they have no real notion of how modern and customer-centred banking might look. Nevertheless, asking customers about their satisfaction levels, wishes and ideas remains an important instrument in bank marketing and belongs in the operative toolbox of every bank. Customer surveys and market research are valuable, because they can provide hints and impulses on product and service innovations, on better processes, or on unknown problems (blind spots such as annoyance about a process). Furthermore they signalise honest appreciation of the customer. Especially in this age of social media and mobile internet, customers see almost everything and talk about almost everything. Annoyed customers who leave a branch office or website turn immediately to their social networks in order to post their frustration about the advisor or bank in question.

A more sensible alternative or extension to conventional customer surveys are customer journeys, which can provide so-called consumer insights (Föll 2007). Customer journey is a marketing term and refers to the individual phases experienced by a customer before deciding to buy a product. From a marketing perspective the customer journey denotes all touchpoints of the consumer with a brand, product or service. These include not only direct points of interaction between customers and companies (advertisements, website, etc.), but also the indirect contacts, from which third-party opinion is gleaned on a brand, product or service (rating portals, user forums, blogs, etc.) (Faulkner 2005). Though still widely unknown in the banking sector, these instruments are tried and trusted in many other areas—such as in the consumer sector. Here, the focus of all observation is on the understanding of the customer (insight). Thus ethnographic market research, for example, can generate further consumer insights by accompanying customers in their everyday lives—what do customers do in the bank? With this form of market research banks get an insight into the everyday lives of their customers. They understand how their attitudes and opinions are formed. The banks experience and observe their customers by observing the everyday actions of these customers in their real environment (bank, office, leisure time, at home, out and about, etc.). Banks also have the opportunity to better understand the ideas and values of customers. This approach provides valuable impulses that depart from the traditional perspective (Spiegel Institute 2013). In that sense consumer insight provides unexpected access to customers' individual human behavioural patterns. It often contains a surprising realisation—a kind of "wow effect"—about what concerns customers with regard to products, services or the entire brand of a bank. Such insights into customer behaviour and comprehensive knowledge of the hidden and previously unknown motives, attitudes, values, views and consumption patterns of customers form the basis and key qualification for a successful customer focus and clearly "understanding and knowing our customers better".

An illustrative example of the benefits and opportunities presented by consumer insight is a case study of property owners with a photovoltaic installation. When asked why they opted for a photovoltaic system, the first response was the possibility to get cheaper credit, to receive state subsidies and to attain high yields. After observing the daily routines of the house-owners, additional, previously unknown motives were detected, such as

- Independence from others (e.g., energy suppliers or price fluctuations on raw materials markets); strength; being regarded by neighbours and friends as particularly modern and ecological (image and status) and
- peace of mind, in other words the good feeling of doing something for the environment and future generations (future viability as a modern lifestyle).

These insights, which are very important not only for the development of products and services, but also for sales processes and consultations, may not have been attained from a conventional customer survey or market research.

Innovation management offers a whole range of other qualitative instruments and tools for intensive interaction with the customer; such as consumer and expert dialogues or consumer diaries or blogs, in order to generate insights and glean inspiration. The next step is to combine the insights gained and to subject them to an initial rough assessment. The classic formats here are creative and concept workshops with or without the involvement of external agents such as suppliers, partners, experts, not-yet customers or customers (Phaydon 2013).

Deutsche Bank is a pioneer in the sector, with its own think tank on Design Thinking. Design Thinking is new innovation tool for developing unconventional approaches and ideas. The method is based on the principle that true innovation can occur only when the customer is placed at the centre of all considerations. The innovation method was developed as early as the 1960s at Stanford University in California (Stanford 2013). It involves customers closely in the innovation process. Teams are deployed for the project work, who act independently during the period of the project—just like a spin-off project. In the initial phase, all solutions are deliberately pursued, including those that appear absurd, in order to approach the topic more openly, rather than restricting oneself. Concentration on realisable results takes place only in the second phase. In each phase the early and cyclical implementation of ideas is pursued with the help of simple yet testable prototypes. Feedback is also integrated into the project work. This work is supported by a comprehensive toolbox composed of a variety of creative and innovative methods, as well as different presentation techniques. Katharina Berger, Head of Design Thinking at Deutsche Bank, said of the objectives and motivation of Deutsche Bank: *"We at Deutsche Bank want to involve the customer in our innovation process in order to be able to better illustrate his needs. Design Thinking helps us to do this. At the same time this method fosters a collaborative work culture, which in turn promotes ideas. Thus in particular the attractiveness of the company for young talented people grows, but also the motivation of the existing employees"* (Berger and Liebetrau 2012). Deutsche Bank has been using this method successfully since 2009 with a series of innovations that have been introduced to market, such as the future planner of Branch Q110 for the private banking sector (Berger and Liebetrau 2012).

As well as individual instruments and tools, entire methods taken from the field of innovation management can also be used in banking, such as:

- Service Design for the development of new services and processes (Koye and Liebetrau 2013),
- Blue Ocean Strategy for the development of completely new services and business areas (Kim and Mauborgne 2005), or
- Business Model Generation for innovative business models (Osterwalder et al. 2011).

1.2.4 Thought Trap: The Customers Will Come to the Bank

Customers are visiting bank branches less often. And indeed why should they? The growing use of online banking and other digital offers allows the customer to receive comprehensive financial advice online, which has led to a constant decline in customer frequency in branches. Customer frequency has even declined slightly in the self-service areas of branches. Cash can be withdrawn much more easily at petrol station tills and in supermarkets. The well-known quote, attributed to Bill Gates: *"Banking is necessary, banks are not"* is becoming more and more a reality (Die Zeit 16.12.2013).

Despite this, the sales and branch concepts of many banks continue to be based on the basic assumption and the possible thought trap that customers like coming into branches, and that they deliberately seek personal contact with their advisor. This assessment is still likely to apply to some customers, even in the future. Nevertheless, particularly in view of the high fixed costs of branches, and in light of the growing online community, it is necessary to reflect critically on the fact that online channels are becoming ever more significant, and to examine how an "omni-channel concept" might look for one's own bank.

Just a few years ago the banking world was simple. There was classic advertising in newspapers, radio and television, and with a bit of luck the advertising worked and customers got in touch with their advisors by telephone or by visiting their local branch. These days, that is very seldom the case. Current touchpoints are in the places where customers spend their everyday lives: in the interplay between the physical and the virtual world, on the one hand in the office or at home, on the other hand online or in social communities. A decisive success factor of modern touchpoint management is to clearly link this wide variety of touchpoints between online and offline, and to create a balance between customer benefits, economic effectiveness and rules.

Another thought trap implies that customers will continue to cover their cash requirements from banks. Cash is a centuries-old foundation of the customer relationship—a sacred bond between the customer and the bank. These days, however, the retail trade is increasingly taking over the supply of cash to the customer.[7] Some banks in Asia and America are already preparing for a future with less cash and time-saving cash services in the retail trade. They have introduced cashless ATMs to their branches and into shopping centres. Coupons are issued instead of cash notes, which can then be used in retail stores to pay for goods or exchange for cash. In addition, it is also possible to make cash lodgements in retail stores (Nextmind 2013). This might seem strange at first glance, but on closer inspection we recognise the logical rethink and the preparation for a future with cash-less banks. In future, cash will be less associated with banks, but instead with the retail trade. At present, however, some banks in Europe are still very passive in the face of this development.

A study by the opinion research institute Forsa on behalf of the fund industry association BVI arrived at a shocking result: Germans prefer going to the dentist than to the bank (Hiller von Gaertringen 2011). 88 % of those surveyed make regular appointments with the dentist. In contrast, only one in 10 meets regularly with his or her bank advisor. This is an alarming finding when we consider that almost all banks regard themselves as being customer- and sales-oriented. Germany's retail bank customers are increasingly dissatisfied with their financial institutions. According to another study by Sinn et al. (2012), customer satisfaction wallows at minus 13 % on a scale from plus 50 % to minus 50 %. Minus values indicate that more customers are dissatisfied than they are satisfied. Other sectors fare much better in comparison. In the automobile industry, customer satisfaction lies at plus 23 %, while even among computer manufacturers it is plus 15 %. The dissatisfaction of the customers certainly indicates a severe crisis of confidence, says the study. Compared to the previous study in 2006, customer satisfaction sank by 10 %. The large banks were a particular focus of criticism. More than 40 % of customers are critical of them, with satisfaction at minus 27 %. Customers of savings banks (Sparkassen, minus 17 %) and cooperatives (Volks- und Raiffeisenbanken, minus 7 %) are somewhat less dissatisfied.

The most satisfied are those customers of direct banks, at plus 13 % (Döring 2012). These values are far removed from the ideal strategic targets aimed at by most banks. We can conclude that customer much prefer and are more satisfied with direct banks without branches and with no personal advisors, and they are more likely to recommend them than local banks from the region. That is a slap in the

[7] In Germany, cash can be withdrawn from a current account at the supermarket chain REWE, for example, with purchases over € 20 (Tarifomat 2013); this is offered in Switzerland by the Migros Bank to their customers in Migros retail stores (Migros Bank 2013).

face for every bank that focuses on personal advisory services. This phenomenon reflects a trend that is already familiar to the banks from the area of self-service. In surveys of their own customers, banks were rated much higher and customer satisfaction grew significantly after they had introduced self-service terminals for cash withdrawals and other transactions. One might be tempted to insinuate that the less contact there is between advisor and customer, the more satisfied the customer is likely to be.

1.2.5 Thought Trap: Sales Take Place Either in the Branch or Online

The boundaries between branch-based and online-based sales are crumbling. The assumption that customers use the physical and virtual channels only sequentially for the same matter is a thought trap. Today customers use these communication options in parallel. The "operated" website with personal advice is transforming from a "nice to have" to a "must have". Wüstenrot Bank is a pioneer in this respect, with an innovative operated online service. In an interview with the authors, Markus Malz, Head of Product Development at Wüstenrot Bank, described the advantages of the operated online service as follows: *"Wüstenrot Bank uses the chat function to conduct the dialogue exactly where the customer's specific questions arise: on our website, while surfing through our product pages or in the completion process. Generally, of course, we try to give the user all the information required for his or her actions on screen. However there may still be details that do not get noticed. All that is needed in such a case is to pose a brief question during a chat—and the user does not have to search for ages for the desired information. The attractiveness of this solution is obvious, especially compared to the telephone: no media break for the customer, real-time communication without waiting times and the preservation of anonymity"* (Interview with Berger and Liebetrau 2012).

The fixed costs of branch-based operations, the removal of the need to visit a bank physically, the boom in social communities and above all in cheaper bank services by direct banks are all forcing banks to engage with operated online services. The idea is to offer customers a differentiated personal contact, also online, with sinking prices. Often, the current configuration of the business models is not yet able to take the necessary steps to adequately and proactively control the conversion of these business models. One key hypothesis is that, in future, customers will be sensitive to price when deciding among basic online services at favourable conditions and value-added advice. In addition, the parallel use of channels will become a necessary element of business models.

At the same time, banks are testing new technological approaches to operation and advice in the operated branches and online as part of developing their operated websites. In future, ATMs and bank statement printers will be used more intensively for pre- or after-sales consultations. The mobile phone or tablet can be used as a consultation tool for simple products without much need for explanation—such as travel insurance—including completion processing. Poster advertising with QR codes can highlight the product in the branches. The customer scans the QR code and is directed to the landing page of the bank with all required information. If the customer wants to buy the product, he or she can do so immediately. "One click" purchasing processes, like those familiar from Amazon, set the benchmark and the underlying philosophy. Where required, customers can receive personal advice directly in the branch, or use the operated website service.

Future-viable approaches for matching customers and advisors use combinations and gradations. They integrate the hybrid customer behaviour and the current situation (context) of the customer. These days, customers still select their channels almost randomly and depending on the situation. It should be noted that customers who switch between different sales channels—so-called "channel hoppers"—are particularly loyal as long as they are provided with a purchase option in every channel (EY 2013).

1.2.6 Thought Trap: The Banks' Internal IT Defines Device Usage

In specialist discussions about the use of IT in banks, the focus is usually placed on the bank's own IT. Talks revolve around the gradual technological advances in banking IT, with tools that support consultation comprehensively in direct dialogue and which have standardised the advisory process.

Yet much more decisive for the future is the development of the use of the latest devices and IT outside the banks by customers and advisors. Enormous technological quantum leaps have been made in the last few years, especially in the areas of mobile phones, mobile internet, tablets and many other forms of technology—and at an increasing tempo. Nowadays the customer has a complete little "mobile bank" in his or her pocket, with a technological performance comparable to that of super computers only very recently. Customer advisors are expected to keep up with this development. They therefore also use the same devices and IT, which are usually much more modern than the current technology of the banks. It is understandable that employees and customers do not wish to forego their "much-loved constant mobile companion" in the bank and during consultations. With the phrase "bring your own device" (BYOD) there are discussions as to how these can be integrated into the banks' IT architecture and then used in advisory dialogues. Connected to this are security concepts and data management systems, which need to be developed in order to ensure the risk-free use of mobile devices. Customers' little technological helpers can already take on the functions of the previously necessary bank IT, the simple processing of transactions and to some degree also the function of personal customer advice, all at the same time.

Banks can exert very little influence on this development. Ultimately, they will be confronted in future with complete and integrated technological solutions for all bank transactions on the customer side. It is likely that we will see a similar development as with travel agencies, which first faced competition from web portals, but not in the field of advice. Now, travel web portals also offer advice and provide the entire service. Furthermore, in future "personal financial management" (PFM; see Chap. 2) will grow in importance for more complex consultations in the area of pre-sales. There have always been well-prepared and informed customers, but this aspect attains a whole new and larger dimension with PFM. Linked to this, beyond device competence, are much greater challenges for the expertise and particularly the social competence of the advisor.

1.3 Wrap Up: Thought Traps

This chapter was concerned with presenting potential thought traps in the digital age. They result from the fact that future customer behaviour is examined using the successful analytical tools of the past. Six potential thought traps were identified and presented. Below are some recommendations for action to avoid these traps, in order to generate added value by integrating them adequately into the strategic control of banks.

▶ **Thought Trap 1: Innovation Is Possible Without Customers** The active involvement of customers (and other external agents) in innovation development can greatly increase the creative potential and initiate change. Correctly understanding the motivation and agendas of the individual customer will become a key competence and the essential factor for successful business models in the digital age. Opening up the organisation is an important step towards a learning,[8] flexible and fluid[9] organisation.

▶ **Thought Trap 2: Customers Are Rational and Informed** The model of the Homo oeconomicus is a tool that helps to understand and interpret the fundamental behaviour of the customer. However, it is not a reflection of reality. Customers do not always act rationally and they do not always have all of the necessary information to hand. In order to better understand customer behaviour, a radical rethink is necessary, integrating the perspective of psychology and other disciplines. These help in interpreting the emotional aspects of customer behaviour. The field of behavioural economics in particular provides new explanatory tools for human behaviour, with its concepts of heuristics, framing effects, aversion and cognitive dissonance. When making decisions, customers are in part rational and in part irrational; at times informed and at other times poorly informed.

[8] Senge (2011) refers to an adaptable organisation that reacts to external and internal stimuli a learning organisation.

[9] Saaman (2012) defines the fluid organisation as a flowing entity. Role categories replace positions or functions, responsibility replaces goals and the key task is to serve the customer, in order to raise competitiveness.

- **Thought Trap 3: Understanding the Customer Is Sufficient for Securing Future Viability** Experience is valuable. Yet it should not misguide one into thinking that one already understands the customer comprehensively. Qualitative tools such as consumer insights or costumer journeys supplement classic market research and are important instruments of innovation development. They expand the view of the direct touchpoints between banks and their customers and provide deeper insights into customer needs. This provides a comprehensive picture of the hidden and/or previously unknown motives, attitudes, values, views and consumer behaviour of the customer. By designing the services accordingly, the resulting customer focus is not only communicated but also generally noticeable, leading to true differentiation in the digital age.

- **Thought Trap 4: The Customers Will Come to the Bank** Customers can conduct most of their transactions, including cash withdrawals, without any personal contact with a bank. They do not actively seek contact with a customer care advisor or a bank. Yet the foundation of the current sales and branch concepts of many banks is the assumption of the personal visit by a customer to an advisor. These concepts must be re-examined due to their questionable effectiveness—they are obviously not working—and lack of profitability—with higher fixed costs for personal advisors and branches. In the medium term, banks should aim for business models in which cash services and other transactions play only a minor role.

- **Thought Trap 5: Sales Take Place Either in the Branch or Online** A new user behaviour is developing among customers. Parallel channel use is becoming state-of-the-art. For instance, customers can inform themselves online while at the same time conducting a personal dialogue by telephone or in person. The winners will be hybrid transaction and advisory concepts that are not only available on all channels, but which can also successfully implement the overlapping of different channels in sales and consultation processes.

- **Thought Trap 6: The Banks' Internal IT Defines Device Usage** "Omni-devicing" with fluid boundaries between private and professional IT infrastructure is a prerequisite for the future viability of business models. Both customers and advisors use devices and IT that have not been developed by the banks—in future, technological standards primarily will be driven externally—and this is a paradigmatic change for banks. At the same time, the demands placed on advisors are growing, as customers use not only the latest devices, but also PFM systems prior to consultations. The advisor no longer has an information advantage—the key competence in the direct contact between the customer and advisor is the tailored evaluation of the available information and the development of solutions with the real-time involvement of the customer.

1.4 Key Message

The paradigmatic change in the banking sector from a buyer's to a seller's market is almost complete. If the business models are to be sustainable, future customer preferences must be anticipated as accurately as possible and applied consistently as guidelines for the transformation. This is possible as long as the thought traps that emerge from continuing previous thought and explanatory patterns are detected:

- Customers are not only rational and informed. They decide on the basis of heuristics, in order to reduce complexity.
- Understanding their needs in the here and now is not a sufficient basis for developing future-viable service configurations.
- In future, customers will visit bank branches much less frequently.
- They interact on all available communication channels in parallel.
- They use the most modern devices and technologies available at the time and expect the same of their advisors. Banks' internal IT can at best (co-) design in part the consulting environment.

References

Berger, K., & Liebetrau, A. (2012, April). Interview: Mehr Kreativität und Kundennähe dank Design Thinking. *Bankmagazin, 2012*(9), 44–46.

Brehm, J. W., & Cohen, A. R. (1962). *Explorations in cognitive dissonance*. New York: Wiley.

Die Zeit. (2013, December 16). *Offline-banking*. http://www.zeit.de/2000/50/Offline-Banking

Döring, T. (2012). *Kunden sind von Großbanken frustriert*. Retrieved September 18, 2012, from http://www.handelsblatt.com/unternehmen/banken/zufriedenheits-studie-kunden-sind-von-grossbanken-frustriert/6929804.html

Eckstein, A., & Liebetrau, A. (2012). Einführung. In A. Eckstein & A. Liebetrau (Eds.), *Insurance & innovation 2012* (pp. 1–4). Verlag Versicherungswirtschaft.

EY. (2013). *Herausforderung Multi-Channel—Neue Wege zu mehr Markterfolg*. Retrieved February 5, 2013, fromhttp://www.ey.com/Publication/vwLUAssets/Gemini_Report_Herausforderung_Multi-Channel/$FILE/Multi-Channel-Report.pdf

Faulkner, M. (2005). *Sense and respond: The journey to customer purpose*. Basingstoke: Palgrave Macmillan.

FAZ. (2011, August 25). *Das Ende einer Ära*. Retrieved September 23, 2013, from http://m.faz.net/aktuell/wirtschaft/netzwirtschaft/steve-jobs-tritt-ab-das-ende-einer-aera-11125153.html

Föll, K. (2007). *Consumer insights—Emotionspsychologische Fundierung und praktische Anleitung zur Kommunikationsentwicklung*. Wiesbaden: Springer.

Ford, H. (2013). *Von Henry Ford lernen heißt siegen lernen*. Retrieved December 5, 2013, from http://www.henry-ford.net/
Fuller, R. J. (1998). Behavourial finance and the source of alpha. *Journal of Pension Plan Investing, 2*(3), 291–293.
Gabler, W. (2013a). *Homo oeconomicus*. Retrieved July 15, 2013, from http://wirtschaftslexikon.gabler.de/Definition/homo-oeconomicus.html
Gabler, W. (2013b). *Heuristik*. Retrieved July 15, 2013, from http://wirtschaftslexikon.gabler.de/Definition/heuristik.html
Gassmann, O., & Sutter, P. (2008). *Praxiswissen Innovationsmanagement: Von der Idee zum Markterfolg*. Munich: Carl Hanser Verlag GmbH & Co. KG.
Goldberg, J., & von Nitzsch, R. (2004). *Behavioral finance: Gewinnen mit Kompetenz*. Munich: FinanzBuch.
Hiller von Gaertringen, C. (2011, May 16). *Lieber zum Zahnarzt als zur Bank*. Retrieved September 18, 2012, from http://m.faz.net/aktuell/finanzen/fonds-mehr/teure-wissensluecken-lieber-zum-zahnarzt-als-zur-bank-1638730.html
Jones, L. W., Sinclair, R. C., & Courneya, K. S. (2003). The effects of source credibility and message framing on exercise intentions, behavior and attitudes: An integration of the elaboration likelihood model and prospect theory. *Journal of Applied Social Psychology, 33*, 179–196.
Jurczyk, B. (2006). *Behavioral finance*. Saarbrücken: VDM.
Kahneman, D. (2003). Maps of bounded rationality: Psychology for behavioral economics. *American Economic Review, 93*(5), 1449–1475.
Kahneman, D., & Tversky, A. (1972). Subjective probability: A judgement of representativeness. *Cognitive Psychology, 3*(3), 430–454.
Kahneman, D., & Tversky, A. (1973). On the psychology of prediction. *Psychological Review, 80* (4), 237–251.
Kahneman, D., & Tversky, A. (1979). Prospect theory: An analysis of decision under risk. *Econometrica, 47*, 263–292.
Kim, W. C., & Mauborgne, R. (2005). *Blue ocean strategy: How to create uncontested market space and make the competition irrelevant*. Boston: Harvard Business Review Press.
Koye, B., & Liebetrau, A. (2013). *Service and solution design: A true game changer in the banking industry, banque & finance*. Retrieved December 7 12, 2013, from http://www.koye-partner.ch/pdf/FF11_4seiter_BanqueFinance_EN_web_04.pdf
Liebetrau, A., & Hirsig, C. (2012). *Mit "Ideen Jam Session" zu Neuem Wissen*. Swiss Future 1/12.
Marsden, P. (2009). *Ideenplattformen—Web 2.0 at its best*. Retrieved August 24, 2013, from https://www.facebook.com/SyzygyGroup/app_326320330789965
Meyerowitz, B. E., & Chaiken, S. (1987). The effect of message framing on breast self-examination attitudes, intentions, and behavior. *Journal of Personality and Social Psychology, 52*, 500–510.
Migros Bank. (2013). *Die multifunktionale Kontokarte für den Alltag*. Retrieved July 15, 2013, from http://www.migrosbank.ch/de/Private/KartenZahlungsverkehr/MCard.htm
Nextmind. (2013). *Wenn's um Geld geht...*. Retrieved September 4, 2013, from http://www.nextmind.de/?p=2006
Osterwalder, A., Pigneur, Y., & Wegberg, J. T. A. (2011). *Business model generation: Ein Handbuch für Visionäre, Spielveränderer und Herausforderer*. Frankfurt a. M: Campus.
Phaydon. (2013). *Kreativ-Workshop Das Potenzial der Zielgruppe nutzen*. Retrieved December 7, 2013, from http://www.phaydon.de/marktforschung-methoden_kreativ-workshop.html
Rapp, H. W. (2000). Der tägliche Wahnsinn hat Methode. In B. Jünemann & D. Schellenberger (Eds.), *Psychologie für Börsenprofis: Die Macht der Gefühle bei der Geldanlage* (pp. 85–123). Stuttgart: Schäffer-Poeschel.
RBS. (2013). *Ideas bank*. Retrieved July 15, 2013, from http://www.rbs.co.uk/global/customer-charter/g1/ideas-bank.ashx
Reichwald, R., & Piller, F. (2009). *Interaktive Wertschöpfung: Open Innovation, Individualisierung und neue Formen der Arbeitsteilung*. Berlin: Gabler.

Rothman, A. J., Salovey, P., Antone, C., Keough, K., & Martin, C. D. (1993). The influence of message framing on intentions to perform health behaviors. *Journal of Experimental Social Psychology, 29*, 408–433.

Saaman, W. (2012). *Leistung aus Kultur: Wie aus "Arbeit-Nehmern" Bestleister werden.* Heidelberg: Gabler.

Senge, P. (2011). *Die fünfte Disziplin: Kunst und Praxis der lernenden Organisation.* Stuttgart: Klett-Cotta.

Shefrin, H. (2002). *Beyond greed and fear: Understanding behavioral finance and the psychology of investing.* New York: Oxford University Press.

Shleifer, A. (2000). *Inefficient markets: An introduction to behavioral finance.* New York: OUP Oxford.

Sinn, W., Vater, D., Lubig, D., & Kasch, M. (2012). *Bain Studie: Retail-Banking: Was Bankkunden wirklich wollen.* Retrieved September 8, 2012, from http://www.bain.de/publikationen/articles/retail-Banking-was-bankkunden-wirklich-wollen.aspx

Spiegel Institute. (2013). *Consumer insights.* Retrieved December 5, 2013, from http://www.spiegel-institut.de/marken-und-konsumentenforschung/consumer-insights

Stanford. (2013). *Homepage.* Retrieved December 7, 2013, from http://dschool.stanford.edu/.

Tarifomat. (2013). *1822direkt Girokonto—Konditionen zum Onlinekonto.* Retrieved July 15, 2013, from http://www.tarifomat24.de/girokonto/1822direkt-girokonto-giroskyline.html

Thaler, R. H. (1991). *Quasi rational economics.* New York: Russell Sage Foundation Publications.

Trend-Report. (2012). *Trend Report 2012. Soziokulturelle Schlüsseltrends für die Märkte von morgen.* Retrieved December 4, 2013, from http://www.trend-update.de/wp-content/uploads/2012/01/Trend-Report_2012-Auszug.pdf

Vahs, D., & Burmester, R. (2005). *Innovationsmanagement: Von der Produktidee zur erfolgreichen Vermarktung.* Stuttgart: Schäffer-Pöschel.

Wilkesmann, U., & Rascher, I. (2005). *Wissensmanagement: Theorie und Praxis der motivationalen und strukturellen Voraussetzungen.* Mering: Hampp R.

2 Newcomers: The Unknown Game Changers

2.1 Introduction

The aforementioned developments are the guide rails for the future-oriented (re-) design of banks' business models. A serious analysis of the consequences can be conducted only specifically to each institute. Yet it is important to realise that time is running out. The reason for this is that a constantly growing number of customers is becoming ever more refractory are willing to switch.

The internet and the digitalisation make it easier for newcomers to the sector to enter the market. They offer innovative products with faster development cycles (time-to-market), as well as greater user-friendliness at lower costs. It is astonishing that even start-ups are considered by conventional bank customers to be sufficiently reliable to be entrusted with their financial means or data. Furthermore, until now digital competitors have had the advantage that they can offer products or services that are not yet subject to any comprehensive state regulation. Above all, however, there are already providers whose business models deliberately exploit the thought traps of the banks, allowing them to acquire step by step those dissatisfied customers who are willing to switch. It is a fact that many new providers have emerged in the banking sector in the last 10 years—even if they do not (yet) dominate the market. Banks are busy trying to meet regulatory requirements, push through cost reductions and optimise processes. The danger here is that customer needs do not form the primary focus of the objectives.[1] The newcomers use these failings of the classic providers in order to position themselves as complete providers or implant themselves in a niche area of the banks' value chain (Insideparadeplatz 2013). One of the main objects of every classic competitor

[1] A study by the Schweizerische Institut für Finanzausbildung (SIF) shows that, according to information provided by Swiss bank employees, around 40 % of banks survey future customer needs less than once a year; when designing/implementing the product range, one third of the respondents believed that customer needs did not form the main focus, but instead other aspects (Auge-Dickhut et al. 2012).

S. Auge-Dickhut et al., *Customer Value Generation in Banking*, Management for Professionals, DOI 10.1007/978-3-319-19938-2_2

analysis is the identification of the success patterns of both the traditional and the innovative competition. The main objective of this chapter, therefore, is to take an impartial look at the business models of these new digital competitors in order to detect the key elements of their unique selling propositions (USP), and thus to lay the second important foundation for the analysis of the possible need for change on the part of conventional banks. The digital competitors can be divided into two clusters: companies that already possess a banking license, and companies without a banking license, but which are starting to offer one or more of the economic functions of banks.

2.2 Newcomers with a Banking License

The providers that can potentially assail the entire business model of banks are either direct banks or new providers from outside the sector, who prepare their entry to market via payment transactions. The basic logic in the age of "big data" is that precise knowledge of the customer's payment behaviour makes it possible to design perfectly tailored solutions to financial needs in real time—as long as the solution components are also available in the background in modular form.

2.2.1 Direct/Online Banks

Direct banks only became possible due to the internet, which therefore also makes them "newcomers", even if they have already been successful in many countries' markets for decades and can boast of steadily growing customer numbers.[2] They allow the customer to cover the entire range of needs, from financing to investments and payments, online at much better conditions—thanks in no small measure to the lack of fixed costs for the branch system. The USP of the direct banks is their permanent 24/7 availability, including transaction processing in real time. In addition, customers who wish to take responsibility for their own actions can use tools to enable them, step by step, to make complex financial and investment decisions and to process these. The "rewards" are much better conditions and a more direct fulfilment of needs. Another difference to classic providers is the fundamental outward classlessness of the customers—the range of services can be used equally by all customers, irrespective of their asset class. On the other hand, not all "premium services" are offered. Conclusion: in the coming years, market share is likely to increase steadily, if we bear in mind the thought traps mentioned in the previous chapter. The direct bank is already the established reply to the decreasing willingness to go to a physical bank branch. By being permanently available via all communication channels, the model exploits two of the thought

[2] For an overview of German-speaking direct investment banks see e.g., Bankentest (2013).

traps of classic banks. It is already the case that the most satisfied customers are those of the direct banks.

2.2.2 Digital Universal Banks

Worldwide we can observe the development of various different digital universal banks, who are aimed rigorously—indeed more rigorously than the direct banks, who merely use the sales channel of the internet for an otherwise conventional offer—at the behavioural and user patterns of the digital generation. They use social media much more consistently and act as a platform, for example for peer-to-peer loans or crowdfunding. Newly-founded banks in the German-speaking area include, for example, Fidor Bank, which already has more than 200,000 customers—these are registered users and do not necessarily have to open an account with a contract (Presseportal 2013). It is aimed at customers who feel at home in Web 2.0, who appreciate digital marketplaces and interacting with other users, and whose user behaviour differs greatly from those of classic bank customers (Fidor Bank 2013). An example from the United States is "Movenbank". It strives to be a mobile bank without any bank cards, paper or branches. Transactions are concluded solely via mobile devices (Moneyland 2013). The "Simple" bank is also on the path to developing and extending this USP (Simple 2013).

2.2.3 Big Data Logic

A key element of the digital age is to hold, obtain and use data in order to segment customers and use the information where necessary for mass customisation. The idea of mass customisation is to try to achieve cost advantages and differentiation by providing customised services using the means of mass production.[3]

In the digital age, big data means that all information about the customer can be used in real time for the precise analysis of customer behaviour, to derive the correlation between results and behaviour, and thus to make perfectly tailored predictions and cluster formations by using all available data sources. Thus the needs and user profiles can be refined permanently, enabling tailored solutions that meet the requirements structure of the customer. In the medium term, providers who are able to offer these perfectly tailored solutions will gradually become trustworthy also when it comes to bank services.

For this reason, companies like Google and PayPal have also already acquired a banking license (Cash 2013). But the focus on payment transactions is also being pursued by other leading internet companies. Facebook cooperates with the

[3] "Mass Customization is more than just a manufacturing process, logistics system or marketing strategy. It could well be the organizing principle of business in the next century, just as mass production was the organizing principle in this one." (Schonfeld 1998, p. 115 f.).

Australian Commonwealth Bank to provide a bank service to Facebook members, allowing payments via Facebook to third parties or to Facebook friends. The security concept is said to be comparable with conventional online banking systems (Finews 2012). The payment system is already being tested online (Tagesanzeiger 2013). Under the name Yapital—and with a banking license in Luxembourg—the Otto Group is working on a payment solution for smartphones and e-commerce. Discussions are underway with stationary retailers such as the Rewe concern about acceptance at the point of sale (Der Handel 20.3.2012).

For industrial companies such as Siemens or MAN, in contrast, the banking license plays a role primarily in sales financing for commercial customers. With a view to the corporate banking sector, this approach represents possible competition for the established banks (FAZ 6.12.2010). In the area of payments via mobile phone, many mobile communications providers are obtaining bank licenses. One of the first in the world was Rogers Telecom, soon followed by European providers (Financial Post 3.5.2013). These include Deutsche Telekom and Vodafone, who offers mobile payment methods in cooperation with Visa. The mobile provider O2 uses the MasterCard platform Paypass for its mobile payment solution. It is also interesting that in 2011 one of the largest concerns in the world, the Japanese telecommunications company NTT Docomo, purchased the publicly-listed German private bank Werther. In Japan this concern already offers payment by mobile phone at free-standing machines (Ernst & Young and University of St. Gallen 2012, p. 17).

2.3 Newcomers Without a Banking License

The providers outlined below exploit the thought traps without possessing a banking license.[4] It will therefore be interesting to observe how these business models will develop. Selected models will be presented from the areas of "payment transactions", "virtual means of payment", "investing and financing", "personal financial management systems", "brokerage and securities trading" and "personal information and decision-making systems".

2.3.1 Payment Transactions

A distinction must be made between the following types of transactions: mobile payment, Near Field Communication (NFC),[5] virtual means of exchange, micropayments and transactions supported by certain additional services. The

[4] No distinction is made below between existing partial or universal banking licenses—as prescribed by German law. Neither Switzerland nor Ireland, for example, make this distinction. For example, PayPal's banking license was issued in Luxembourg and applies throughout Europe.

[5] NFC is a non-contact payment method via mobile phone or credit card. Its main area of use is in paying smaller sums such as parking metres or ticket systems. But NFC can also be used for areas such as access control (Tipps 2013).

following forms of payment, in descending order, are expected to be dominant in the year 2025:

- Smartphones with NFC chips in combination with eWallets[6]
- Mobile payments via online services such as PayPal
- Customer cards
- Credit cards
- Cash (Kearney 2012)

Providers of payment transaction services, whether online or via eWallets, are in contact with their customers on a daily, and sometimes even hourly basis. This allows them to collect relevant data about customers and their transactions. The loss of customer data can lead to the loss of the customer relationship. If banks lose their access to the traditionally low-margin payment transactions business, they then become dependent in future on the data of other service providers. In extreme cases, the bank becomes nothing more than the processor of transactions on the system platforms. The customer interface can be occupied successively by new competitors and, again in extreme cases, the traditional providers become invisible to the customer. The traditional provider's brand fades progressively, while the brand of the new competitor is recharged.

The flow of start-ups of mostly mobile providers in the area of electronic payment transactions is therefore relentless. Along with the well-known service PayPal by eBay, other providers are Paymate and Propay. Yapital (www.yapital.com), by the Otto Group, is a special case. It offers point-of-sale (POS) payments and is a pioneering cross-channel payment provider. Small business owners, such as market stall operators or delivery services, can easily use iZettle (www.izettle.com) to transform their smartphone or tablet into a POS payment terminal with the help of a card reader.

Providers like Euro2Cash (www.euro2cash.de) offer a mixture of old and new payment methods. They allow users to transfer money online to recipients abroad who do not have a bank account. The transferred sums are then paid out by regional paying agents. Other systems such as BillGuard (www.billguard.com) analyse users' credit card payments. Once read-only access is granted for a credit card account, all credit card payments by the user are examined. The payments are checked for hidden fees, booking errors, etc., using more than 100 automated security tests (BillGuard 2013).

Holvi (www.holvi.com) is a Finnish software company. It soon plans to open a Europe-wide innovative bank that offers not only internet-based investments, but also an entire programme encompassing all financial payment flows. The business

[6] It is predicted that by 2014–2016 every fifth smartphone will be equipped with NFC. The volume of transactions processed directly via mobile phone in 2015 is estimated at around 670 billion US$ (Juniper Research 2011).

will be managed exclusively by the customers themselves. The philosophy presupposes that people work in other dimensions these days, and act in networks.

Social micropayment services such as Flattr (www.flattr.com) offer user accounts into which a certain sum is deposited monthly. The user can then click on a payment button on the websites of various different media providers, which then receive a donation from the account.

2.3.2 Virtual Means of Payment

Bitcoin (www.bitcoin.org/de) and Opencoin (www.opencoin.com) are forms of virtual money that are based on the ideas and values of the open source movement. The demands on virtual currencies are that they can be divisible as required, and that they are absolutely forgery-safe, anonymous and untraceable. The virtual currency is formed out of a calculated, encoded character string that meet certain mathematical conditions. This is done in a network of connected computers. Thus one single virtual currency does not consist of a constant character string, but is variable. The string shows the history of the individual virtual currency and the transfer from one owner to the next. This approach ensures that virtual coins cannot be forged, as each individual currency has its own code (Stöcker 2011).

It is already possible to buy mobile phones or ebooks on auction platforms using digital coins, or to play poker with them on specially designed websites. Organisations such as the Free Software Foundation (www.fsf.org) accept donations in virtual currencies. Various platforms offer to exchange digital money into US dollars or other currencies, at constantly updated—and at present, steadily growing—exchange rates (Stöcker 2011). At the moment, however, digital currencies appear to present more of a problem—if at all—to real currencies and their associated economies than to banks. The Chinese central bank, for example, is already worried that the "QQ" coin, which is issued by Tencent, the most important Chinese instant messaging provider, might influence the value of the Yuan. The central bank is considering introducing regulations for the virtual currency, respectively for the transactions in which they are used (King 2010, p. 333).

Digitalisation is penetrating real life in ever more aspects, and therefore currencies that exist only online are greatly increasing. The growing importance of social networks reinforces this trend even further. There are already trading centres for virtual currencies, such as Mt. Gox, and marketplaces in which only virtual currencies are accepted for payment, such as Flowplace (Menn 2011).

2.3.3 Investing and Financing

Conventional banking advice with regard to savings and financing activities faces competition from specialised, web-based advice given by various different providers. This web-based advice, or decision-making support, ranges from the replication of the share portfolios of start investors to the analysis of successful private investors and the replication of these portfolios as exchange traded funds (ETF), right up to the financing of loans by means of a wide range of private persons via special online platforms. Increasingly, customers are managing their own portfolios, and they compare their investment decisions with those of other investors. It can be expected that the willingness of investors to shift their money to other, cheaper and more comfortable providers, will continue to grow.

Peer-to-peer lending and borrowing is based on a similar business model to that of eBay. In each case, the customer is provided with a platform for exchange relationships without the involvement of classic intermediaries. Peer-to-peer lending enables direct bank transactions between private investors who wish to invest money and those who require credit; no bank is involved. As the term is quite cumbersome and long, the acronym P2P is mostly used.

The English company Zopa (www.zopa.com) is a pioneer in the area of online lending. Private individuals can borrow and lend money here quickly and easily. Customers determine the sum and the conditions under which they wish to invest. Borrowers do the same, and as soon as the conditions intersect at a "zone of possible agreement" (hence Zopa), the transaction can take place. For the sake of security, each investment sum is divided among at least 50 borrowers, and a credit reporting agency check is made. Lenders can choose between debtors with different credit rating categories, and receive more or less interest accordingly. Zopa is financed by a fee amounting to 1% of the loan sum, which is paid by the debtor, and a 0.5 % charge for investors. The interest margin required by banks is twice as large (Zopa 2013).

The advantage for the participating parties is the partial omission of the bank margin. The anonymity and simplicity of the transactions can also be an attraction. Many customers are not keen on telling their bank about their financial difficulties in order to get money. Others do not even have the opportunity of receiving money from a bank. In patchwork careers it is not uncommon for phases of good earnings to alternate with other phases in which little or nothing is earned. Those who find themselves in need of money during a phase of low income often cannot expect to receive a bank loan due to a lack of security and no regular income. And even if it is possible, the conditions are very poor. Under certain circumstances, internet platforms solve this dilemma.

The attractiveness of P2P lies not only in the cheaper conditions. While Zopa aims to make a profit, the American internet platform Kiva (www.kiva.org) has a different approach. Here, start-up founders and young entrepreneurs in developing countries can be supported with loans to help them out of poverty. The importance and necessity of such concepts was made very apparent by the awarding of the Nobel Peace Prize to the economist Muhammad Yunus. In 1983 he founded the Grameen Bank (www.grameen-info.org) in Bangladesh, in order to improve the situation of the poor. After a famine he realised that the poor people required only very little capital in order to buy materials for their craft businesses. Yet despite this small capital requirement, hardly any profit was left over. They paid usurious interest rates to moneylenders or were dependent on suppliers. Established banks refused them loans because of a lack of security. Yunus developed a system in which the borrower felt obliged to repay the money due to personal solidarity. His bank paid out loans only when small groups joined together in the villages and vouched for each other. The model now supports people in more than 60 developing countries.

Thus an old idea is revitalised: P2P is not a new phenomenon. As early as 300 AD people in China loaned and borrowed money by organising themselves into groups. The idea remained successful for hundreds of years. Now there are Rotating Savings and Credit Associations (ROSCA) in many countries and cultures. These are alliances between people who save jointly and equally and give loans to members. Zopa developed this idea further, taking it to its logical conclusion with Web 2.0 technologies.

Other new financial instruments in combination with social media and social communities are crowdinvesting or crowdfunding, microfinancing and donation. With crowdinvesting or crowdfunding, a large number of people directly finance a single project. As well as repayment and interest, investors also receive, for example, the finished work, individual gifts or supporting advertising with the help of the cooperation partner.

In donation or rewards-based funding the idea of financing is combined with a donation. On the platform Indiegogo (www.indiegogo.com), for example, donations can be given to a wide range of projects, many of which provide some kind of return.

2.3.4 Personal Financial Management (PFM)

The change currently being experienced by the classic service offer from banks can be seen very clearly in the area of personal financial management. Every person conducts many hundreds of financial transactions each year. Only a fraction of these transactions are conducted via the principle bank. They also include payments with credit and debit cards, second bank connections, cash transactions and many other types of transaction. It seems very difficult to maintain control of this huge amount of data. And if we include the large number of contracts with banks, insurance companies, social insurance funds, etc. of every single customer and his or her family, the task is almost impossible. PFM solves precisely this dilemma to a large degree. It allows customers to maintain an overview and control of their own financial transactions and contracts.

PFM is based on a highly automated, web-based software and is characterised by a high level of user-friendliness with regard to the social dimensions of Web 2.0. PFM applications automatically categorise transactions from customer accounts and credit cards, present this information visually and allow the user to monitor, manage and control his or her finances with the help of intuitive tools. Training videos are often available to users, to explain the first steps of the application possibilities (see e.g., Meniga 2013).

Well-known providers include the American company Mint (www.mint.com) and Meniga (www.meniga.de). They support the customer with, for example, a highly precise, automatic categorisation of transactions, a possible budget overview for spouses or partners and account consolidation. The systems learns with each use and therefore improves constantly. This soon rewards the initial time investment required for PFM.

Furthermore, PFM provides customers with the opportunity to inform and prepare themselves prior to or after a consultation with an advisor, or indeed to manage completely without the help of an advisor. This technological "upgrade" in the area of self-advice, which is relatively easy to achieve—though certainly nowhere near completely adopted by all customers as yet—threatens to present banks with similar changes as those faced in the past by travel agencies or bookshops. It is not necessary to be an expert or a visionary to recognise the future of online banking. Supplemented by mobile applications on smartphones, PFM can become the focal point of personal financial management: always in the customer's pocket, accessible with only a few fingertips, and at the technological level of the best bank IT.

One special feature—and a clear competitive advantage over classic online banking—is the possibility to compare one's own financial conduct (e.g., spending behaviour) anonymously with others (peers) with similar behavioural patterns. Recommendations from the same reference group (similar lifestyle, same financial situation, etc.) are particularly decisive factors when opting to purchase. From the banks' perspective PFM extends the classic value chain with information about one's own user behaviour and with the possibility to glean even more information in this regard. The necessary data is usually available. One of the first major providers in Switzerland was PostFinance with its "Cockpit". The Cockpit offers private customers an automatic categorisation of their income and spending, the creation of budgets and savings goals, and notification whenever budget goals have been reached or exceeded (PostFinance 2013). By now most main providers have caught up. PFM is also offered by digital banks in the context of their customer care (see e.g., Fidor Bank, www.fidor.de or Banksimple, www.simple.com). As well as the direct offer as a platform in itself, "white label" solutions are now also being offered for European banks. Meniga, a well-known provider, refers explicitly to the additional benefits of PFM tools: a demonstrable increase in customer loyalty and the growth and optimisation of cross-selling with individual products and recommendations by using the information obtained (Meniga 2013).

2.3.5 Personal Information and Decision-Making Systems

Beyond the strengths of PFM—which is focussed on customers and their data—personal information and decision-making systems have the advantage that external information from internet platforms can be used for the purpose of personal decision-making. The functionalities include rating portals on the quality of financial service providers, capital market information and tool-supported investment decision aids and portfolio management systems. For example, on the internet platform whofinance (www.whofinance.de), potential customers can read the customer ratings for individual financial advisors. And in the network XING, Fidor Bank already presents more than 1000 ratings on the advisor scene.

One of the most innovative capital market information systems is stocktouch (www.stocktouch.com). It provides a system that help investors—by means of an intuitive iPad app, among other things—to monitor the stock market. At present analyses of 900 American stocks can be accessed (Stocktouch 2013). Alphasys (www.alphasys.ch) is a Swiss company that offers software solutions for portfolio management systems. These are specially tailored to the requirements of asset managers, private banks and pension funds.[7]

There is a large number of providers of tool-based investment decision systems. What they all have in common is that they seek to acquire investors on the basis of their individual theories and recommendations for action. These are based on the use of data via stock trading by executive or supervisory boards that are subject to reporting, or on the identification of reports on securities on the internet.

StockPulse (www.stockpulse.de) is concerned with the analysis of digital social networks and is a navigator for financial markets that delivers real-time analyses on moods and trends on the stock market. StockPulse follows tweets and the posting of messages worldwide about the financial market and can thus provide trading ideas and signals. Inside analytics, on the other hand, uses the findings that can be attained from the trading behaviour of company insiders such as executive boards. They analyse this behaviour for the entire European market (Inside-analytics 2013). Yavalu (www.yavalu.com) conducts risk analysis for private investors and recommends investments in exchange traded funds (ETF). The investment solutions are analysed in the process. Justetf (www.justetf.com) is also aimed at internet-based asset management for private investors via ETF.

2.3.6 Brokerage and Securities Trading

Brokerage is the web-based trading of securities, raw materials and currencies. The main focus here can be on either cheap, internet-based trading or on the receipt of information about the strategies of successful traders. Zecco (www.zecco.com) is a California-based online trader that was founded as early as 2006. It is characterised by extremely cheap trading conditions and contains a social community platform for people who trade securities via this platform. Facebook users can use Zecco thanks to a cooperation with Trade King (Zecco 2013).

---

[7] The programme Netfolio has numerous functions with which portfolios can be managed, rated, calculated, compared and monitored. The modular structure of the software allows asset managers to carry out calculations and presentations of the portfolio in accordance with the individual wishes of their customers (Alphasys 2013).

Most newcomers offer social trading services. Social trading is a new possibility to access financial markets in a simple and cheap manner. In social trading, traders are connected to each other worldwide in a social network. This means that individual traders can benefit from the experience of other members and act jointly. Since the collective knowledge of the community is available to each trader, completely new possibilities emerge. Social trading or investing is also known as mirror trading. Among those active in the German-speaking area are: Ayondo (www.ayondo.com), Etoro (www.etoro.com/de), Twindepots (www.twindepots.de), Wikifolio (www.wikifolio.com), United Signals (www.united-signals.com) and Moneymeets (www.moneymeets.com). The basic principle of these platforms is similar. A trader opens a portfolio and his or her activities are visible to the users of the platform in question. If investors are convinced by the trader's strategy, they can invest their money with a broker in a manner that duplicates the trader's strategy. Other providers, such as Moneymeets, disclose their members' trading strategies, but other users are not obliged to adopt them. Here the focus is more on the exchange of information about the various investment strategies chosen. With United Signals, Etoro and Ayondo one can follow traders, but their identities are usually not disclosed. It is up to the investor to research which trader pursues the optimum risk-yield profile for his or her needs.

On many platforms it is also possible to duplicate certain portfolios without investing real money, and to follow these virtually to see how a real capital investment would have developed (see NZZ 24.12.2012 for an overview of mirror trading). Tracking communities often examine in retrospect how successful a stock recommendation was. Sharewise (www.sharewise.com) is such a stock community for investors, who can communicate there with other, like-minded investors and check who made correct prognoses in the past. This retrospective analysis of recommendations is claimed as an essential advantage of this community. The information is available free of charge. At the same time, Sharewise automatically checks all recommendations with the help of a professional ratings system and shows who the best investors are or who has managed to beat the benchmark index STOXX Europe 600 in the long term (Sharewise 2013).

Investory (www.investory.eu) acts in a similar manner to Sharewise and offers registered members an insight into the portfolios of successful independent traders, the ongoing monitoring of their own portfolio, a shares blog and other services connected to securities trading (Investory 2013). Waytrading (www.waytrading.de) is a free, interactive online site on which interested investors can exchange views and publish virtual investment decisions.

The American company Loyal3 (www.loyal3.com) goes a step further with its new service. It offers customers the chance to buy the shares of their favourite companies directly on Facebook. While in classic banks this would involve a comprehensive and time-consuming advisory documentation and annoying fees, Loyal3 offers easy-to-use purchase with only three clicks. And it is all completely free to the customer. Companies that wish to sell shares to their "fans" install the relevant app on their company website or Facebook page. Fans can then subscribe to the shares in batches from 10 US dollars per month. The advantage for the companies is not only the direct and cheap financing, but also the resulting strong customer loyalty. The customer who owns part of the company is usually a loyal customer who buys more and recommends the services of the company to others (Nextmind 2013). Friends of the customer see their activities on Facebook and become curious. By these means, friends also become new customers and part-owners of the company.

Some newcomers supplement social trading with gamification. Gamification is the use of game-like elements and processes in non-game contexts. Integrating game-like elements is intended to increase the motivation of the customer, who would otherwise have to conduct less challenging, too monotonous or too complex transactions.

2.4 Speed Matters: Innovation Competence

Along data management, another challenge is presented by generally much-reduced innovation cycles. The growing speed of innovation is in contrast to the more traditional and wait-and-see culture of banking. Banks must examine how they can increase their innovation speed. There are a number of possibilities available, from the implementation of their own spin-offs with a high degree of autonomy to the delegation of development tasks to external suppliers or with innovative partners in a network.

A large number of smaller companies demonstrate innovative ability, thus assailing a classic area of retail banking, traditional payment transactions. Quick and safe electronic and mobile payment methods, combined with eWallets and innovative tools for managing financial means, are changing the function and dominance of cash and credit cards.[8] Naturally one can argue that the margins in classic payment transactions are low, unless the customer is willing to pay for special services. Competitors like PayPal appear to demonstrate that e- and m-payment solutions can nevertheless be profitable. The loss of income from payment transactions is not the only risk for banks. Whoever loses payment transactions—and thus also the associated financial management of their customers—will no longer have any access to the growing and competitively decisive volume of data that is available for every customer. The possibilities for dealing with this will be presented in Part III: The path to a customer-centred banking architecture.

[8] When surveyed, 35 % of all consumers stated that they would like to use their mobile devices as eWallets (Kearney 2012).

2.5 Wrap Up: Game Changers

2.5.1 The Newcomers

This chapter was concerned with understanding how new competitors exploit thought traps in order to develop future-viable business models. The competitors include newcomers with and without banking licenses. What consequences does the market entry of this large number of new competitors have for the established banks?

Newcomers with a Banking License Essentially three types of new provides of bank services in the digital age were identified:

1. Direct banks offer classic bank services without branch operations.
2. Digital universal banks focus on the internet generation by rigorously using new communications channels and platforms.
3. Many internet and telecommunications providers (still) focus on payment transactions, as it allows the generation of "big data"—the perfectly tailored user profile of the customer with regard to financial transactions and consumer behaviour allows an equally well-tailored offer of financial services and solutions. An analogy here would be the predictive product suggestions introduced by Amazon, based on previous user behaviour. This illustrates clearly the potential effect of new technologies on the banking sector. Get ready now, but how?

Classic banks are being threatened by all three groups of competitors: the fact on the one hand is that the established direct banks already demonstrate much higher customer satisfaction. It is likely that the pull effect will lead to the customer basis of the traditional providers being hollowed out, so that the profit margins of the established business models will continue to decrease further.

A future threat, on the other hand, is presented by the options created for customers by the digital universal banks. Some providers—for example Fidor Bank—are already positioning themselves as a platform on which customers can advise themselves and invest directly, due to the rigorous use of modern forms of communication and a partial "withdrawal" from the role of mere platform provider for various financial transactions.

In addition, the "big data" strategies of Google and PayPal pose an extremely large threat, because these providers also hols banking licenses and can create perfectly tailored offers for individual financial needs in the coming years by the rigorous use of customer information and the payment, search and information behaviour of the customer. Banks find that they are confronted with the danger that they are being cut off increasingly from the data basis. To this day not all of the available data appears to be utilised to its full potential. The integration of the different sales channels and the associated information has not yet been fully achieved. It is very likely that a not inconsiderable number of customers would find this offer very attractive. In contrast to newly-founded digital universal banks that still need to build up their customer basis from the beginning, the internet concerns already have an abundance of customer information and a considerable user basis. It is therefore highly probable that they can achieve the necessary number to trigger a "critical mass effect", thus degrading classic banks to the role of a processor in the background, with no control over the customer interface. However: the reputation of banks, which is based on the factors trust, privacy protection and data security, can be a strong asset. The ability to guarantee data security possibly ensures a comparative competitive advantage and can be a successful business model.

> **Newcomers Without a Banking License** In future consultation situations in which standardised products form the core of the solution, customers can not only advise themselves, but can also complete the transaction online without requiring any advice from the bank. The entire sales process will become possible via the media, without the involvement of a personal advisor. Online forums or private advice from peers can help in the event of problems.

In the case of more complex advisory needs, PFMs will grow in significance in the area of pre-sales. Well-prepared and informed customers have existed for a long time, but this aspect takes on a whole new dimension with PFM, as customers can analyse in precise detail their own financial behaviour. This presents a great challenge to the expertise and the social and methodical competence of the present-day advisor. Personal information and decision-making systems help the customer to gain easily accessible external information that is relevant to their transactions. For the most part the information advantage and the associated power previously held by banks is being eroded. A new trend is to also use the knowledge and assessments of other customers (the wisdom of many) along with information from experts. The accumulation of information in customer groups can lead to joint decisions that are sometimes better than the approaches of individual customers or the bank. Virtual means of exchange do not in themselves pose a direct threat to classic banking services. However, should these parallel currencies ever establish themselves in the long terms as a means of payment, this could represent a new form of competition for banks from companies that manage such currencies. Internet companies in particular appear to be open to the creation of virtual currencies. If 1.1 billion Facebook (www.facebook.de) users were to start using their own currency, for example, this would become one of the most important currencies in the world, on an equal footing with the US dollar, Euro and yen.

There are two possible future scenarios as to how the further development pattern of business models in the banking sector might look with regard to competitors without a banking license, who cover only part of the value chain of the established banks.

One hypothesis is that the existing providers will integrate the USPs of those providers without a banking license into their own value chain as soon as a critical mass has been achieved in terms of demands from existing customers. Such a pattern has often been observed in the past. The integration is carried out either by buying up smaller competitors or by copying the relevant technologies.

The alternative hypothesis is that the competitors, who are strong in their niche services, will cause an erosion of the value chains of the banking services and will integrate customers by means of technological possibilities into the partial services of separate providers, in a kind of "plug and play" manner.

It can be seen from the example of consumer loans just how far the fragmentation of the value chain has already progressed and how individual service aspects can be taken on by providers unconnected to the sector. Market analysis can be conducted with the help of comparative portals. Here, the price and often—with the help of communities—also the quality and characteristics of loans offers are displayed. One the purchase decision has been made, an analysis of the financial means can be made using PFM—for example, the number of instalments to be financed for a required consumer loan. Then, via a credit platform, a finance request can be placed online. If the financing has been cleared, the purchased product can be ordered and paid for via the internet. The same is easily conceivable and achievable for the purchase of securities, including the accompanying investment advice, or for the financing of property purchases (Vater et al. 2012, p. 12).

2.5.2 Outlook: Are Game Changers Just a Hype?—Bank Management in the Digital Age

Just a decade ago, some exponents decried the significance of the digital age as pure hype after the bursting of the dotcom bubble (Spiegel 2013). Using the same logic, one could now also express the view that the new competitors are merely a brief occurrence. This assumption must be disproved and—if that succeeds—suitable analytical and design instruments must be developed.

The next chapter, therefore, will show the fundamental forces of change presented by digitalisation with regard to the business models of banks, as well as the instruments of successful bank management.

It will become clear that these developments demand a fundamental change in business models and that the willingness of classic banks to analyse the medium and long-term consequences and to make their business models network-compatible from the inside will be key to success in the coming years. It will not be possible to defend against future competitors by clinging on to old business models or by imitating the new rivals. Banking in the private sector requires a tailored, customer-centred business model.

References

Alphasys. (2013). *Alphasys—der Software-Partner für die Vermögensverwaltung*. Retrieved February 03, 2013, from http://alphasys.ch/presse.html

Auge-Dickhut, S., Hemmo, M., Koye, B., Sidler-Gisler, B., & Willimann, A. (2012). *Kundenorientierung in Banken*. Zürich: compendio Bildung.

Bankentest. (2013). *Bankentest*. Retrieved December 16, 2013, from http://www.bankentest.org/tester-Stiftung+Warentest+Finanztest.html

BillGuard. (2013). *Grey charges in America*. Retrieved January 16, 2013, from https://www.billguard.com/greycharges

Cash. (2013). *Wenn der Kunde die Bank nicht mehr braucht*. Retrieved December 17, 2013, from http://www.cash.ch/community/forum/politik-und-wirtschaft/wenn-der-kunde-die-bank-nicht-mehr-braucht

Der Handel. (2012, March 20). *Otto Group will PayPal Konkurrenz machen*. Retrieved July 13, 2013, from http://www.derhandel.de/news/technik/pages/M-Payment-Otto-Group-will-PayPal-Konkurrenz-machen-8368.html

Ernst & Young, University of St. Gallen. (2012). *Retail banking 2020*. Retrieved September 29, 2013, from www2.eycom.ch/publications/items/banking/2012_retail_banking_2020/2012_EY_Retail_Banking_2020_d.pdf

FAZ. (2010, December 6). *Siemens erhält seine eigene Banklizenz*. Retrieved September 23, 2013, from http://www.faz.net/frank-furter-allgemeine-zeitung/wirtschaft/siemens-erhaelt-seine-eigene-banklizenz-11078933.html

Fidor Bank. (2013). *Banking mit Freunden*. Retrieved December 4, 2013, from https://www.fidor.de/

Financial Post. (2013, May 3). *Rogers gets closer to starting banking business*. Retrieved July 13, 2013, from http://business.financialpost.com/2013/05/03/rogers-gets-closer-to-starting-banking-business/?__lsa=3fbe-e9df

Finews. (2012, July 19). *Facebook mutiert auch noch zur Bank*. Retrieved January 26, 2013, from http://www.finews.ch/news/banken/9046-facebook-commonwealth-bank-online-banking

Inside-analytics. (2013). *Providing the most accurate and fastest insider/director dealing data*. Retrieved February 3, 2013, from http://www.inside-analytics.com/

Insideparadeplatz. (2013). *Liebe Banken: Aufwachen*. Retrieved December 7, 2013, from http://insideparadeplatz.ch/2013/09/11/liebe-banken-aufwachen/

Investory. (2013). *Strategien von Profis*. Retrieved February 10, 2013, from https://investory.eu/investory/web/home.html

Juniper Research. (2011). *Mobile payment strategies—Opportunities & markets 2011–2015*. Retrieved June 27, 2013, from http://www.juniperresearch.com/reports/Mobile_Payment_Strategies

Kearney AT. (2012). *Inside tomorrow's retail bank*. Retrieved September 29, 2013, from https://www.atkearney.com/de/financial-institutions/ideas-insights/article/-/asset_publisher/LCcgOeS4t85g/content/inside-tomorrow-s-retail-bank/10192

King, B. (2010). *Bank 2.0: How customer behaviour and technology will change the future of financial services*. Singapore: Marshall Cavendish Business.

Meniga. (2013). *Warum PFM einsetzen?*. Retrieved February 12, 2013, from http://www.meniga.de/pfm-loesung/warum-pfm-einsetzen

Menn, A. (2011, July 14). *Warum Internetwährungen den Staat nervös machen*. Retrieved July 13, 2013, from http://www.wiwo.de/technologie/cyber-geld-warum-internetwaehrungen-staaten-nervoes-machen-sei-te-2/5155564-2.html

Moneyland. (2013). *Movenbank wird Bankenindustrie revolutionieren*. Retrieved December 17, 2013, from http://moneyland.ch/de/brett-king-movenbank

Nextmind. (2013). *Aktien kostenlos mit drei Klicks in Facebook kaufen*. Retrieved September 4, 2013, from http://www.nextmind.de/?p=1830

NZZ. (2012, December 24). *Mirror-trading geklonte performance*. Retrieved February 10, 2013, from http://www.nzz.ch/finanzen/uebersicht/private_finanzen/geklonte-performance-1.17901327

PostFinance. (2013). *E-Cockpit. Für den finanziellen Durchblick*. Retrieved July 13, 2013, from https://www.postfinance.ch/de/priv/prod/eserv/cockpit/offer.html

Presseportal. (2013). *200.000 registrierte Nutzer: Fidor Bank Community setzt Meilenstein*. Retrieved January 30, 2014, from http://www.presseportal.de/pm/64229/2567544/200-000-registrierte-nutzer-fidor-bank-community-setzt-meilenstein

Schonfeld, E. (1998, September 28). The customized, digitized, have-it-your-way economy: Mass customization will change the way products are made forever. *Fortune*, 115–116. Retrieved September 23, 2013, from http://money.cnn.com/magazines/fortune/fortune_archive/1998/09/28/248738/

Sharewise. (2013). *Ihre Vorteile*. Retrieved July 13, 2013, from http://www.de.sharewise.com/

Simple. (2013). *Welcome to better banking*. Retrieved December 17, 2013, from https://www.simple.com/#welcome

Spiegel. (2013). *Don't believe the hype!* Retrieved January 28, 2014, from http://www.spiegel.de/spiegel/print/d-16525474.html.

Stocktouch. (2013). *Homepage*. Retrieved January 03, 2013, from http://stocktouch.com/

Stöcker, C. (2011, May 31). *Hacker-Währung Bitcoin: Geld aus der Steckdose*. Retrieved July 13, 2013, from http://www.spiegel.de/netzwelt/netzpolitik/hacker-waehrung-bitcoin-geld-aus-der-steckdose-a-765382.html

Tagesanzeiger. (2013). *Facebook testet Bezahlsystem*. Retrieved December 17, 2013, from http://www.tagesanzeiger.ch/digital/internet/Facebook-testet-Bezahlsystem-/story/31249460

Tipps. (2013). *NFC—Mit dem Smartphone bezahlen*. Retrieved July 13, 2013, from http://www.tipps.net/nfc-mit-dem-smartphone-bezahlen.html

Vater, D., Cho Y., & Sidebottom, P. (2012). *Bain brief: Retail-banking: Die digitale Herausforderung*. Retrieved September 28, 2013, from http://www.bain.de/publikationen/articles/the-digital-challenge-to-retail-banks.aspx

Zecco. (2013). *Welcome to the new tradeking*. Retrieved July 13, 2013 https://www.zecco.com/

Zopa. (2013). *Peer-to-peer lending: How Zopa works*. Retrieved July 13, 2013, from http://www.zopa.com/about-zopa/peer-to-peer-lending

Part II

From Classic Business Models to a Customer-Centred Banking Architecture

3 What Now for Banks?

In the previous section the thought traps of the classic understanding of banking services were discussed. The USPs of innovative providers of financial services in the digital age were also made clear. It is therefore high time for banks that have been successful until now to ask themselves how their business models can be transformed in the future. Are the existing business models still suitable? What instruments can banks use in order to successfully manage the metamorphosis of their business models?

First of all, the framework for the necessary changes must be built. Therefore we shall address the impact of the information or network age—as the key trigger of the pressure to transform. While Part I focussed on current trends, it will be now be shown—following on from that—that the current developments are not merely "hype", but instead that much more profound forces of change are at work. In the foreground is no longer the question of "whether", but of "how" individual banks can shape this change. The central architectural framework elements for present-day business models will be explained. This includes an examination of the concepts of "bank" and "financial intermediation", as well as essential framework conditions under which previous business models have developed.

The key question then is how the business models can be transformed in such a manner that a bank's right to exist is confirmed—also by the markets—by the satisfaction of effective customer needs with attractive price/performance configurations, thus leading to a win-win situation: satisfied customer needs and successful banking in the digital age. The necessary management "tools" will be presented, at first prior to the information/network age and then with the necessary modifications for the digital age. Following an overall overview of the spectrum of the "toolbox" for shaping business models, the individual components—strategy, structure and culture, as well as the business models as a combination—will be presented.

S. Auge-Dickhut et al., *Customer Value Generation in Banking*, Management for Professionals, DOI 10.1007/978-3-319-19938-2_3

It will become clear that there will be winners and losers and that the line of separation in the next few years will run along the innovative power of individual banks. The findings of this section will form the conceptual "toolbox" for the transformation of banks and for the development of future-viable business models.

4 Change Frameworks

Whoever wishes or needs to change must fully understand the levers of the reality to be changed in order to be able to make precise corrections. In this chapter, therefore, we shall examine the framework conditions of banks' present-day business models.

Starting from the findings of the previous chapters, it is first essential to understand the digital age in its key aspects as a trigger of change—only by doing so can the willingness to take the necessary steps arise (see Sect. 4.1).

Following on from that, the fundamental "levers" of banks' present-day business models will be outlined briefly. For the management of the banks these are the factors against which their success to date has been assessed and towards which they have been and continue to be oriented—and it is therefore important for successful change to once again call these to mind (see Sect. 4.2).

The chapter ends with the outlining of the fundamental factual and technical levers of financial services—since these are being challenged by the innovations of the digital age, respectively it is here that the innovations that challenge previous business models in the long run are manifested (see Sect. 4.3).

4.1 The Digital Age

4.1.1 Patterns of Change Processes

Nothing is as constant as change. Change accompanies the life cycles of individuals and organisations. In retrospect, however, the reasons why change processes were triggered can be understood logically. That which appears to us today as new and stimulating is soon integrated into our individual world view after a phase of adaptation and usually without any cognitive effort. At the levels of the individual, a subsequent behavioural adjustment is usually possible without any severe consequences.

S. Auge-Dickhut et al., *Customer Value Generation in Banking*, Management for Professionals, DOI 10.1007/978-3-319-19938-2_4

At the corporate level, on the other hand, failure to set the right course can threaten the very existence of a company. The fundamental question is how banks can adapt to a changing environment if they have only limited advance knowledge about the changes ahead. During the industrial era we have repeatedly observed the phenomenon that the decision-makers of large and successful companies could not master substantial changes, despite their expertise and the intensive analysis of development trends (Christensen and Overdorf 2000). Thus in order to define the successful change strategy for one's own bank, understanding the patterns can help in managing change and innovation processes.

Empirical studies show that most economic growth at every stage of development has been the result of technological innovations (Solow 1957). Kondratieff found in 1926 that economic development occurs in cycles. These economic cycles encompass not only the short and medium term, but also the long term, lasting between 40 and 60 years. He identified three such long cycles since the beginning of the nineteenth century (Kondratieff 1926). The Kondratieff cycles show how the sequence of innovation cycles developed in an S-shaped manner. The basic revolutionary innovations that formed the basis of cycles one to four were the steam engine and cotton wool production, steel and the railways, electrical technology and chemistry, as well as the automobile and petrochemicals.

In the fifth Kondratieff cycle, information and knowledge play the decisive role as a foundation for growth for the first time.[1] These immaterial raw materials, which have guided the economy onto new paths of growth, lead constantly to new applications of the basic innovation, information technology. Thus the energy-driven structural change has been replaced by an information-driven structural change. This has wide-ranging consequences for all information intermediaries—and therefore also for banks, as financial information intermediaries. That is the deeper significance of the digital age and the answer to the question of its importance (Fig. 4.1).

4.1.2 Levers of the Digital Age

The fundamental paradigmatic change from the industrial to the digital age (Koye 2005, S. 5 ff.) has placed great long-term pressure on the successful position of many industries, including banks, and at the same time, while at the same time presenting opportunities to develop new potential.

The transformation process began at the beginning of the 1990s—with the attainment of the critical mass of users of the internet (Koye 2005, p. 13 ff.)—

[1] The sixth Kondratieff cycle has begun in parallel with the intensification of the fifth. An empirical analysis has shown that health, in the holistic sense of the bearer, will be the next long cycle. The main bearers of the sixth Kondratieff are psychosocial health and biotechnology (on the further developments of the Kondratieff cycles see Kondratieff 2013).

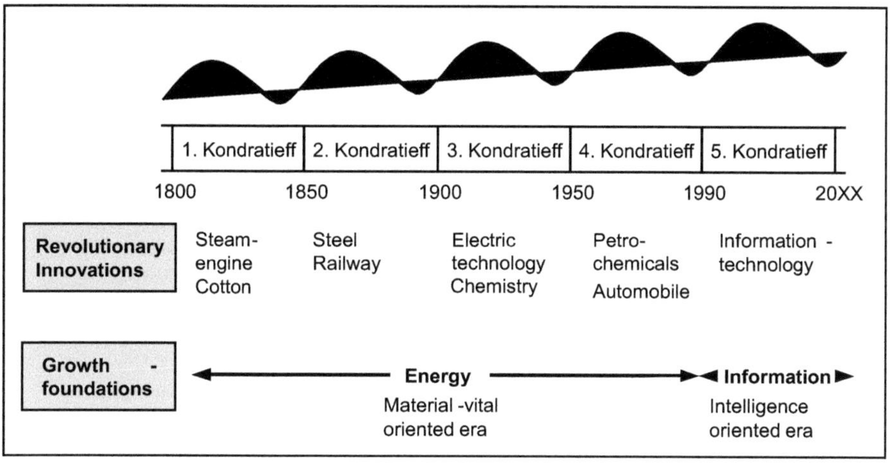

Fig. 4.1 Kondratieff cycles (*Source* Koye 2005, p. 24)

and has now reached the concepts of Web 2.0 and Web 3.0.[2] The internet has not only made it possible to present comprehensive information to a wide audience simultaneously, but also to link users to each other with their respective communication needs. During the industrial age it was possible only to reach a broad public with one general message—for example through television advertising—or else only to reach a limited public with deeper information—such as in a telephone conversation, a letter or a meeting. The internet suspends the previous limits on information and at the same time enables all connected users to have access to the same comprehensive information at the same time, to communicate, and furthermore to follow new paths in analysing digital user behaviour (digital footprint). The information advantage held by previous information intermediaries—such as banks—is being eroded (Evans and Wurster 1998, p. 52).

In the digital age the competitive advantage gained through technological advances erodes within months. On the other hand, customers expect their providers to adopt current technological innovations immediately.

Therefore, technology-based competitive differentiation is hardly possible anymore. This dynamic enables the customer step-by-step to achieve access to and feedback from information about the entire spectrum of offers in real time. The consequences, respectively challenges, are expectations of better service, greater price transparency and lower prices. The benefit, from the customer's point of view,

[2] The term Web 2.0 describes the altered use of the internet and emerged with the strong growth of community sites at the middle of the last decade. Web 2.0 offers not only the mere dissemination of information or product sales, but also enables the participation of the user, which leads to the generation of additional benefits (Gabler Wirtschaftslexikon 2013). Web 3.0 is based on the semantic web. The information on the internet can be ascribed with clear meanings, which allows the mechanical processing of the information gathered on the internet, leading to more efficient search engines and the generation of new web services (Wikipedia 2013; Swisscom 2013).

	Industrial Economy	Information Society
	Hierarchy	**Network**
Hierarchical levels	Many	Few
Employee makeup	Interchangeable, obedient, conformist	Committed, loyal ,informed, independent
Networking	Low	High
Work processes	Strictly regulated, rigid responsibilities	Flexible, ad hoc, short-term project organisation
Influence and power	Dependent on hierarchical level	Depending on knowledge and skills
Extend of Participation	Low	Large
Organisational orientation	Business management	Own interest, company and community
Most important goal	Output maximisation	Benefit optimisation

Fig. 4.2 Company structures in the industrial and information society (*Source* Nefiodow 1999, p. 2)

decides the success rate of each individual bank. Forms of management and cooperation are becoming more vertical; speed and prototyping are increasingly decisive success factors. Figure 4.2 shows a comparison of the most important aspects of the industrial and information society with regard to organisations:

In the industrial age, the most prevalent form of organisation was a hierarchical division of labour with little interlinking. The distribution of power and influence, as well as the work processes, were clearly regulated. In the digital age, the previous hierarchy is being replaced by networked forms of organisation in which the individual members complete their partial processes for the most part independently, and contribute these to the network—thus enabling more efficient price/performance configurations. Increasingly, knowledge and ability are decisive when it comes to influence and power. Previous positions of success are being replaced to the same degree as the previous structures for providing the price/performance configuration.

While it remains the case in the digital age that effective delivery is absolutely necessary, the entire value chain for information-based products can be processed electronically. Furthermore, customers inform themselves thoroughly online and question the price/performance configurations of providers very closely. The possibilities provided by information technology mean that customers are exerting an ever more active influence and pay only for those services that can give them an added value that they cannot themselves provide. A veritable "collapse in time and distance" is taking place (Geiger 1999, p. 1). Information technology is the cause of this collapse—it has become the key design factor for business models.

Thus network systems are replacing top-down hierarchies. They are referred to as critical mass systems, because they prevail in the market only when they have attained a certain number of users (Weiber 1992, p. 19). Three effects are connected to the critical mass systems (Koye 2005, p. 35):

1. Benefit of the installed basis: the number of persons connected to the network is known as the installed basis. The benefit to each participant and the willingness to adapt on the part of customers grows in line with the size of the installed basis. Examples include Facebook or Twitter as social media applications, which become more interesting for each individual user, the more users there are overall.
2. Juncture of diffusion development: if the installed basis is too small, the system is threatened with failure due to lack of interaction. If a minimum number is reached, however, it is likely that the system will continue to be used, thus securing long-term market success. Attaining the critical mass becomes the so-called juncture of diffusion development. Until the critical mass is achieved the system goes through an unstable phase, with the danger of an absence of market success. Once critical mass has been reached, on the other hand, the installed basis has a diffusion-promoting influence, leading to a phase of stability with probable market success. This influence is also known as positive feedback (Shapiro and Varian 1999).
3. Positive and negative feedback: Critical mass systems are shaped additionally by the expectations of the users, which lead to feedback. The more positive the expectation of a potential customer with regard to the willingness of other potential customers to participate in the installed basis, the more likely it is that he or she will also be willing to join. Thus the installed basis plays an important role in his or her decision. At the beginning of the diffusion, therefore, more negative feedback is to be expected, becoming more exponentially positive with progressive development. After reaching the critical mass, this inherent self-reinforcing process eases a chain reaction with very likely market success (Weiber 1992).

Sooner or later all sectors—thus also banking—must address these developments as the basis of future-viable business models.

4.1.3 Reaction Patterns

Political, social and economic systems react to innovations with varying adjustment speeds (Fig. 4.3).

Technology is the trigger of change. Purely technological further development requires "only" intellectual development input. No human-emotional hurdles must be overcome, as is the case subsequent to the spread of innovation. Younger people are generally more open to technology than older generations, so that the adjustment of the social systems takes place with a time delay. At the aggregated level of economic and political systems, there tends to be even more of a time lag in adjustment because in democratic societies the process of opinion-making at an individual level follows acceptance of new developments at the political level (as in democratic societies, the acceptance of new developments at the political level is

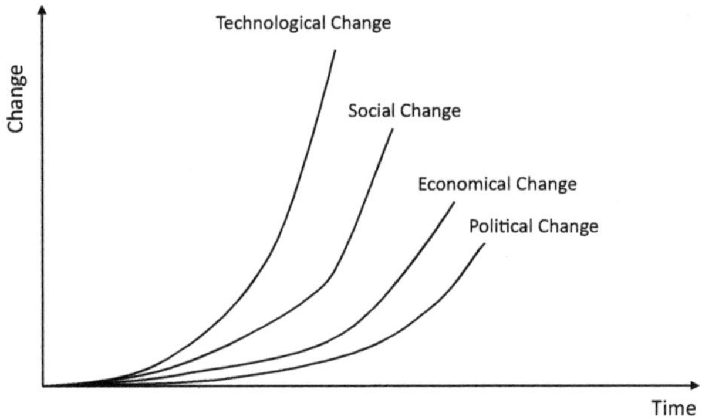

Fig. 4.3 Adjustment speeds of different systems in the digital age (*Source* Koye 2005, p. 116)

preceded by the opinion-making process at a personal level). That takes some time, because economic systems are oriented towards the predominant customer needs.

This transformation leads to the gradual erosion of existing positions of success, as informed customers increasingly begin to question the margins and added value of purely brokering services, and become gradually more open to new business models without brokerage fees. Price/performance configurations come under pressure as a result, making structural changes necessary. Only networked organisational forms in which individual members complete their partial processes independently and make them available to the network, can face these developments with continued competitive price/performance configurations, for if every provider were to continue providing partial processes alone, he or she cannot offer a competitive price/performance configuration on the market. Banks must direct their attention to this feature, for the question of the gradual change in customer needs among different age groups is key to the successful reorientation of banks' business models.

Schumpeter observed innovations from the process perspective: for him, the "process of creative destruction" (Schumpeter 1942) was the switch between static and dynamic phases. He regarded economic evolution as a disruption of a static state of equilibrium, which could, through destruction—i.e., innovation—cause a reaction towards a new state of equilibrium (Schumpeter 1911). He expanded on Kondratieff's research and saw innovation as the cause of longer economic cycles (Schumpeter 1961)—and called them Kondratieff cycles.

Nefiodow calls innovations that trigger a new Kondratieff cycle, thus assuming the function of a locomotive for the entire economy for many decades, revolutionary basic innovations.

- They are deemed revolutionary because entail a network of technological and economic innovations and change in the long term the business foundations of entire sectors.
- They are regarded as basic innovations because they are based on a fundamentally new technological development. Established companies can survive only if they introduce the necessary transformation processes at the right time.

Building on the findings of Kondratieff and Schumpeter, Nefiodow summarised three conditions for revolutionary basic innovations (Nefiodow 1999):

- At the technological level, the direction and speed of the innovation process are determined by innovation.
- At the economic level, the entire economic growth during an upturn phase is borne considerably by innovation.
- At the social level, wide-ranging reorganisation is triggered.

The digital age quite clearly has this character—we only need to think of the emergence of e-mail, mobile phones, the iPhone or the establishment of business models such as Google. The challenge is that there are actually three different groups of customers whose behaviour influences the balance between the old and the new business model—the traditional consumer, the digital convert and the digital native. The intersections of the three curves are important elements for changing the current business models of banks. Accordingly, from 2020 the majority of customers of bank services will be composed of digital natives (Fig. 4.4).

Industrial development therefore occurred in thrusts of innovation. Phases of substantial new developments with "disruptive technologies" alternated in the long term with phases of the improved efficiency of the existing standards (sustaining technologies) of basic innovations, which could slowly be perfected while maintaining current business models. A distinction is made, therefore, between sustaining and disruptive technological developments. Sustaining developments refer to the operative further development of existing applications. Disruptive technological developments redefine the status quo of all market participants and create new applications (Christensen 1997). The response profiles of established companies can exhibit both sustaining and disruptive technological developments.

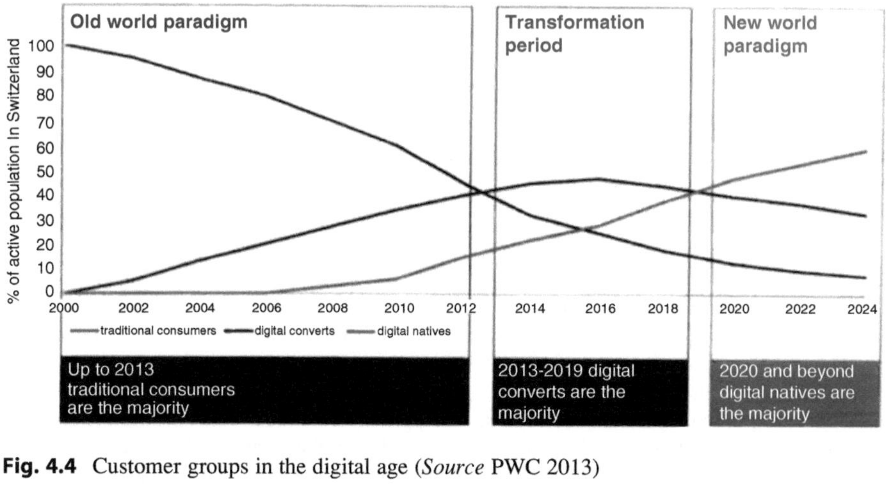

Fig. 4.4 Customer groups in the digital age (*Source* PWC 2013)

The following phases are distinguished:

- In the development phase, new applications are created on the basis of revolutionary technological developments, which lead to further new product innovations.
- In the transitional phase, progressive standardisation allows increased concentration on product improvements. The product innovation rate sinks with a growing process innovation rate. Product variety declines. Dominant product types evolve.[3]
- In the specialisation phase the innovation rates of both products and processes decline. Management focus is placed on cost reduction, productivity improvement and capacity utilisation.

According to the evolutionary theory of institutional survival, the most efficient company in each phase will prevail on the market during that respective phase; the less efficient companies will be pushed successively out of the market. Efficiency in the economic system can be explained by technological advances, as being a result of dismantling behavioural constraints (e.g., deregulation) or by increasing competitive pressure. Specifically this means the elimination of too high margins and profits, from an efficiency perspective, due to the intermediation systems—customers are optimally informed, can compare services, and thus pay the economically justifiable price for the effective provision of the service, without additional premiums due to a lack of information (North 1990; Bisignano 1998).

If we view innovation processes from a product perspective, it becomes clear that in the case of increasing revenues it is not the best technology that wins through on the market, but rather a quickly developed solution that creates path dependency.[4] Solutions that are technologically perfect but have been developed later can no longer prevail. The speed of innovation development and the implementation of the innovation in concrete products are key to the successful evolution of technological developments and institutions (Arthur 1990).

In the process, the substantial new developments are often devised by market entrants who have no existing product or process infrastructure. Frequently the fundamental significance of a disrupting technological development—one speaks

[3] Utterback speaks of "dominant design", meaning "*the design that wins the allegiance of the marketplace, the one that competitors and innovators must adhere to if they hope to command significant market following*". Utterback (1994, p. 24).

[4] An example of path dependency is the IT equipment of large companies. If the entire company uses Microsoft products, a change of system to Apple involves much time, effort, and expense, even if the quality of the Apple products is often better that that of Microsoft. The initial fundamental decision to install the Microsoft Windows system led to the path dependency of the company in later years.

of a "killer application" (Downes and Mui 1998, p. 4)[5]—is not apparent to established market participants at the time of development,[6] as is the case today in banking.

The main reason for the disappearance of companies is that they cling to their strategy of gradually improving existing products or processes. Such an improvement to the efficiency and quality of existing products to maintain attractiveness and extend life cycles is known as a "burst of improvement". The motivation for this behaviour has been identified as the economic and emotional bond (Utterback 1994) that arises from investments that have already been made in the existing production plants and processes.

In addition, there can be resistance from employees who regard the withdrawal of resources from previously successful activities or areas as unnecessary. Change potential is also often blighted by the fact that management objectives tend to concentrate on maintaining the existing success position (Christensen 1997). Culturally, the foundation of a new, separate unit is often seen as the best possible organisational option (Foster 1986). But even then conflicts can arise between organisational units, with the withholding of important information or the refusal of support or the sharing of experiences. Frequently, change processes are not addressed, or much too late (Utterback 1994). Yet the new applications are superior to the services based on the old technology, at least in the medium term. Established companies therefore have two main obstacles to managing these revolutionary changes (Koye 2005):

- Awareness of the threat to the company's existence posed by the revolutionary applications and awareness of the company's vulnerability due to its own reactive behavioural pattern.
- Willingness to implement operatively the necessary organisational adjustments to the new application.

Information-based business models experience a permanent process of evolution: the introduction to market is the beginning of a process of continuous adaptation to further technological developments. "Thinking in versions" has become established: the first version of a business model addresses only the early adapter customer group. A wider customer group is attracted later by further developments. The learning process of the provider is accompanied by a parallel learning process on the part of the customer (Brynjolfsson and Hitt 1998). Providers with a first-mover strategy are not automatically successful (Arthur 1994). In early innovation

[5] At first, the PC was underestimated by all makers of mainframes. They did not believe that existing customers would be interested in these devices. That was true, but a much larger market emerged with new customer segments, which was occupied by new manufacturers.

[6] When the PC was invented, not many market participants realised just how revolutionary the changes to the working environment would be. The mainframe computer industry, which dominated at the time, was completely obliterated. Only IBM managed to adapt to the PC age (Downes and Mui 1998).

phases, competitors develop different product types before a dominant product type emerges (Utterback and Abernathy 1978). Once a critical number of users has been reached, a self-reinforcing process begins. Only then do economic rewards emerge as a result of the positive feedback and the so-called superstar effect—according to which the three most dominant business models in the digital age attain a disproportionately large share of the turnover pie (Shapiro and Varian 1999).

Due to self-reinforcing network effects, economies of scale experienced by providers due to mass customisation, the ever better informed customer—who is less willing to pay for mere intermediation but instead expects truly needs-oriented advice at very competitive prices—and the sinking costs for customers of switching, oligopolistic sector structures are likely to occur in the network economy, in which only a few information-based products, business models and providers will manage to establish themselves.

4.2 The Banks' Right to Exist: The "WHAT"

The purpose of companies—and thus also of banks—in a capitalistic economic system is to provide market-appropriate services—the "what"—in the chosen business fields. Services are market-appropriate when customer benefit is created by satisfying customer needs with products or services of an expected quality at competitive prices and at the desired time, to an extent that customers are willing to purchase those products and services. Market economy systems are controlled by prices, which in turn are determined by supply and demand. Companies that do not offer a marketable range of services have no right to exist. It has been proven empirically that the orientation of core competencies towards the changes of the digital age is the key factor for the competitiveness of companies and banks (Koye 2005).

4.3 Organisational and Coordination Forms of Service Provision: The "HOW"

As well as the "what"—the marketable provision of services—companies are also faced with the question of "how"—i.e., the execution of the individual activities required for bank services. Positioning the activities and the costs of each single activity also determines the price/performance ratio of the service being provided—an essential element of the competitiveness of banks in competitive markets.

In principle, the question is which configuration of individual steps in providing a service allows the optimum price/performance mix. The important factor is deciding which share of performance provision a company wishes to provide itself—because it attains a very good price/performance quality or the step is seen as strategically important—while others provide better quality and/or lower prices for these partial performances. As long as the provision of a partial performance can be done at a lower price or with better quality within the company, then it will be provided within the company—otherwise it can be outsourced.

In the information/network age, this relationship has shifted dramatically. Therefore it is worthwhile presenting the conceptual foundations of this development, in order then to be able to derive the right conclusions for one's own bank.

The optimum design of business models is a subject that has preoccupied the field of organisational theory for a long time. Coase (1937) posed the question as to why companies exist at all, and why everything isn't always processed afresh via the market. He formulated his reply in terms of economic transaction costs theory, which is concerned with the regulation of the exchange of goods and services between suppliers and demanders. The use of resources must be coordinated in a collaborative economy, and this leads to transaction costs. Where there is equally large benefit from a variety of work stages, the cheaper version is chosen (Picot 1991).

The examination unit of transaction costs theory is the individual transaction or activity by a company to provide a service. In detail, transactions costs represent the costs of information and communication related to the initiation, agreement, processing, control and adjustment of an exchange of performances. They are the efficiency standard for evaluating and selecting different institutional agreements. Coase (1937) identified two coordination alternatives, market[7] and hierarchy.[8] Conducting a transaction within the company makes sense as long as its marginal costs correspond with the market price. The transaction price is the key criterion. Transaction costs are "the operational costs of an economic system" (Arrow 1969, p. 48). They justify the existence of companies and the internal execution of all necessary partial steps to provide a service. Hierarchical organisational forms often have lower transaction costs than market organisational forms. Figure 4.5 shows both extreme coordination alternatives, market and hierarchy, as well as the transaction costs as a decision-making criterion.

Market Transaction Costs are the costs of using the market mechanism to conduct the economic exchange of services. Specifically, they refer to information and contract costs[9]:

---

[7] *"In the extreme manifestation of market coordination, all transactions in an economic system between individuals are processed on the basis of individual contractual rules; no multi-person economic units participate in the transaction process."* (Freese 1993, p. 203).

[8] *"If companies are founded, then transactions are removed from the market and processed in companies. [...] Outside of companies, price movements control production; it is determined by a series of exchange transactions on the market. Within companies the market transactions are suspended and complicated market transactions with exchange transactions are replaced by coordination by the company owner, who controls production."* (Freese 1993, p. 204).

[9] Coase (1960, p. 15) describes market transaction costs as follows: *"In order to conduct a market transaction, one must find out with whom one wishes to transact; inform people that one wishes to transact with them, and under which conditions; conduct negotiations that will lead to a conclusion; draw up the contract; install the requisite controls to ensure that the contractual conditions will be observed."* Somewhat deviating, but substantially similar categorisations can be found, for example, in Freixas and Rochet (1998), Fuchs (1994) and Picot (1991).

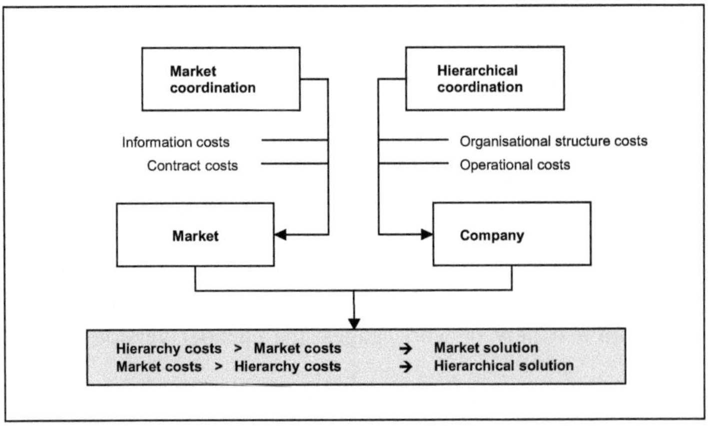

Fig. 4.5 Coordination forms of economic exchange relationships (*Source* Koye 2005, p. 121)

- **Information costs** arise in the context of seeking and selecting contractual partners, the communication and search costs of gaining information about available providers and price structures, and the expense of acquiring information about specific partners (Stigler 1961; Hirshleifer 1973; Hirshleifer and Riley 1979).[10]
- **Contract costs** comprise negotiation and decision costs. The influencing factors are the time until the decision is made, the preparation of information[11] and legal advice (Richter and Furubotn 1999)

Added to these are the possible costs of monitoring and asserting delivery deadlines, quantity and quality control, as well as collection, operational and bankruptcy costs. Theoretically, additional opportunity costs can arise from the difference between theoretically the best available offer on the market and the one that has been effectively chosen (Cocca et al. 2001).

Hierarchical Transaction Costs are generated by the fulfilment of longer-term contracts within existing organisations:

- **Organisational structure costs** are the costs of establishing, maintaining and adapting the organisational costs, and are thus usually fixed costs.
- **Operating costs** are the costs for decision-making processes, performance measurement, business management and instruction monitoring, as well as

[10] In the service provision sector, the search for suitable employees, for example, is a complicated process (Richter and Furubotn 1999).

[11] Kreps (1999) notes that inefficient results can arise from information asymmetries (if one partner has more, perhaps private information).

physical company services. These are usually variable costs (Williamson 1990; Richter and Furubotn 1999) (Fig. 4.5).[12]

The digital age is now transforming these transaction costs heavily in favour of the attractiveness and necessity of market forms of organisation, as search and information costs have decreased sustainably, the margins of existing business models are declining steadily, and the organisational structure costs of existing hierarchical systems are too high—this is the scientific basic of all business-related discussions relating to the industrialisation of the banking sector. It is no longer a question of whether, but rather of how the transformation of business models should be shaped in the digital age.

4.4 Shareholder Value as a Central Control Concept

The business models of banks therefore have a right to exist only if they meet customer needs (the WHAT), and do so with the price/performance ratio that customers also consider to be attractive (the HOW). The third essential framework element in designing a bank's business model is the question as to how companies can measure their success in fulfilling the first two aspects.

Against the background of the development—since the 1980s—of dynamic methods for calculating company value, the principle of shareholder values, defined by Alfred Rappaport, has established itself as the central measuring parameter for the performance of management based on the generation of added financial value (Rappaport and Klien 1998). According to this principle, the objective is to maximise the value of the company for shareholders.[13] The market value of equity can be calculated using the DCF (discounted cash flow) method or, in the case of listed companies, by deriving the company value[14] from the stock market capitalisation. Departmental, team and individual employee goals in publicly listed banks are derived from the superordinate profitability target and are decisive in evaluating performance, granting bonus payments, and reaching career targets (Volkart 2006).

In recent years there has been increasing criticism of this concept of success, calculated purely using financial criteria, with high profitability targets[15] and correspondingly high bonus payments to management. One main objective of economies is to safeguard the optimised cycles of goods, services and finance:

[12] These costs will also be addressed in detail in the context of the process costs analysis.

[13] In the 1980s (equity) capital was a scarce commodity and therefore the focus was placed on shareholders' profitability, which had been somewhat neglected in previous years.

[14] The total capital value from DCF minus the market value of the borrowed capital produces the market value of equity.

[15] 25 % equity profitability was an established measured and target value prior to the outbreak of the financial crisis in 2008.

this leads to criticism of the work carried out by management in publicly-listed companies and banks, whose success is measured primarily according to short-term profit targets. Such an approach unilaterally prioritises the interests of the investors, neglecting those of other claimants and target levels (ecological, social, ethical and socio-political)[16]—this discussion is essential to the transformation of present-day business models.

4.5 Financial Intermediation, Banks and Financial Services

This section will describe the economic function of banks, their commercial business areas, and the concept of financial services.

4.5.1 Economic Functions of Banks

A bank can only become and remain successful if the financial services it offers satisfy a customer need so much that the price/performance configuration on offer will also be purchased effectively. So what are the fundamental customer needs with regard to financial services?

From an economic perspective, a functioning money-and-goods exchange system is a decisive competitive factor and thus an essential means for optimising the wealth of all citizens. A successful financial intermediation system achieves optimum capital allocation between all economic agents, at lower transaction costs and with fewer risks in comparison with other financial intermediation systems. Financial intermediaries fulfil five key functions, from an economic point of view (Bernet 2004, p. 8 ff.):

- Transfer function: safeguarding of efficient payment transactions
- Transformation function: period, lot size and life cycle transformation of money flows (saving, investing, financing)
- Risk balancing function: risk management to reduce uncertainty—as an intermediary between providers and receivers of savings, investment, financing and transfer services of money flows
- Logistics and service function: efficient processing mechanisms for financial exchanges
- Information function: preparation and provision of financial information of all kinds for all participants in the financial market.

Banks are financial intermediaries that make a key contribution to fulfilling the above functions. In accordance with the German Banking Act (KWG), a company

[16] On the discussion in Switzerland, which also includes Germany, see also Handelszeitung (2013).

is considered to be a credit institute if it conducts bank transactions commercially or in a manner demanded by a commercially-oriented business. According to Swiss legal practice, this includes for example the commercial acceptance of public deposits and the public recommendation to provide finance; large-scale refinancing of third-party companies or persons, as well as offering to acquire securities and providing services in the primary market (Bernet 2003, p. 25).

4.5.2 Commercial Business Management Areas of Banks

The specific business fields of banks can be categorised as follows (Bernet 2003, p. 29):

- Retail banking: retail and private banking as investment advice, depending on the amount of assets
- Asset management: the management of significant sums of assets belonging to private or institutional customers in different asset categories
- Financing business: financing private or corporate customers by means of mortgages or loans, sometimes also called commercial banking
- Investment banking: support for companies in raising capital and IPOs, and the trading of securities on financial markets with large sums

4.5.3 The Concept of Financial Services

Services are generally independent, marketable and immaterial benefits that are made available by a provider (Bruhn and Meffert 1995, p. 27, other definition approaches Hotz-Hart et al. 2001; Büschgen 1994; Süchting 1991; Corsten 1990). In contrast to real goods, services cannot be stored. They become obsolete if they are not used within the time period in which they are available. The result of a service process, on the other hand, can be storable.

Thus, an asset manager can give advice only during office hours, otherwise it is forfeited. However the financial products purchased on his or her recommendation can be stored in a depot for an unlimited period (Bruhn and Meffert 1995; Büschgen 1991; Corsten 1990). Financial services are marketable, intangible benefits that are easy and quick to imitate. Their development time is relatively brief, and they can be "protected legally against imitation only in exceptional cases" (Bächtold 2003, p. 24). They do not emerge per se, but rather are linked directly to the need for a certain good, and are therefore a means to an end. For instance, loan financing becomes necessary upon the realisation of the desire for property (Büschgen 1998, p. 19).

The lack of shelf life that is mentioned in terms of services in general also applies to financial services. The capacities required vary considerably over time. While certain cycles can be observed, customer demand often cannot be planned. Reacting flexibly to the demand for financial services can present a problem to providers: shortfalls can lead to the loss of potential customers to the competition, while overcapacity can cause an increase in fixed costs. Therefore, overcoming the restricted storage and transport capability is a key objective of the financial service provider (Kotler and Bliemel 1992, p. 667).

The distinction between standardisable and non-standardisable financial services is important to the extent that they determine the scope of consulting requirements. Standardised financial products—such as payment transactions—can be marketed relatively easily as a mass product with a high degree of homogeneity. Retail banking services, on the other hand, are very heterogeneous—due to the customers' intensive need for advice and integration—and could barely be standardised prior to the digital age. Here, not only the needs of customers determine the results of the process, but also the experience and education of the advisor (Zöllner 1995, p. 38). The complexity and degree of abstraction of consultation-intensive financial services entail a significant amount of explanation. Because of its immateriality, it is difficult for customers to make a quality assessment of a service prior to its purchase. These factors make financial services trust-based goods or "credence qualities" (Platzek 1996, p. 10).[17]

Due to the large share of consultation and the great significance of the trust component, human capital—i.e., the competence of the advisor—plays a key role (Büschgen 1994, p. 19). From banks' own perspective, and based on these characteristics, the strategies of financial service providers are focussing increasingly on developing a positive image and a good relationship of trust between customers and institutions (Kotler and Bliemel 1992, p. 664), as customers usually do not—or did not—have the same degree of knowledge as their advisor.

Theoretically, information-based services have an unlimited life span, as the information is not used up by consumption. The time value of the information, on the other hand, is indeed limited. A rapid loss in value often occurs as soon as the novelty of the information creates the added value. Share prices, for example, can become immediately valuable due to fast communication. Over time, however, additional information, such as the overall market development, becomes more important. Conclusion: the value depends first on the speed, and later on the comprehensiveness of the information (Whinston et al. 1997).

Information items are intangible in nature, so that there are hardly any storage problems, and the physical storage site is technologically insignificant as long as access is secured. The items can be used by a number of people simultaneously. There is no competition in terms of direct use (Cohen et al. 2000).[18] Different consumers can derive a different benefit at different times from the same

[17] In addition to these there are "search qualities", which can be assessed analytically prior to the conclusion of a transaction, and "experience qualities", which can be assessed after the conclusion of a transaction (Bruhn 1997; Bruhn and Meffert 1995).

[18] Thus many users can read the online version of a daily newspaper at the same time. The freedom of financial products from competition is limited, however. The danger of insider trading and the delayed forwarding of information are just two examples of possible conflicts of interest when it comes to financial products.

information. The possibility to exclude third parties from using the ideas contained in the information is limited. A monopoly position can be maintained through patent and copyright protection, but only for a certain time period. The ability to separate the idea from the protected information item[19] means that information can be replicated at low cost (Arrow 1962).

Prior to the beginning of the digital age, the cost of switching between information-based products was high due to the amount of learning and familiarisation that was involved. These days, systems are user-friendly, and at the same time quality can be better assessed by reading the opinions of other users online. The new media have expanded people's horizon of activity, enabling social and economic contacts with ever fewer limitations to time or space. This should be considered when designing a service.

Despite their growing knowledge and the easier availability of information, customers are still attracted to relationships of trust, even in the digital age. Purchase decisions are made under greater ex-ante uncertainty than is the case with physical products. Following purchase, customers cannot judge conclusively whether the expected added value has actually occurred. Yet the ex-ante price depends on the ex-post benefit, which can lead to a potential conflict between buyers and sellers (Arrow 1962). If the provider cannot send a sufficient signal in the form of reputation or reports by other customers, the customer will perceive the risk as being high.[20]

The cost of the initial production of immaterial goods is high, while the costs of reproduction are low (Arrow 1962). There are almost no production-related limitations to what can be offered, as information can be reproduced at will (Shapiro and Varian 1999). This determines a corresponding pricing and the aspiration for a critical mass of turnover.

4.6 The Consequence of the Impact of the Digital Age for Banks

The statement that existing positions of success are no guarantee for future success has been proven scientifically. Time and again—and across all industries—those revolutionary developments described in the previous section arise, which upset the established business models. The developments in banking in the twenty-first century are definitely a revolutionary basic innovation that is based on the knowledge society and which suspends the previous rules of the industrial society. The key problem from an innovation perspective is that established banks are currently situated in the specialisation phase of their business models and technologies, while

[19] Internet Explorer by Microsoft, for example, is a protected object, but a browser in general is not, which is why there are a number of products that are based on the same idea.

[20] See Nelson (1970) on trust-based goods. From this perspective, the importance of brand management for asset managers is understandable.

new technologies and competitors are appearing on the horizon, the clear significance of which has perhaps been underestimated for too long. This leads to the erosion of the existing position of success and possibly to the disappearance of many of today's providers. Thus the banks' problem in introducing measures now is that they are stagnating in the specialisation phase of their existing business model, while new revolutionary business models are already in the development phase. The innovation dilemma of many banks is therefore further developing the current service form while at the same time anticipating and integrating the revolutionary changes, with the same resources.

However, the consistent strategic orientation towards the circumstances of the digital age is essential for survival, in order to be able to be counted among the best-in-class providers. Google demonstrates this with its business model: for 20 years it has been possible to use Google free of charge, and Google's worldwide share of the advertising pie is clearly growing. As the considerations on critical mass show, the consequences of a delayed orientation towards innovative developments should not be underestimated. The self-reinforcing powers can lead to a negative spiral effect if the time point of positive feedback is missed.

Banks are definitely faced with the challenge of addressing the necessity for change. The duality of the further development of existing success positions and the revolutionary development of new ones is a key task for the management of banks. Existing customers desire evolutionary support, while "digital natives" will adopt the emerging revolutionary models immediately. Established banks are in danger of misreading the actual—disruptive—signs of the times by focussing on incremental process improvements to existing business models, and might thus make wrong decisions with regard to their own future viability. The balance between maintaining and further developing existing success positions and developing new potential will be decisive—and it should not be forgotten that it is not the technically perfect solutions that prevail in the market, but rather the speedily developed prototypes with a rapidly growing number of new users.

Understanding the disruptive logic—we find ourselves in the development phase of new revolutionary innovations—and actively addressing the question of the balanced design of business models within each bank is a necessity, both from the previous control paradigm of the shareholder perspective—otherwise the market capitalisation of a bank will also suffer greatly—and from the future-oriented win-win perspective outlined in Chap. 7, which in itself represents a disruptive change at the level of the customer-bank relationship. The decisive question is whether there are management principles that allow established banks to survive these revolutionary changes and even to contribute actively to their design.

4.7 Wrap Up: Change Frameworks

This chapter examined the framework for the analysis of the redesign of banks' business models—building on the dangers identified in Part I, which are presented by the thought traps and the new providers in the digital age.

▶ **The Digital Age as the Key Driver of Change** It is essential to include the regularities of the digital age in the redesign. It is accompanied by a ground-breaking change. Thanks to the internet customers are questioning the price/performance configurations offered by banks due to their much improved information situation, and they converse online about the quality and the experience of dealing with the bank in question. Gradually they are becoming less willing to pay for the mere communication of financial information by banks.

Successful business models will be "critical mass systems", which will succeed in reaching a large number of users. Structures must become more networked in order to attain the necessary flexibility and reaction speed, and to continue to facilitate attractive price/performance configurations. It will become less and less possible to provide all components of the value chain in one's own bank. The transformation will take place gradually, as individuals decide at a different speed to adopt new models—the ability to keep a gradual balance between maintaining things for existing customer groups and changing things for those customers who desire change will be the decisive core competence when rebuilding banks' business models.

▶ **Customer Benefit as a Central Determinant of Successful Bank Services (WHAT)** When providing bank services—the "what"—the fundamental question is that of customer benefit. Only when this is provided to a satisfactory degree from the customer's perspective will the services be demanded and the medium and long-term survival of banks be possible—if customers no longer have this impression, there is no longer a right to exist.

▶ **Structural Configuration of the Provision of Bank Services (HOW)** Not all components of bank services must be provided from within one bank. The coordination of these services is a decisive competitive factor; the tailored combination of the configuration is a potential distinguishing feature. As long as the transaction costs of the market procurement of partial steps are higher than the costs of providing the component themselves, banks' business models are based strongly on the principle of "everything from one source". Prior to the beginning of the digital age, the market costs of gaining information, drafting contracts and then asserting these were often higher than the hierarchical costs for organisational structure and operation—which is why almost all business models of banks provided the partial steps themselves until now. In the digital age, search and information costs have decreased drastically, which means on the one hand that customers are better informed and margins are sinking, and on the other hand it is becoming more attractive to buy additional partial services on the market in order to complete the full service provision; indeed it is necessary in order to keep the price/performance configuration at an attractive price for the critical customer.

▶ **Shareholder Value as a Decisive Financial Control Factor** In the last 20 years the management of publicly-listed banks was always measured on the maximisation of surplus value to the shareholder. Since the financial crisis of 2008 there is growing concern that the ever more one-sided focus on this financial success and the ever greater risks taken by banks to increase profitability contradict economic goals. What is decisive from a business perspective is whether customers continue to be willing to buy the services on offer at the defined price, because they regard their financial needs as being satisfied. If this changes, that would be a business-driven reason for managers of banks to change sustainably the control objective for the management of the business models. It is in the customers' hand; customer behaviour makes the difference.

▶ **Core Parameters of Financial Services** Financial intermediation meets five basic financial needs (transformation, transfer, risk balance, service and logistics, and information functions). It is important to understand precisely the prerequisites for bank customers to demand these functions from a bank. In other words, only when bank customers have the impression that their transformation, transfer, risk balance, service and logistics and information needs with regard to financial flows will be satisfied in a trustworthy manner by a provider with an attractive price/performance configuration, will they take up the offer.

If other providers can produce these functions more cheaply and/or with better quality and/or with greater trustworthiness, the existing business models of banks will be eroded. Only when the service offered by the individual bank—the price/performance configuration including the question as to which services a bank should provide itself and which it should procure—is attractive to customers will they effectively buy these services from this bank and not from the competition.

Existing success positions can erode completely in the digital age, but not overnight. Understanding changes in customer needs is the central competence when it comes to transforming the existing success position of banks in the future—with ground rules that are themselves changing enormously.

References

Arrow, K. (1962). Economic welfare and the allocation of resources for innovation. In National Bureau of Economic Research (Ed.), *The rate and direction of incentive activity: Economic and social factors* (pp. 609–626). Princeton, NJ: Princeton University Press.

Arrow, K. (1969). The organization of economic activity. The analysis and evaluation public expenditures: The PBB-system. In R. Richter & E. Furubotn (Eds.), *Neue Institutionenökonomik*. Tübingen: JCB Mohr.

Arthur, W. (1990, February). Positive feedbacks in the economy. *Scientific American, 262*, 92–99.

Arthur, W. (1994). Path dependence, self-reinforcement and human learning. In W. Arthur (Hrsg), *Increasing returns and path dependency in the economy* (S. 133–158). Ann Arbor, MI: University of Michigan Press.

Bächtold, R. (2003). *Marketing für Finanzdienstleistungen*. Bern: Eigenverlag.

Bernet, B. (2003). *Institutionelle Grundlagen der Finanzintermediation*. Oldenbourg: München.

Bernet, B. (2004, Juni 13.). zit. In F. Pfiffner (Ed.), Keine einfache Liaison. *NZZ am Sonntag*, S. 47.

Bisignano, J. (1998). *Towards an understanding of the changing structure of financial intermediation – An evolutionary theory of institutional survival*, SUERF Studies, Nr. 4, Amsterdam.

Bruhn, M. (1997). *Marketing – Grundlagen für Studium und Praxis*. Gabler: Wiesbaden.

Bruhn, M., & Meffert, H. (1995). *Dienstleistungsmarketing*. Wiesbaden: Gabler.

Brynjolfsson, E., & Hitt, L. (1998). Beyond the productivity paradox. *Communications of the ACM, 41*(8), 49–55.

Büschgen, H. (1991). Prinzipien, Aufgaben und Teilbereiche der Organisation. In J. Stein & J. Terrahe (Hrsg), *Handbuch der Bankorganisation* (S. 27–58). Wiesbaden.

Büschgen, H. (1994). *Bankbetriebswirtschaftslehre*. Stuttgart.

Büschgen, H. (1998). *Bank-marketing*. Wiesbaden: Gabler.

Christensen, C. (1997). *The innovator's dilemma—When technologies cause great firms to fail*. Boston: Harvard Business School Press.

Christensen, C., & Overdorf, M. (2000, March). Meeting the challenge of disruptive change. *Harvard Business Review, 78*(2), 66–76.

Coase, R. (1937). The nature of the firm. *Economica, 4*, 386–405.

Coase, R. (1960). The problem of social cost. *Journal of Law and Economics, 3*, 1–44.

Cocca, T., Linner, F., Podlewski, M., & Stapfer, P. (2001). Finanzportale—Die neuen Konkurrenten der klas- sischen Universalbanken? *Österreichisches Bankarchiv (ÖBA), 03* (2001), 229–234.

Cohen, S., Delong, J., & Zysman, J. (2000). *Tools for thought: What is new and important about the Economy* (BRIE Working Paper Nr. 138). Berkeley: BRIE.

Corsten, H. (1990). *Betriebswirtschaftslehre der Dienstleistungsunternehmungen*. München.

Downes, L., & Mui, C. (1998). *Unleashing the killer app—Digital strategies for market dominance*. Boston: Harvard Business School Press.

Evans, P., & Wurster, T. (1998). Die Internet-Revolution—Alte Geschäfte vergehen, neue entstehen. *Harvard Business Manager, 2*, 51–60.

Foster, R. (1986). Innovation: The attacker's advantage, New York. In J. M. Utterback (Hrsg), (1994) *Mastering the dynamics of innovation: How companies can seize opportunities in the face of technological change*. Boston: Harvard Business School Press.

Freese, G. (1993). *Organisationstheorie*. Wiesbaden.

Freixas, X., & Rochet, J. (1998). *Microeconomics of banking*. London: MIT Press.

Fuchs, W. (1994). *Die Transaktionskostentheorie und ihre Anwendung auf die Ausgliederung von Verwaltungsfunktionen aus industriellen Unternehmen*. Trier.

Gabler Wirtschaftslexikon. (2013). *Web 2.0*. Zugegriffen September 18, 2013, http://wirtschaftslexikon.gabler.de/Definition/web-2-0.html

Geiger, H. (1999). *E-Commerce und die Banken*. Soft(net) Update, 02/1999b, S 1.

Handelszeitung. (2013). *Die Abzocker-Initiative.* Zugegriffen February 10, 2013, from http://www.handelszeitung.ch/die-abzocker-initia-tive
Hirshleifer, J. (1973). Exchange theory: The missing chapter. *Western Economic Journal, 11*, 129–146.
Hirshleifer, J., & Riley, J. (1979). The analytics of uncertainty and intermediation—An expository survey. *Journal of Economic Literature, 17*, 1375–1421.
Hotz-Hart, B., Dümmler, P., Mäder, S., Schmuki, D., & Vock, P. (2001). *Volkswirtschaft der Schweiz.* Zürich.
Kondratieff, L. (1926). About the question of major cycles in the conjuncture. In C. Freeman & F. Louca (Hrsg), *As time goes by—From the industrial revolutions to the information revolution* (S. 384). Oxford: Oxford University Press (2001).
Kondratieff, L. (2013). *Der sechste Kondratieff.* Zugegriffen September 25, 2013, from http://www.kondratieff.net/19.html
Kotler, P., & Bliemel, F. (1992). *Marketing-management: Analyse, Planung, Umsetzung und Steuerung.* Stuttgart.
Koye, B. (2005). *Private Banking im Informationszeitalter.* Bern: Haupt Verlag.
Kreps, D. (1999). A course in microeconomic theory. New York. In R. Richter & E. Furubotn (Hrsg), *Neue Institutionenökonomik* (S. 52). JCB Mohr: Tübingen.
Nefiodow, A. (1999). *Der sechste Kondratieff—Wege zur Produktivität und Vollbeschäftigung im Zeitalter der Information.* St. Augustin.
Nelson, P. (1970). Information and consumer behavior. *Journal of Political Economy, 2*(78), 311–329.
North, D. (1990). *Institutions, institutional change and economic performance.* Cambridge: Cambridge University Press.
Picot, A. (1991). Ökonomische Theorien der Organisation—Ein Überblick über neuere Ansätze und deren betriebswirtschaftliches Anwendungspotential. In D. Orderheide, B. Rudolph, & E. Büsselmann (Hrsg), *Betriebswirtschaftslehre und ökonomische Theorie* (S. 143–170). Stuttgart.
Platzek, H. (1996). Perspektiven des Vertriebs von Finanzdienstleistungen. *Bank und Markt, 25* (2), 10–13.
PWC. (2013). *Profitable growth in the digital age.* Retrieved May 5, 2015, from https://www.pwc.ch/user_content/editor/files/svcs_adv/pwc_profitable_growth_e[1].pdf
Rappaport, A., & Klien, W. (1998). *Shareholder Value: Ein Handbuch für Manager und Investore.* Stuttgart: Schäffer Pöschel.
Richter, R., & Furubotn, E. (1999). *Neue Institutionenökonomik.* Tübingen: JCB Mohr.
Schumpeter, J. (1911). *Theorie der wirtschaftlichen Entwicklung.* Leipzig: Duncker and Humbolt.
Schumpeter, J. (1942). Capitalism, socialism and democracy. In C. Freeman & F. Louca (Hrsg), *As time goes by.* (S. 48). Oxford: Oxford University Press.
Schumpeter, J. (1961). *Konjunkturzyklen: Eine theoretetische, historische und statistische Analyse des kapitalistischen Prozesses.* Göttingen: Vandenhoek & Ruprecht.
Shapiro, C., & Varian, H. (1999). *Information rules—A strategic guide to the networked economy.* Boston: Harvard Business School Press.
Solow, M. (1957). Technical change and the aggregate production function. *The Review of Economics and Statistics, 39*, 312–320.
Stigler, G. (1961). The economics of information. *Journal of Political Economy, 69*, 213–225.
Süchting, J. (1991). Die Theorie der Bankenloyalität—(noch) eine Basis zum Verständnis der Absatz- beziehungen von Kreditinstituten? In J. Süchting & E. van Hooven (Hrsg), *Handbuch des Bankmarketing* (S. 1–42). Wiesbaden.
Swisscom. (2013). *Zuge-griffen Okt.* 10, 2013, from www.swisscom.ch/de/ghq/innovation/forschung/trends/. . ./web-30.html
Utterback, J. (1994). *Mastering the dynamics of innovation: How companies can seize opportunities in the face of technological change.* Boston: Harvard Business School Press.

Utterback, J., & Abernathy, W. (1978). Patterns of industrial innovation. *Technology Review, 80*, 40–47.

Volkart, R. (2006). *Corporate finance: Grundlagen von Finanzierung und Investition*. Zürich: Versus.

Weiber, R. (1992). *Die Diffusion von Innovationen in der Telekommunikation—Probleme der kritischen Massen*. Wiesbaden: Gabler.

Whinston, A., Stahl, D., & Choi, S. (1997). *The economics of electronic commerce*. Indianapolis, IN: Macmillan.

Wikipedia. (2013). *Semantisches Web*. Zugegriffen November 28, 2013, from http://de.wikipedia.org/wiki/Semantisches_Web

Williamson, O. (1990). *Die ökonomischen Institutionen des Kapitalismus*. Heidelberg.

Zöllner, G. (1995). *Kundennähe in Dienstleistungsunternehmen*. Wiesbaden: Deutscher Universitäts-Verlag.

Management Tools 5

5.1 Introduction

It is clear from the previous chapters that only a rigorous examination and reorientation of services and business models towards the digital age will enable future success potential beyond the next couple of years. Tools suited to the digital age are required for this purpose, and that is the subject of this chapter. Business management instruments that allow firms to detect trends that are relevant to success and to derive the right consequences for their own business model, will first be shown in their classic form, before being expanded by the dimensions that are necessary for the successful analysis of the trends of the digital age.

5.2 The St. Gallen Management Model as a Reference Model

By examining in a structured manner the potential impact of current and future trends on their own business model, banks can derive the necessary consequences for their future success positions. Even if gut feeling often rules in successful periods, neat strategic work makes a difference.[1]

The control of the "WHAT" and the "HOW" of the activities of companies can be substantiated by means of different models, which illustrate the level of knowledge with regard to the best practices of business administration. The reference framework for this book is provided by the St. Gallen Management Model (Fig. 5.1).

It distinguishes between four trend dimensions (society, nature, economy and technology). As well as the trend dimensions there are stakeholders, who are

[1] IBM, for example, was the only company that managed to adapt successfully to the changes in the computer industry with two relevant technological advances—thanks to an intelligent linking of trend analyses and implementation in the current business environment (Downes and Mui 1998).

S. Auge-Dickhut et al., *Customer Value Generation in Banking*, Management for Professionals, DOI 10.1007/978-3-319-19938-2_5

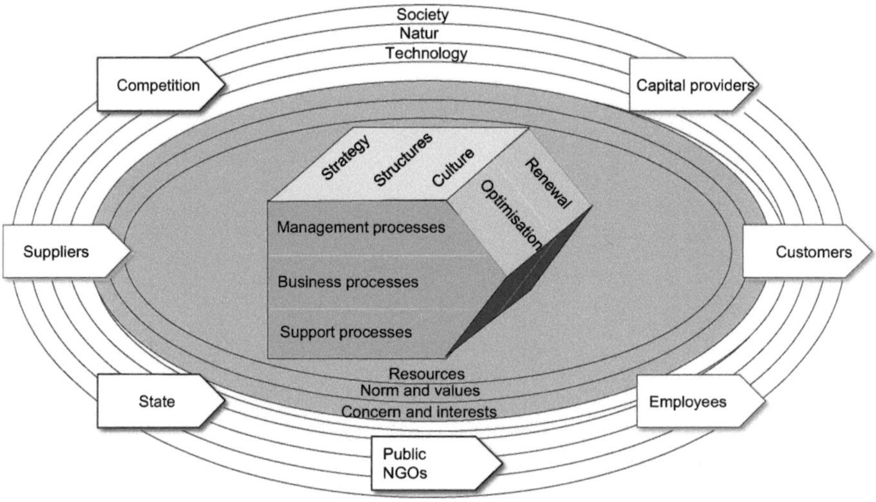

Fig. 5.1 The new St. Gallen management model (*Source* Rüegg-Stürm 2003, p. 22)

significant for a bank. Aside from competitors there are other stakeholders who influence the development of the bank: governments and states, the public, customers, suppliers, employees, investors and society. The activities, values and norms of these groups are also essential influencing factors. Thus, for instance, a change in regulations can restrict a bank's scope of activity just as strongly as the better strategic work by a competitor or a change in values among a relevant customer group.

Trends and stakeholders influence the current and future success positions for banks. The St. Gallen Model explains a company's provision of the price/performance configuration in three ordering dimensions: strategy, structure and culture. Strategy deals with the question "where do we want to go?" The structural design addresses the coordination of resources for providing the price/performance package. Ultimately, the company culture—with the sum of the embodied norms and values in providing the service—can be the decisive difference for customers, for only that which can be perceived in reality can be appreciated by the customer. With regard to culture, the St. Gallen Management Model distinguishes between phases of change and renewal and gives different recommendations for action with regard to managing the necessary changes (Rüegg-Stürm 2003).

The individual dimensions of this model will be outlined below and applied to banks. Section 5.3 is concerned with strategy, and Sect. 5.4 with structure.

5.3 Strategy

5.3.1 Concept

The object of strategic management (the WHAT) is the question as to how companies can use competitive advantage to gain added value for shareholders or simply to maintain their right to exist. Strategic management is therefore concerned with the targeted orientation of companies. Strategies are measures to secure long-term success. From an economic history perspective, long periods of evolutionary development of competitive positions are repeatedly replaced by breakthrough phases with strategic changes in course as a result of technological innovations. The challenges faced by companies are, on the one hand, the evolutionary preservation of their competitiveness in phases of stable development, and on the other hand timely agenda-setting and the adaptation of the organisational form to revolutionary innovations, otherwise survival is seriously endangered (Mintzberg 1987; Mintzberg et al. 2012).[2]

The concrete strategy—which impels the direction of the company's action—consists of a sufficiently precise description of the target situation, the necessary activities and a time horizon. The activities are a decision pathway, and not an exact plan. They are prepared by means of an environmental and a company analysis, which allow a specific business model to be conceived.

5.3.2 Environmental Analysis

The environmental analysis focuses on analysing the influential factors external to the company and derives from this the opportunities for and dangers to the success position of a bank. This market-based view of strategy considers three possible reasons for permanent success (Porter 1980, p. 4 ff.):

- Industry structure
- Strategic behaviour of competing companies
- Positioning along the value chain

The industry structure is heavily determined by the intensity of competition. The greater the competitive intensity, the smaller are the chances of success in an industry. Five competitive forces have been defined: potential new competitors, suppliers, buyers, threats from substitute products and existing competitors. Competitor analysis focusses on the strategy and possible behavioural changes of individual competitors within the industry. The third element defined, the value chain, will be addressed in Chap. 7.

[2] Understanding this innovation dynamic is essential for the successful transformation of the existing business models of banks.

Three generic types of strategy can be distinguished for industry-specific success positions:

1. The objective of the **cost leadership strategy** is to achieve the lowest unit cost. Despite this low-cost strategy, the service quality must remain positive. Thanks to the lower costs, this strategy protects the bank against all five competitive forces, as the competitor will always be the first to experience difficulties in the event of declining profitability. There can only ever be one cost leader in any industry (Porter 1980, 1985).
2. The **differentiation strategy** aims to achieve a distinction from the competition by offering unique customer benefits. Customers are prepared to pay a higher price compared to that of a rival company, if the singularity means more to them. It is possible to achieve a higher-than-average profit only if the surplus price is not exceeded by the differentiation costs. This strategy can be selected by many providers within one industry, as long as different differentiation features are possible (Porter 1980, 1985). Both of these strategies are oriented towards the entire banking sector.
3. By focussing on one single market segment, a **focussing or niche policy** can be pursued. Both cost leadership and differentiation strategies are conceivable within the niche.

5.3.3 Company Analysis

Company analysis places the focus on the internal life of a bank—what are the bank's strengths, where is there improvement potential? The main goal here, too, is the permanent economic success position—from this perspective, from the ability of a bank to concentrate a unique and inimitable combination of resources into defensible core competences (Rühli 1994). Future-viable core competences are those that are anchored in the company culture and developed from the inside through organisational learning. They cannot be easily acquired by competitors, but instead must be developed independently by means of an organisational learning process. Due to their uniqueness they are very difficult to imitate and help the bank to gain a noticeable competitive advantage, as customers recognise the benefits and therefore avail of the service (Prahalad and Hamel 1990).

5.3.4 Strategically Relevant Key Elements for Banks' Business Models

5.3.4.1 Key Trends

In recent years, pressure has grown from the EU and the OECD for greater transparency in designing business models. The reason for this is the combating of tax evasion, in order to improve the financial situation of all states, which has become more precarious as a result of the various financial and debt crises since

2008, by raising the tax base. One element in this is the ever more rigorous regulation of banks at European and gradually also international level, as the digital age has also substantially increased transparency—even in totalitarian states like China (see Tagesanzeiger 23.01.2014). The growing regulation costs are increasing the cost structure of the banks to a very large degree.

Globalisation also influences banking: financial markets are facing rapidly growing competition. National financial system have become global financial systems to an extent, which leads to easier comparability between bank services and the competitive dissolution of regional monopoly positions. Structural differences between national systems are balanced out. Furthermore, the individual lifestyles of many wealthy private persons have changed, resulting in greater international mobility and international diversification in property and company holdings. This increases the need for international tax advice and special services, which are being included more intensively in international legislation.

Finally, the technological developments and the informed customers of the digital age, also known as "digital natives" or "Generation Y", form the core of the pressure of change generated from the environment. The point in time of convergence can be anticipated from the developments observed—as soon as the "digital natives" form the largest customer group, traditional business models will become obsolete. A gradual and yet rigorous reorientation is absolutely necessary.

Until now, financial institutes gathered information into knowledge, which then informed the financial services and thus created additional benefits for all parties. The price of this service was justified by the more efficient allocation of means and the lower transaction costs for the customer in acquiring and processing information, thanks to the support of the intermediary. In the past there were information asymmetries in the retail banking sector, both between the provider and the customer and between different customer groups with regard to the quality of information on investment opportunities and risks.

With the reduction in search and information costs, accompanied by an increase in the availability of information, the bank has lost its information advantage. Customer are less and less willing to pay for this kind of intermediation. The physical distance between provider and customer is also being overcome technologically. The cost to a customer of switching banks is sinking, which leads to diminished customer loyalty. New providers can operate on the market with lower costs and more efficient processes thanks to slimmer structures and thus exert pressure on the classic providers of financial services. The previous strategic positioning of each banking provider erodes successively. These days, customers are very well informed—increasingly, previous price/performance configurations are no longer competitive enough, and margins are sinking.

5.3.4.2 Environmental Analysis

The negotiating and market power of customers has grown in the digital age. There is increasing threat from potential substitute products, and new competitors are entering the banking sector, thus intensifying competition between current rival companies. Competition is being led increasingly by price, which has triggered a downward price spiral. It is becoming ever more difficult to protect unique offers; average profits are declining. The greatest advantages of the internet—comfortable access to information and easier interaction—make it difficult, at the same time, to convert them into profit. Porter (2001, p. 69) thus speaks of the paradox of the internet.

5.3.4.3 Company Analysis

The central objects of examination in company analyses are core competences. Schäli (1998) studied core competences in banking and discovered that they arise from a value-creating combination of knowledge, human, technological and material resources. Image focussing, customer care, the customer loyalty structure, information transfer and the use of technology fulfil all core competence requirements (Koye 2005).

- The image of a bank is determined by the combination of its market presence and its corporate culture. Thanks to constant discretion and reliability, banks have created institutions with a positive image for customers. The image has become the expression of the corporate culture as a result of company-specific processes, some of which have lasted for centuries. To maintain this image, employees in customer care must constantly exceed the expectations. Added value can be generated from the image factor through good advice, because this increases the credibility of the bank in the eyes of the customer. Image is also of key importance for competitive advantage, as the basic products and services of asset management are in principle interchangeable. The subjectively perceived customer benefit and the resulting willingness to pay a higher price are often based on the image of the bank.
- The customer care approach chosen by the bank consists of focussed customer segments, determining customer needs, coordinating marketing instruments (service, pricing, products, distribution) and deriving a clearly defined consultation and product package. Implementing such a customer support approach requires analytical, segmenting and differentiation skills, so that the selected customer segments can be served with differentiated offers. As each institution has an individual customer and employee base, the competitive starting position of each market participant is different. Value creation can be improved by the targeted use of company resources, because customers then receive services that meet their needs and the intensity of support is adapted to the customer potential and profitability. Ideally, customers will believe that the services and conditions offered have been tailored precisely to their expectations and needs, leading to high satisfaction.
- Customer loyalty structure, or relationship management, is the ability to build customer loyalty by means of providing support in a service-oriented corporate culture. On the one hand this reduces customer losses, and on the other hand a good service improves internal cooperation and resource usage. Both activities have a positive effect on value creation. While measures such as the poaching of advisors or the adaptation by competitors of customer loyalty strategies might be

conceivable, the implementation of an excellent relationship management system requires a lot of time and management effort, which makes it almost impossible to imitate comprehensively. The competitive advantages that arise from the recommendations of satisfied customer is the basis for market success.
- Information transfer is also a core competence of the bank. Added value arises from the professional exchange of information and the transfer of information across all adequate channels. The knowledge of specialist departments (portfolio management, law, taxation, pensions, insurance solutions, etc.) is pooled and passed on to the customer advisor or PFM, who then passes it on to the customer in a tailored package. A contribution can be made to value creation by choosing the most efficient organisation of the information chain. The efficiency assessment also encompasses a review of the cost-oriented outsourcing of individual parts of the information chain.
- The use of information technology plays a decisive role in the structural development of banking. Early assessment of the potential of new technologies and their rapid integration must occur in parallel with the willingness to adapt or redefine existing business processes. Prior to the digital age, technology was a merely supporting element in customer communication, decision-making and process optimisation. The digital age has opened up new forms of market processing for banks; it includes semi-independent transaction processing by the customer and allows the provision of cost- and needs-oriented offers as well as an optimised use of resources.

Competences that do not fulfil all requirements are not core competences. For example, a conditions policy might be related to value creation and it may contribute to a consulting concept by being directed towards a certain target group, however it can be imitated very quickly and therefore cannot achieve a competitive advantage in the long term. Equally, the product range can also be copied quickly. Management systems, promotion systems and organisational structure are basic operative prerequisites for a successful business. Employee training is an operative measure to anchor the core competence of information transfer. Performance and existing customer base are the results of the core competences customer care and information transfer.

In the digital age, core competences arise from collective organisational learning as an optimum combination of different resources and the integration of different technologies (Prahalad and Hamel 1990). In the future, knowledge, brand and image will be the decisive competences; IT competence will once again return to being a mere "enabler". This can—and must—be used profitably in combination with the other core competences by developing problem-solving expertise, for example along the configuration of online and offline sales channels, as demanded by the customer, and also with regard to the perfect analysis of existing data on customer needs, as well as the provision of the optimum information portfolio for customers.

Due to the rapid rate of change, knowledge-based resources would appear to be best suited to adapting dynamically to the challenges of the digital age, as they can learn from and react to environmental changes (Miller and Shamsie 1996). Employees' educational levels therefore offer the best chances, while the brand and the image are also rare resources in the digital age, which are difficult to imitate (Hall 1992). The core competences of customer care and loyalty need to adapt to the new regulations and to changed customer needs. For this reason, the highest priority should be given to identifying future customer needs and attaining the best position in the value chain (Geiger 2000). It is essential to utilise segment-specific knowledge when using various different sales channels for the purpose of establishing contact. To maintain customer relationships, or to build new ones, the brand and the image of the company are very important. If established providers miss important developments and no longer meet image expectations, opportunities arise for competitors. However, if a company manages to harmonise the component of trust with the need for modernisation in the digital age, it supports its image and brand and therefore continues to have future-viable and difficult-to-imitate successful resources at its command. In terms of image, the long-established attributes of trust, security and reliability continue to play an important role in the digital age—however under new conditions in the "critical mass systems". These attributes are supplemented by the imperative competence of adding partial performances to networks in the digital age.

The use of technology as the foundation of the information transfer from the bank to the customer is a central prerequisite of success. While information cannot be equated with knowledge, technology is changing both the economic basis and the production and distribution foundations of banking, therefore either questioning the previous core competences of information transfer or dismissing them completely. The physical distance between providers and demanders is being overcome technologically, so that it no longer seems necessary to maintain a branch-office structure, which in turn leads to reduced customer loyalty (Llewellyn 1999).

Due to the possibility to rapidly imitate innovative technological systems, the use of ICT (information and communication technologies) is a necessary, but not entirely sufficient condition of long-term success. Thus the combination of resources into a customer-centred approach, which is also optimised for Web 2.0 or 3.0, is probably the most decisive core competence.

5.4 Structure

5.4.1 Concept

In the St. Gallen Model the structures (structural and process organisation) are the second element of order alongside strategy, as the specific provision of services is performed via structures—and their optimum configuration can also be used to gain a competitive advantage over rivals. Structural organisation consists of permanent organisational units such as positions and departments and forms the hierarchical framework of an organisation. It defines the framework conditions: Who bears what hierarchical responsibility? Who has what decision-making competence? Process organisation regulates the working and information processes: Who contributes which steps towards providing the service? The focus of this process-oriented organisation is the optimum satisfaction of the customer's needs with an efficient use of resources and, where possible, without any interface problems. Communication and coordination when providing the service package runs vertically.

The concept of the value chain analyses the individual phases of a company's provision of services and identifies potential cost or differentiation advantages that might be reached based on the configuration of different activities in the context of the operational service-provision process (Porter 1985). The value chain is composed of two different types of activity:

- Primary activities: these are directly involved in the provision of the service. They are also known as business processes or central value-creation processes: this is where the key market-related activities are carried out. These are customer processes: customer acquisition and loyalty, brand leadership. They also include market research, market processing, the development and intensification of customer relations management (CRM);
  a. Provision of services (procurement, logistics, production) and
  b. Service innovation (life cycle management, research and development).
- Supporting activities: these take care of the operational environment in which the primary activities are carried out. Supporting activities are, on the one hand, management processes—all fundamental management tasks that are concerned with planning, guidance, control and development within the organisation. On the other hand they are also support processes—securing the infrastructure; providing internal services that are necessary to complete the business processes (HR, infrastructure, IT, communication, risk management, law).

The added value created by the bank is measured on the amount that the customer is willing to pay for the service. A profit margin results when this amount is higher than the costs. Competitive advantages arise either through a cheaper or a more differentiated execution of the activities, which allow a greater margin (Porter and Millar 1995; in detail Porter 1985).

5.4.2 The Value Chain in Banking

The key activities of banking are the development and maintenance of customer relationships, the provision of financial advice, product development and provision, and the processing of transactions. The supporting activities, which must be carried out across all phases, are in part sector-specific (risk management, compliance and regulation, and financial analysis) and in part generic (HR, IT, management). The

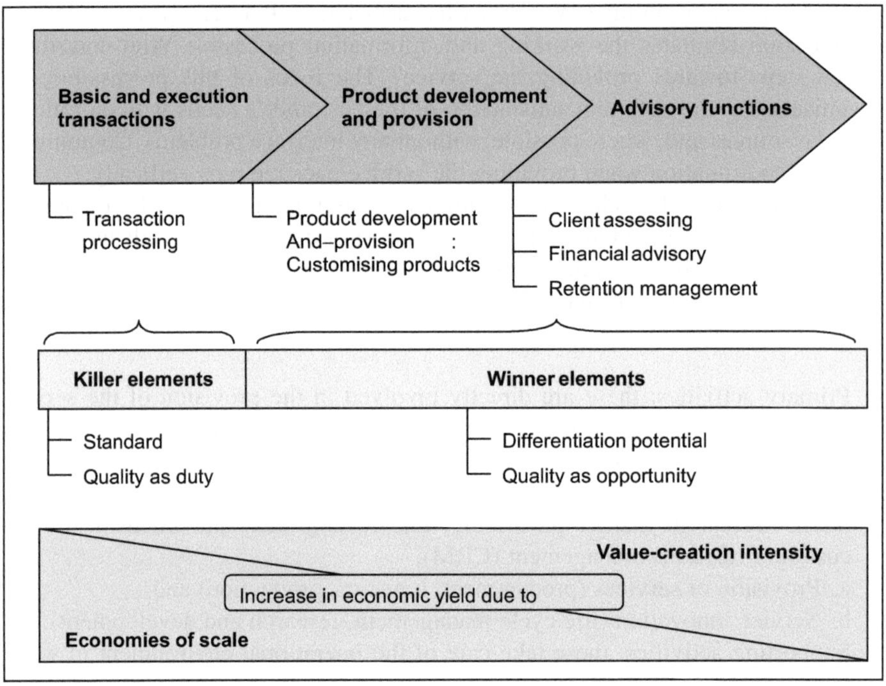

Fig. 5.2 The value-creating potential of the core competences of banking (*Source* Koye 2005, p. 101, based on Gehrig 1996, p. 25)

key processes can also be summarised in terms of their value-creating potential (Gehrig 1996, p. 25) (Fig. 5.2).

1. Basic and implementation transactions guarantee the processing of transactions. Customers demand the perfect processing of the basic and implementation transactions of bank business. For this reason, a processing error can only lead to a negative differentiation in terms of the competition, which is why it is also known as a killer element. Transaction processing is fixed-cost intensive and allows an increase in economic benefits only via economies of scale, as long as a sufficient volume can be processed. Smaller providers cannot achieve these economies of scale with their own customers—or only to a limited degree—so that greater emphasis is placed on fixed costs. Larger providers are better able to cover their fixed costs with a high transaction volume.
2. Asset allocation comprises product development and provision, and asset management. A good asset allocation leads to a quantitatively measurable good performance. A qualitative differentiation becomes possible, and asset allocation is a potential winner element.
3. The advisory functions combine the activities of developing and maintaining customer relationships and the provision of financial advice. A good advisory

process generates a feeling of trust among customers. Therefore the greatest differentiation potential can be found in this area. Gehrig (1996) defines the advisory functions as the primary winner element. They are based above all on personal know-how. Once the capacity limit of an employee has been reached, no further increase in performance is possible without appointing new staff. The starting point here is identical for both small and large providers.

5.4.3 Bank-Relevant Structural Trends in the Digital Age

5.4.3.1 Industrialisation, Network Organisation and Virtualisation

From the perspective of transaction cost theory, financial institutions represent a hierarchical solution to the coordination problem of financial services. They turn information into knowledge, which then flows into the financial services. Until the end of the last millennium, there were information asymmetries between providers and customers, and also between different customer groups with regard to the quality of information on all functions of financial intermediation (see Sect. 4.5.1). Prior to the digital age, the price for these services was justified by the more efficient allocation of resources and the low transaction costs for customers in procuring and processing financial information.

The traditional understanding of a bank is based on a vertical, integrated organisation, which makes and provides products and services; all process components to manufacture and sell the products are completed internally by the company itself (Llewellyn 1999, p. 23). Prior to the digital age, the models were aimed at the customer in the classic sense—the interface with the customer was defined by the account and deposit relationship—customers could choose their "advisory institution", open their accounts there and avail, where necessary, of individual products from other providers, usually for a larger fee. If a customer wanted a number of bank relationships simultaneously, they had to aggregate these themselves, as the relevant technical possibilities did not yet exist—otherwise they revealed their overall situation to their advisor. Only with this step, or by cooperating with an "independent asset manager" who was concentrated solely on the advisory capacity, could the customer aggregate between different providers and maintain an overview. It was not possible, in contrast, to choose different product providers and/or processing institutions. Previously, almost every bank produced each step of the service configuration itself (Egli and Rüst 1997). The reasons given were the guarantee of a confidential treatment of customer data and the protection of privacy. Involving third partied was seen as a weakness (Geiger and Hürzeler 2003). Now, the technology of the digital age has clearly changed this situation. Information can be sent and distributed to every place in the world within seconds. Customers can get share price information on the internet in real time, exchange opinions, observe the behaviour of "star traders" and conduct their stock exchange transactions via online platforms, without requiring the services of a bank as an intermediary.

Because of the key strategic trends—see Sect. 5.3.4—more efficient structures must be set up—this is also logical from the perspective of transaction costs. Until now, financial institutions provided an almost purely hierarchical solution to the coordination problem when satisfying customer needs. Gradually, transitional forms of coordination between companies and markets are being developed, such as network organisations, cooperative networks or virtual organisational structures. When the reduction in transaction costs due to modern information systems exceeds the increase in coordination costs (Picot et al. 1996), the result is a modification of previous forms of coordination.

The modern organisational principle, therefore, is the integration of business processes and the orientation towards customer benefit, as well as the minimisation of lead times with the involvement of one or more partners. An integrated organisational principle must ensure that the structural organisation of a bank is aligned with the business processes, which leads to a powerful and agile organisational form within each individual bank.

At the same time, the growing division of labour and specialisation increases the demands on coordination and thus also transaction costs. In contrast to the traditional organisation according to development and operation, process-oriented organisational design places the main focus on the special demands of an optimum operation of value-creating processes (see Waser and Peter 2013, p. 39). "*The objective is to design, where possible, continuous processes between the procurement and sales markets, without any interface. [...] The key words "customer orientation" are meant seriously, because an immediate feedback from the customer becomes possible.*" (Osterloh and Frost 2006, p. 33) The core processes must be directed rigorously towards the strategic goals of the company (see Osterloh and Frost 2006, p. 36). Each process contains many individual activities, which together produce a result. However, only a few activities can increase the value of the result. Therefore, all activities that do not increase value should be reduced to a minimum. Füermann and Dammasch (2012) categorise all activities into effective, supporting, blind and erroneous performance. Figure 5.3 shows the proportion of their overall performance in processes.

Effective performance refers to those activities that lead to an increase in value from the customer's perspective. This might be the advisory process, for example, or also marketing measures. These activities are planned and should be optimised continually.

In contrast, **supporting performance** contributes only indirectly to an increase in value. It supports the effective performance, for example by preparing meetings or approving loans. These activities are not noticed by the customer, yet they generate costs. Therefore, such activities should be reduced as much as possible and optimised to be economically effective.

Blind performance is unplanned and does not contribute either directly or indirectly to increasing value. It includes, for example, multiple entries due to media disruption or the rejection of loan applications due to missing documents. These activities are not noticed by the customer and they drive up costs. They must be eliminated.

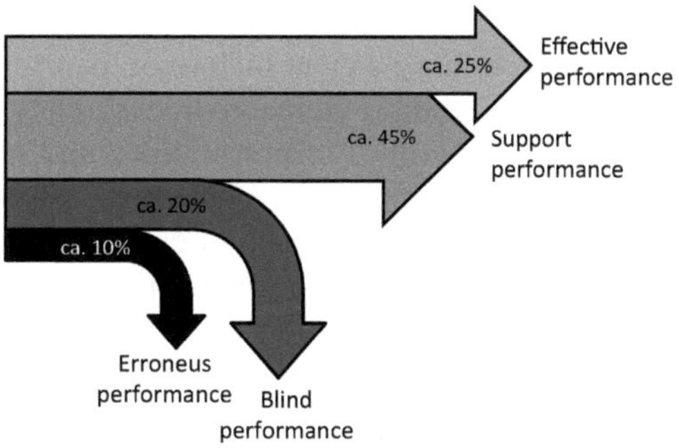

Fig. 5.3 Allocation of performance (*Source* Füermann and Dammasch 2012, p. 54)

Erroneous performance covers those activities that were perhaps planned as effective or supportive performance, but which could not be utilised due to errors. These activities must be avoided by means of improved planning, training or process optimisations.

A critical review of processes based on these aspects should increase the share of value creation within the process. Concentration is placed on the activity that increases customer benefit. Unnecessary activities should be identified and reduced or eliminated (see Füermann and Dammasch 2012).

Here, the use of technology becomes a key existential question. Even in the information-intensive banking sector, the previous linear value chains are breaking up into value networks. This new form of cooperation different partners in network structures is also known as collaborative commerce (Kyburz 2001). It involves the deconstruction, disintermediation and reintegration of business processes (Evans and Wurster 1998; Keller 2000). First the internal processes are divided analytically into their individual parts. Then a gradual disintegration takes place.[3] Increasingly, partial components are carried out by specialised third parties. Due to the diverse range of information and as a result of the suspension of the conflict between comprehensiveness and range, the customer is able to circumvent previously established intermediaries. The result is disintermediation (Hürzeler 2000; see also Geiger and Hürzeler 2003).[4] New and more efficient value creation processes emerge. Reintegration[5] takes place on a networked basis (Keller 2000). A further result of the digital age is that it allows communication between all network participants (Evans and Wurster 1998). Hierarchies become networks—and virtualised business models (Janssen and Vanini 1999).

Coordination between the individual partners in a network—whether within the bank or cross-company—is done by defining roles. A role involves responsibility

[3] *Disintegration* means that in the event of sinking transaction costs, procuring (intermediate) products externally is cheaper than their internal production.

[4] *Disintermediation* means that the direct contact with a third party—due to the lower transaction costs—is cheaper than involving an intermediator.

[5] *Reintegration* means that efficient providers compile individual components of the formerly integrated value chain into value networks.

for one process and is defined in the role description. This helps managers and employees to have a clear picture of their main tasks, and clear responsibilities are defined. The result is increased transparency and orientation—for management and staff—with regard to responsibilities and interfaces. The so-called RACI matrix (responsible, accountable, consulted, informed) is often used to illustrate the dependencies and responsibilities. In the process, the roles mesh together like gear wheels. "Holding responsibility" means being measured on agreed work results and reaching targets within the defined action frameworks. Responsibility consists of tasks, authorisation, and accountability.

The providers integrated earlier must share the declining value creation. The reduced transaction costs change both the production structure of the entire sector and the form of customer relationship with regard to an industrialisation of banks.[6] "*If the automobile industry had the same production depth as banks or insurance companies do, they would breed cattle to produce leather for the seats themselves.*" (Gillardon 2010, p. 22). The previous prototype of the integrated bank, which covers all parts of value creation, is an obsolete model. Financial intermediaries can produce according to industrial principles: customer orders are on the "conveyer belt", the raw materials consist of information, the goods are money, precious metals and securities.

In the network-based value chain, the integrated value chain has disintegrated into a virtual network, without the customer having noticed. Bank advisors remain the contact points for the customer, and at the same time coordinate the network partners. They define the standards for the cooperation, advise the customers and trigger transactions by buying and selling products and services. Research and investment guidelines can be provided by external partners, just as product manufacture, trading and transaction processing can. The creation and operation of networked systems pose a large challenge to banking providers. Different third-party systems must be integrated into the bank's own platform, in order to be able to access the relevant customer data from the external system. For this purpose, standardised methods are used, which allow data transactions between different companies and enable the conversion of these data to executable orders in other companies. It is absolutely necessary to introduce security instruments for the different access authorisations to the partner systems and to transfer sensitive data in coded form. Finally, CRM systems are needed, which can enable communication across channels and the management of the preferences, behaviour and interactions of customers, while observing the regulatory requirements.

---

[6] One used to speak of "*looming paradigmatic changes, a fundamental redefinition of the economic function and responsibility of the bank and thus of the concept of banking*" (Bernet 1997, p. 33) and of the industrialisation of the business models through networked banking (Evans and Wurster 1998).

5.4.3.2 Outsourcing as an Essential Element of Industrialisation

Transaction costs are the key determining factor in selecting hierarchical or market forms of organisation and thus in the matter of outsourcing. In efficient markets, a company will completely outsource all activities that do not belong to the core competences if the market costs of searches, contracts and controls are lower than the hierarchical costs. Outsourced competences can also be those that were traditionally seen as integral parts of each company, but for which there is no strategic necessity or no specialist skills. The following factors can be seen as drivers of the amount of transaction costs (Bösch 2004, p. 125 f.):

- Degree of uncertainty with regard to the future and the outsourcing service providers
- Specificity of the production factors deployed, which are tailored precisely to the company in question. The relative costs of outsourcing partial activities increases with the factor specificity. Market solutions become ever more expensive due to organisational and contractual safeguards in the face of growing uncertainty.
- State regulations allow only a gradual development of technological potential. It is often obligatory for legal reasons to produce some steps within the bank, even though outsourcing would make better economic sense.
- From the resources perspective, the incentive to involve others in partial activities sinks in accordance with how strategic the activities are. Nobody is keen to surrender strategically significant know-how.

In summary: a high degree of factor specificity, great uncertainty, regulation and large strategic significance favour in-house production. Figure 5.4 presents the outsourcing alternatives and also intermediate forms from the perspective of transaction costs.

The artificial word coopetition was coined for the mixture of cooperating in networks and competition, and means the strategy of trustworthy cooperation between competing providers to the advantage of both partners and the customer (Nalebuff and Brandenburger 1996). The concept of coopetition follows a game-theory approach that combines the advantages of cooperation with the advantages of competitive pressure. Although two or more companies might be battling for customers in their sales markets, they cooperate with each other in certain areas, to the benefit of both (Dathe 1999). There are different control and flexibility variations, such as with regard to arranging the relationship with network partners.

There is a permanent trade-off between flexibility and control. Due to the increased complexity, the improved technological flexibility, the changed transaction costs and the associated higher specialisation, outsourcing has become more attractive in principle. Specialised providers can often produce competences at lower costs and with greater added value.

Understanding outsourcing and network partnerships is an important competence for every company in the digital age and an integral part of every business model (Quinn and Hilmer 1994).

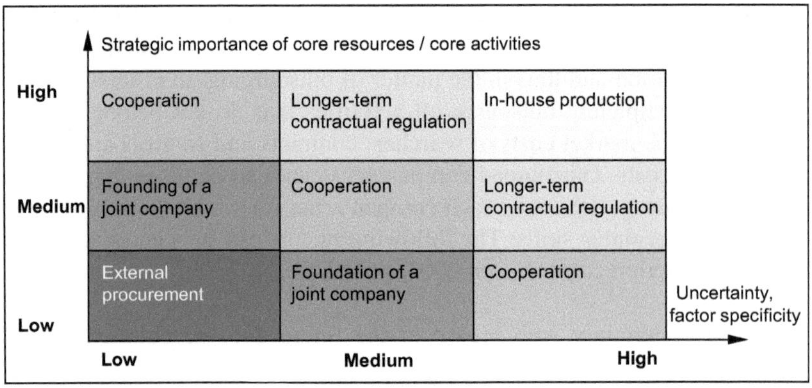

Fig. 5.4 Characteristics of outsourcing based on key resources and factor specificity (*Source* Bösch 2004, p. 127)

The time required to launch a new products and services can be reduced significantly by cooperating with best-in-class network partners. The advantage of this strategy is the realisation of efficiency potential, including cost reductions. Prior to the outsourcing decision, any potential vulnerability due to dependence on external partners and the surrender of key competences should be clarified. A loss in flexibility in product development and innovative capability may arise due to the difficulty of combining many competences in a differentiated manner (Quinn and Hilmer 1994).

Three effects can be distinguished in efficiency potentials (Hürzeler et al. 1999):

- **Economies of scale** enable a reduction in costs by producing larger quantities. Large companies can gain competitive advantages particularly in transaction-intensive processes by means of automation. In the field of consulting, great value is achieved by means of individual support. This means that economies of scale tend to be small in such personnel-intensive work. In an age of technological change, negative economies of scale might even emerge, as size is no guarantee of survival in innovation-intensive phases.
- **Synergy effects** enable cost savings through the joint use of infrastructure or via cross-selling. In the digital age, the possibilities of cross-selling have grown, with an increase in integral optimisation and an objective choice of best-in-class products.
- **Knowledge effects** allow the exchange of know-how in networks. The specialisation of each network partner on his core competence and the exchange of experience within the network means allows the value chain to be examined for optimisation potential and the specialist knowledge to be integrated into the overall context.

Many company execute their own activities internally only because this was always common practice or because these activities appear to be integral parts of the end product. However, a more realistic market comparison can show if the internal efficiency lies well below that of the best-in-class company and whether or not outsourcing might be a sensible alternative. In markets with many providers and mature structures, it seems possible to attain lower transaction costs through outsourcing. Therefore, the critical question for each company when it comes to focusing on core competences and on outsourcing is: Which parts of the value chain should be produced in-house in order to best deploy the quality of the core competences? The following derived questions are paramount:

- What potential does the analysed core competence have to achieve a strategic competitive advantage under consideration of the transaction costs?
- How great is the potential vulnerability caused by surrendering central core competences and the dependency on partners, or by the development of incorrect core competences in the event of a decision to outsource?
- Which measures can be taken to reduce this vulnerability by means of precise agreements with network partners?

5.4.3.3 Solution-Finding Competence as a Differentiation Factor for Banks

The availability of information in the digital age does not automatically increase the level of knowledge among investors. Information cannot be equated with knowledge. Information is data that have a purposeful reference (Müller-Merbach 1995, p. 4). These data encompass an almost unlimited amount of available facts, statistics, texts, pictures, audio and video sequences in existence. The danger is that such easy access to more and more information will lead to the generation of information giant, yet people will understand less and less of it. The knowledge advantage held by banks cannot be caught up on immediately, as it is so-called implicit knowledge. Acquiring and transferring this implicit knowledge is bound up with the experiences and internal contexts of those who have the knowledge and often demands a context transfer: analytical skills and expertise are required to understand and convert the information into knowledge. From a banking perspective, this means that while all investors have access to the same raw data of the capital markets in the digital age, these can still only be assessed based on specialist knowledge and financial market models. For this reason, financial intermediaries still have a right to exist to provide complex advice, as this creates real added value for the customer. The competitive opportunities of financial intermediaries are large wherever banks' integration and solution-finding competence is in demand.

5.5 Culture

Whereas strategy and structure are the "hard" components of the St. Gallen approach towards illustrating business models, culture, as a "soft" component, is a frequently underestimated dimension. The St. Gallen Management Model speaks of change and renewal.

As shown clearly in Sect. 4.1, the digital age is shaped by an acceleration of developments and the need for change. Purely hierarchical business models withdraw into the background, while the process-related and networked perspective become ever more important. This also leads to whole new challenges for corporate and management culture. The focus is on the perfectly tailored solution—and not on hierarchical loyalty. Traditional competence models and management patterns are eroding, resulting in collective insecurity among traditional companies.

Studies show that 75 % of important projects in companies are planned and conceptually prepared, yet they are not implemented because the internal service providers are not convinced and power struggles between departments prevent a consideration of the big picture (Koye 2011; Boston Consulting Group 2009). The critical mass of effective advocates is not reached and the project peters out over time.[7]

Effective competence is always paramount in career models. Cross-company network orientation and working with and in flat hierarchies are skills that need to be learned—and yet it is precisely these competences that are required at an individual and collective level for the successful metamorphosis of business models.

5.6 Business Model as an Interlocking of Strategic and Structural Analysis

The fusion of the results of the strategic and structural analysis lead to the business model of a company. This section presents both classic business models and those of the digital age. Building on this, the bank-specific reference will be addressed in detail in Chap. 6.

5.6.1 The Classic Economic Concept of the Business Model

The concept of the business model originated in the process and data modelling by means of information technologies (Dottore 1977). It was used to distinguish between companies (Huff and Beckow 2000) and also transferred to corporate models.

The concept of the business model is formed as a combination of the results of an internal and an external strategic analysis and the derivation of suitable structures and thus the integrated development of prerequisites that allow a company to be economically successful in the long run. The specific components of business model development are:

[7] By now this has also been recognised in conventional consultancy firms, as shown by the study "Organisation 2015—Designed to Win" by the Boston Consulting Group (2009).

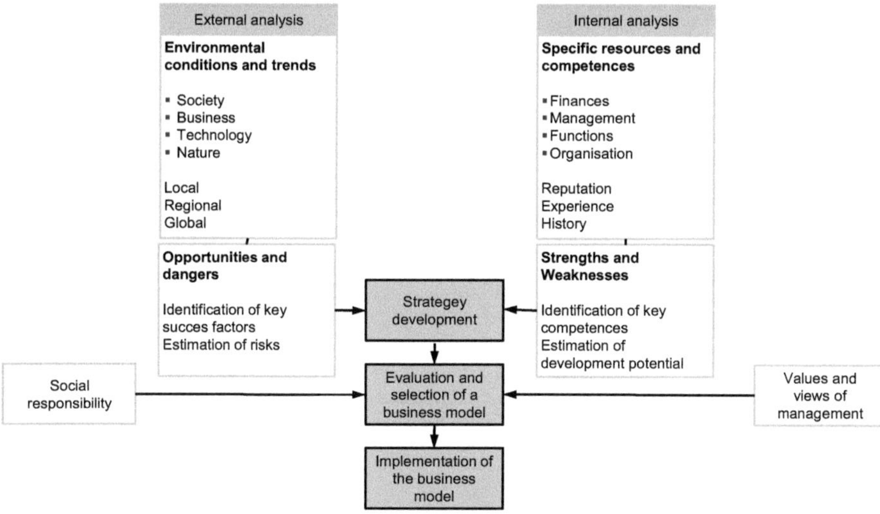

Fig. 5.5 Business model development (*Source* Koye 2005, p. 97)

- Goal formation (vision and mission, key figures)
- Environmental analysis (market, competition, chances/risks)
- Company analysis (strengths/weaknesses, performance and management potential, resources, value chain according to Porter)
- Choice of strategy (portfolio analyses—e.g., BCG, Ansoff, 7-S) and structure definition/adjustment
- Planning models and strategy implementation (budgeting, balanced scorecard)
- Strategy control

The environmental and company analyses are combined to make a SWOT analysis (strengths/weaknesses/opportunities/threats). On this basis a concrete strategy and structure can then be derived and implemented (Fig. 5.5).

The business model therefore enables:

- Clarity about the relevant stakeholders
- A definition of the service range
- The determination of the focus of value creation and production depth
- The definition of cooperation partners
- An analysis of already existing core competences

The answers to these five questions produces the configuration of the success position of the business model to be aimed for in the future.

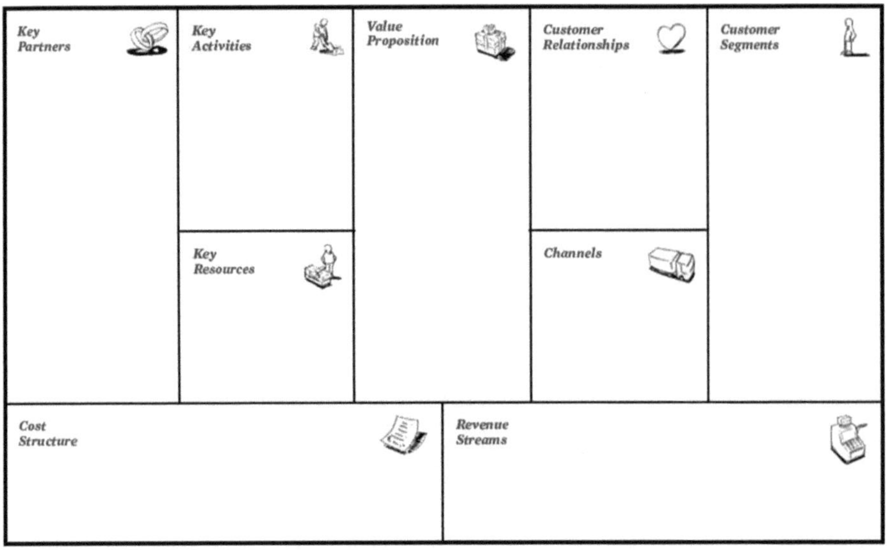

Fig. 5.6 The CANVAS business model (*Source* Osterwalder et al. 2011, p. 44)

5.6.2 Economic Concept of the Business Model in the Digital Age

The concept of the business model in the digital age—as an extension of the classic model—can best be described by means of the Canvas Model. It supplements the classic concept with components relevant to the digital age. These include cooperation partners in the network, and channel management (Osterwalder et al. 2011). In principle it consists of nine components, against which a business model can be compared and a foundation can be laid for optimisation and survival. The components are (Fig. 5.6):

1. Customer segments: these are customer groups that the company wishes to reach and serve. Only profitable customers can secure long-term survival.
2. Value offer: this defines the service offered to customers that will provide the best possible solution to their needs. It is all the customer is willing to pay for.
3. Channels: this describes how the customer segments are addressed and how the value offer is made to them.
4. Customer relationships: this defines the type and intensity of the customer relationship.
5. Sources of income: how much are customers willing to pay for which services?
6. Key resources: this defines those resources that are imperative for the company and its "success". These could be persons, machines or methods, which expand or change the value offer well beyond that of the competitor.
7. Key activities: these are the most important activities that a company must execute in order to be successful. They differ from business model to business

model and, like the key resources, shape the value offer of every single company.
8. Key partnerships: this is more than just the surrounding network of suppliers and partners. These are the decisive contacts that allow a transfer of knowledge and thus help to orient business models successfully towards dynamic customer needs.
9. Cost structure: here, all costs incurred by the business model are analysed. This makes the cost structures clearer and allows the detection of hidden costs.

5.7 Wrap Up: Management Tools

The key result of this chapter was the overview of the relevant instruments for controlling companies—and therefore also banks—strategically and structurally, and the application of these tools in the digital age.

> **Instruments** Strategically, the permanent analysis of environmental developments is essential in order to detect changes to the existing business model or the emergence of new influencing factors and the significance these might have. Then the questions of "what" and "how" must be clarified. A clear analysis of the future trends, expectations and activities of the stakeholders, as well as of market developments, is a necessary factor for survival.

The digital age is changing the foundations of financial intermediation in the long term, as the knowledge advantage that banks held over customers is eroding and the entry barriers for new market participants sinking. The informed customers place pressure on margins in the network age. In addition, there is growing regulatory pressure on banks as a result of the global financial and debt crises and growing transparency; this also increase the metamorphosis pressure.

> **Structure** Future-viable success positions depend on the competence not only to recognise effective customer needs in an open dialogue, but also to translate these into modern solution packages with attractive price/performance configurations. There are three core process steps in banking: the provision of customer advice, product allocation to meet customer needs, and transaction processing. Banking does not differ from any other sector in principle, so that analysis of the price/performance configuration can also be conducted in every bank according to usual standards and thus contribute to increased competitiveness.

The basic form of implementation is the interwoven exchange between those with responsibility, which should be regarded as motivating and sensible. By creating an agile process structure, the process costs can also be optimised rigorously by means of lean management. Existing bank services can be offered more efficiently through network-like price/performance configurations, new services become possible, and economies of scale in the processing areas increase. Organisational and functional boundaries are shifting successively and becoming more permeable, or are disappearing altogether. The organisational form of the future is based on the clear understanding of responsibilities along the individual steps of the performance configuration, which are being conducted increasingly in networks—with each individual concentrating on his core skills.

Industrialisation is a necessary answer to the key trends of the digital age for every bank—economies of scale and an improvement to the price/performance configurations are merely the admission ticket to the further metamorphosis of banks' business models. This requires a shifting of the previous, often purely vertical view of the organisational structure to a primarily horizontal (process-focussed) perspective and a merging of both by means of role and job profiles. This process-oriented view also allows the analysis of the question as to which competences should be provided in-house and which should be procured externally.

▶ **Business Model** The concept of the business model arises as a fusion of an external and internal strategic analysis and the derivation of suitable structures. In the digital age the classic concept is supplemented by the dimensions of the cooperation partner network and adequate channel management.

▶ **Outlook: Customer Focus and Change Management as Key Success Factors** Even if the significance of trends and expectations is assessed correctly and the right strategic decisions are made, success is still not guaranteed, for success arises solely from successful business activity on the market. Resources are scarce and their proper use in the price/performance configuration decides its success or failure. Therefore, following a clear analysis, three factors are crucial for the future success of a bank in the digital age:

- First the precise understanding of one's own business model and the adjusting screws for changing these—this will be addressed in Chap. 6.
- Then, how this is implemented into actual customer experience, in order to develop and maintain customer trust by fulfilling service promises. This key success factor will be analysed in detail in Chap. 7 of this book.
- On the other hand, the question of how this strategically, structurally and culturally complex transformation process is at its infant stage in many banks. If it is to succeed, future-viable change management will be the central success component. This topic will be addressed in detail in Part III.

References

Bernet, B. (1997). Banking im 21. Jahrhundert—Gedanken zu den langfristigen Entwicklungstendenzen im schweizerischen Bankwesen. In C. Schmid & B. Varnholt (Eds.), *Finanzplatz Schweiz—Probleme und Zukunftsperspektiven* (pp. 333–345). Zurich: Verlag Neue Zürcher Zeitung.

Bösch, M. (2004). Outsourcing im Transaction Banking: Theorie, Praxis und Ausblick. *Die Bank, 2*, 125–129.

Boston Consulting Group. (2009). *Organisation 2015—Designed to win*. Munich.

Dathe, J. (1999). Coopetition—mehr als eine Mode. *Harvard Business Manager, 6*, 22–29.

Dottore, F. (1977). Data base provides business models. *Computerworld, 11*(44).

Downes, L., & Mui, C. (1998). *Unleashing the killer app—Digital strategies for market dominance*. Boston: Harvard Business School Press.

Egli, S., & Rüst, L. (1997). Banken und die industrielle Revolution. *Geldinstitute, 10*, 90–92.

Evans, P., & Wurster, T. (1998). Die Internet-Revolution—Alte Geschäfte vergehen, neue entstehen. *Harvard Business Manager, 2*, 51–60.

Füermann, T., & Dammasch, C. (2012). *Prozessmanagement*. Munich: Carl Hanser.

Gehrig, B. (1996). *Private Banking—Aktuelle Probleme und neue Herausforderungen*. Zurich: Verlag Neue Zürcher Zeitung.

Geiger, H. (2000). Die Transformation von Banken. In H. Österle & R. Winter (Eds.), *Business engineering—Auf dem Weg zum Unternehmen des Informationszeitalters* (S. 289–304). Springer: Berlin.

Geiger, H., & Hürzeler, H. (2003). The transformation of the Swiss private banking market. *Journal of Financial Transformation, 9*, 93–103. Retrieved December 20, 2003, from http://www.ccfz.ch/files/j09art15.pdf

Gillardon. (2010). *News 2/2010*. Retrieved February 3, 2014, from http://www.msg-gillardon.de/uploads/media/msgGillardon-Kun-denmagazin-NEWS-2-2010.pdf

Hall, R. (1992). The strategic analysis of intangible resources. *Strategic Management Journal, 13*, 135–144.

Huff, S., & Beckow, D. (2000). Homegrocer.com—a case study. *Ivey Business Journal, 64*(5), 90–95.

Hürzeler, H. (2000). *Das Internet und der Niedergang der Seidenstraße*. Schweizer Bank 5:46.

Hürzeler, H., Basler, S., & Gatti, A. (1999). *Disintegration of the value chain in private banking*. Case Study am 1st International Private Banking Retreat der Swiss Banking School, Interlaken.

Janssen, M., & Vanini, P. (1999, Sommer). Preference-based asset & liability-management for private investors: The strategy to win the future. *Finance & Technologie, Les Magazins de l'Agefi*, 94–97.

Keller, M. (2000). *Virtual Private Banking—Vision oder Illusion*. Diplomarbeit an der Swiss Banking School, Haupt, Bern.

Koye, B. (2005). *Private Banking im Informationszeitalter*. Bern: Haupt.

Koye, B. (2011). *Organisch Wachsen*. Retrieved July 15, 2013, from http://www.koye-partner.ch/pdf/11_KN_Journal_doppel_SGS.pdf

Kyburz, C. (2001). *Finanzportale—Kundensicht ist entscheidend* (Insight Financial Services No. 4).

Llewellyn, D. (1999). *The new economics of banking* (SUERF Studies, No. 5). Amsterdam.

Miller, D., & Shamsie, J. (1996). The resource-based view of the firm in two environments: The hollywood film studios from 1936 to 1965. *Academy of Management Journal, 39*(3), 519–543.

Mintzberg, H. (1987). Crafting strategy. *Harvard Business Review, 65*(4), 66–75.

Mintzberg, H., Ahlstrand, B., & Lampel, J. (2012). *Strategy Safari: Der Wegweiser durch den Dschungel des strategischen Managements*. Munich: FinanzBuch.

Müller-Merbach, H. (1995). Die Intelligenz der Unternehmung. Management von Informationen, Wissen und Meinung. *Technologie und Management, 44*(1), 3–8.

Nalebuff, B., & Brandenburger, A. (1996). *Coopetition—kooperativ konkurrieren*. New York: Campus.

Osterloh, M., & Frost, J. (2006). *Prozessmanagement als Kernkompetenz: Wie Sie Business Reengineering strategisch nutzen können*. Wiesbaden: Gabler.

Osterwalder, A., Pigneur, Y., & Wegberg, J. T. A. (2011). *Business model generation: Ein Handbuch für Visionäre, Spielveränderer und Herausforderer*. Frankfurt a. M: Campus.

Picot, A., Rippberger, T., & Wolff, B. (1996). The fading boundaries of the firm: The role of information and communication technology. *Journal of Institutional and Theoretical Economics, 152*, 65–79.

Porter, M. (1980). *Competitive strategy: Techniques for analysing industries and competitors* (1st ed.). New York: Free Press.

Porter, M. (1985). *Competitive advantage: Creating and sustaining superior performance*. New York: Free Press.

Porter, M. (2001). Bewährte Strategien werden durch das Internet noch wirksamer. *Harvard Business Manager, 5*, 64–81.

Porter, M., & Millar, V. (1995). How information gives you competitive advantage. *Harvard Business Review, 63*(4), 75–98.

Prahalad, C., & Hamel, G. (1990). The core competence of the corporation. *Harvard Business Review, 68*(3), 79–91.

Quinn, J., & Hilmer, F. (1994). Strategic outsourcing. *Sloan Management Review, 35*(4), 43–55.

Rüegg-Stürm, J. (2003). *Das neue St. Gallen Management-Modell*. Bern: Haupt.

Rühli, E. (1994). *Die Resource-Based View of Strategy—Ein Impuls für einen Wandel im unternehmungspolitischen Denken und Handeln?* Wiesbaden: Gabler.

Schäli, S. (1998). *Kernkompetenzen im Private Banking aus der Perspektive großer Bankinstitute in der Schweiz*. Bern: Verlag Paul Haupt.

Tagesanzeiger. (2014). *Banker tun alles fürs Geld*. Retrieved January 22, 2014, from http://www.tagesanzeiger.ch/wirtschaft/Banker-tun-alles-fuers-Geld/story/22511061

Waser, B., & Peter, D. (2013). *Prozess- und Operations-Management*. Zürich: Versus.

Business Models of Banks

6

6.1 Classic Business Model Concept of Banks

With regard to conventional banking business models, a fundamental distinction can be made between major banks, retail banks, private banks and independent asset managers (Koye 2005a). Classically, the business model of a bank consisted of a price/performance configuration, which was usually provided entirely by the same bank. Only the independent asset manager focussed solely on providing customer advice and drew all other services from other banks.

Major banks are characterised by a high market capitalisation and the ability to pursue capital-intensive strategies. An example in Germany is Deutsche Bank, while Switzerland has Credit Suisse and UBS and, with some qualifications, the Zurich Cantonal Bank. These model types differ from retail banks in their orientation towards all customer segments. As well as private customers without many assets, whose needs are generally covered by a retail division, the wealthy customer segment is also served by a specialised division. In addition, all elements of the value chain of corporate business, asset management, and investment banking are also offered equally. The large customer base allows both economies of scale for basic transactions and more intensive value creation in advisory functions. Asset management and investment banking are usually conducted at a global level. Customer care and loyalty concepts are treated with different levels of intensity for each individual customer group. With private customers without many assets, these institutions are at a disadvantage, compared to retail banks, in that they are not present regionally to the same degree. Therefore, their image focus is on the financial strength and variety of a globally active institution that can guarantee the entire information transfer of its worldwide experience across all business areas with the most up-to-date technology.

The traditional image of a retail bank builds on reliability and often also on its fixed position in the local region in question, and creates trust among private customers without many assets as the main target group of the customer care and loyalty concept. Examples in Germany include the Postbank, the Sparkassen

S. Auge-Dickhut et al., *Customer Value Generation in Banking*, Management for Professionals, DOI 10.1007/978-3-319-19938-2_6

(savings banks) and the Raiffeisen and cooperative banks. Examples in Switzerland include Migros Bank, the COOP Bank, PostFinance, the Raiffeisen Group, the Clientis Group, the Valiant Group, the regional banks and also almost all cantonal banks. Customers are offered the entire product range, with a focus on standard products, which are produced in-house, mostly without any manual modification, and distributed via physical locations. With regard to the information transfer to customers and the supporting use of technology, this model is no different to other banking providers. Although the focus of the business activity often lies in the margin-sensitive retail and corporate customer business, all elements of the banking value chain are also offered. The regional, Raiffeisen and cooperative banks have created synergies through cooperation, in order to achieve economies of scale in the area of basic transactions. As the needs of the main customer groups of these institutions are in the area of basic services and investments, the value creation intensity of the advisory function is lower than in other institutions.

Private banking service providers offer the entire value chain with a strong focus the advisory function for the most intensive value-creating customer group: wealthy clients. In Germany these include the Berenberg Bank, Hauck & Aufhäuser private bankers and the banking house Lampe; in Switzerland, Vontobel, Julius Bär, Lombard Odier Darier Hentsch and Pictet. They offer tailored solutions for financial planning and portfolio management and thus an individual information transfer. The business areas of asset management and investment banking are operated only as an extra, and not by all institutions. Technological developments were mostly adopted only when they had established themselves as standard, as the focus was on the personal relationship with the customer. The core competence is individualised service, in combination with an image of trustworthiness, discretion, and long-standing tradition.

The independent asset manager supports and advises customers in all finance-related matters (Bernet 2000). He does not develop any products himself, but rather compiles the services of third parties. Within the value chain this model concentrates solely on providing advice for value chain-intensive customers and cooperated with external specialists in the areas of asset allocation and basic transactions. Individual or target group-specific solutions are found with the help of information technology. The image focus is on the personal relationship of trust between the asset manager and the customer. Customer care and loyalty are also shaped by the relationship, which often lasts for many years. Technological developments are adopted as soon as they have prevailed on the market.

6.2 The Modern Concept of the Business Models of Banks

In this section, first the pervious findings on the digital age and its effect on the "what" and "how" of business models is substantiated (see Sect. 6.2.1.), before the concrete business model options of the digital age are then presented (see Sect. 6.2.2).

6.2.1 The Success Factors of Digital Business Models

6.2.1.1 Fundamentals

Banks fulfil various intermediating functions (see Sect. 4.5.1) as hierarchical forms of organisation. The costs of fulfilling these functions via the market mechanism have sunk dramatically in the digital age (see Sect. 5.4.3). That means that customers can become informed about all relevant development at any time in any place, real-time and almost free of charge. The previous intermediary functions of banks—such as lot size and deadline transformation (aggregation of the money of different customers via savings accounts and the granting of loans or mortgages to borrowers) or in part also risk transformation[1]—are of very little value to the customer anymore. That is the main reason for the margin-related and industrialisation pressure on banks.

How can banks now adapt their business models to the new situation in the medium and long term? In order to be able to manage this development, the business models must become more efficient—focussing on core competences and task distribution along the value chain will become necessary elements of future-viable business models. For this reason, the positioning in the value chain network and the active management of the customer interface are the key factors of current business models. Analysing the perfectly tailored participation in value chain networks is a central task of management. In a virtual network, companies avail of both their own knowledge and outside knowledge, as well as internal and external resources, in providing their services. In short, virtuality is defined as the competence required in order to participate in company networks (Wüthrich and Philipp 1998, p. 42).

The traditional analytical units of market and company must be expanded to include the new circumstances—the "virtual network structures" and the "redefinition of the customer interface" (see Hamel 2000 and Tapscott et al. 2000 for alternative approaches).

6.2.1.2 Value Contribution (WHAT)

So the previous instruments for strategically analysing the existing success positions of banks must be supplemented by the "value creation network" and "customer interface" aspects. Here the concentration on the bank's own effective core abilities is unavoidable, and the reference to previous services or the passing on of intermediate in-house parts of the service provision to the (end) customer as well as an exact analysis in accordance with the nine factors of the CANVAS model is necessary.

The concept of the three value disciplines by Treacy and Wiersma (1995) gives an orientation for possible value contributions, which arose from studies of the success of large companies. According to the concept, market success is only really

[1] A smaller denomination of investments might be possible via the market, thus reducing the risks. However, these are then borne by the market participants.

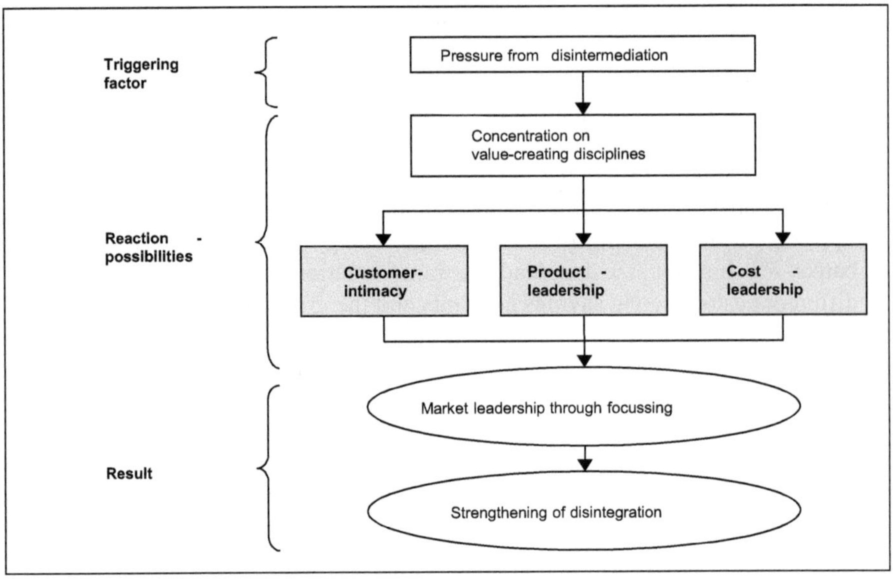

Fig. 6.1 Concept of the three value disciplines based on Treacy and Wiersema (*Source* Koye 2005a, p. 149 based on Treacy and Wiersema 1995, p. 45 ff.)

possible by focussing on one, or maximum two value disciplines. With customer intimacy, the focus is on the customer interface, while with product or cost leadership it involves concentrating on those parts of the value chain that are not immediately apparent to the customer (Fig. 6.1).

Thus, the following strategies are possible:

- Concentration on cultivating the external customer interfaces
- Positioning at the product level as a product specialist
- Positioning at the processing level as a transactions specialist, and offering this service package as a cost leader to the customer-oriented network partners

A combination of all three areas within a company leads to economic and cultural conflicts. Management is forced into efficiency-reducing compromises. Once, such compromises had to be made because of the high transaction costs of market solutions (see Sect. 4.3). In future, according to this model, no company can afford to be the long-term market leader in all three disciplines. This means that maintaining the previous proprietary models will become gradually more problematic. Increasingly, customers are expecting "best-in-class services" in each area, at cheaper overall conditions.

6.2.1.3 Organisational Form of the Network Cooperation in Providing Bank Services (HOW)

As a consequence, virtual forms of organisation emerge, in which individual partners can work together beyond the company boundaries of network partners.[2] Companies are oriented towards integrating the output of the core competences of other companies into the value chain. The main motivation for the formation of virtual organisations is the concentration on one's own strengths under consideration of cooperation, in order to keep the price/performance configurations attractive. The business processes are designed in such a manner that the individual competences are coordinated to create more value for all network partners. The concentration entails a dependency on external competence providers for those network partners involved (Sieber 1999, p. 245).

As shown in Fig. 6.2, a so-called focal company unit forms the centre of a virtual company, which controls the network and selects the partners. A unified front is presented to the customers, and the value chain is optimised with the use of ITC technology. The prerequisites for the effective realisation of the efficiency gains are a culture of trust and the IT networking of the independently acting partners.

Depending on the speed of change within the network and the complexity of the knowledge and information demands, one speaks of an internal, stable or dynamic network (Keller 2000, p. 36 f.):

- Internal networks are formed by decentralised units within a company. The provision of services is coordinated internally, as it concerns the management of complex knowledge and information demands.
- In stable networks, external partners are involved. Here the service provision is guided by a focal company that covers most of the key value creation itself. The knowledge and information demands of the components outsourced to partners are not as complex as those in internal networks.

  The focal company at the customer interface completes the value chain by procuring some elements and products externally. Network partners who were once competitors before the information age can now be both competitors and partners. The focal partner usually also has the contact with the customer.

[2] A virtual organisation (VO) is a form of organisation in which legally independent companies and/or individuals join together virtually into a business partnership (usually via the internet) for a certain period of time. The virtual company presents itself to third parties or clients as a unified company. A distinction can be made between intra-organisational and inter-organisational forms of virtual organisation. While in the first case, the virtualisation occurs within a single legally independent company, the (often time-limited and project-related) inter-organisational form for virtual organisation is composed of a number of legally independent companies (Gabler Wirtschaftslexikon 2013). The concept of the virtual company has not been defined uniformly. The main discussion points are: the duration of the connection, the extent of the contractual regulation, and the safeguarding of key functions solely based on information and communication equipment. See Keller (2000), Sieber (1999), Mertens and Faisst (1995) and Wüthrich and Philipp (1998).

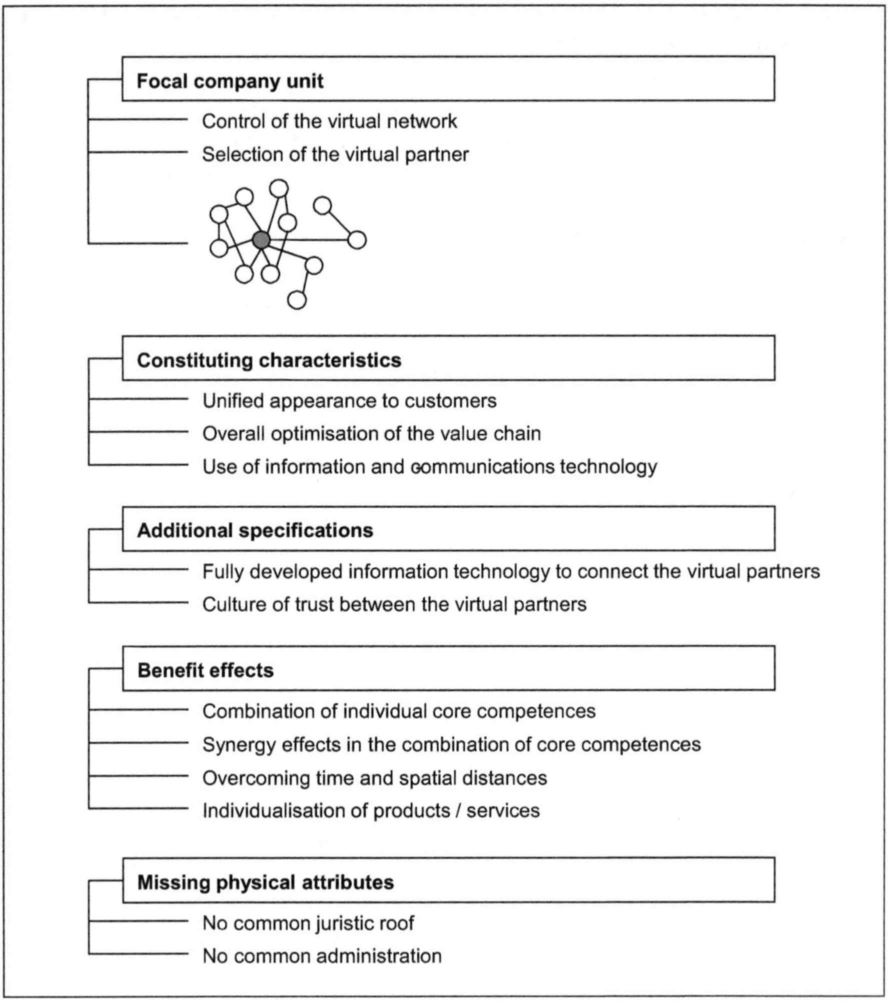

Fig. 6.2 Features of network-oriented/virtual organisations (*Source* Koye 2005a, p. 185)

- Dynamic networks are situation-dependent and composed of different partners, with the aim of using current market opportunities. Both partners are leaders in their own areas in parts of the key value creation.

These three network positioning options are open to all banks. If a major bank decides to organise individual divisions as independent units, a quasi-externalisation or externalisation of individual units is possible. In the case of quasi-externalisation, these remain connected with each other in an internal network (on the basis of service level agreements). The involvement of smaller providers, where at the same time major banks take on the role of the focal unit,

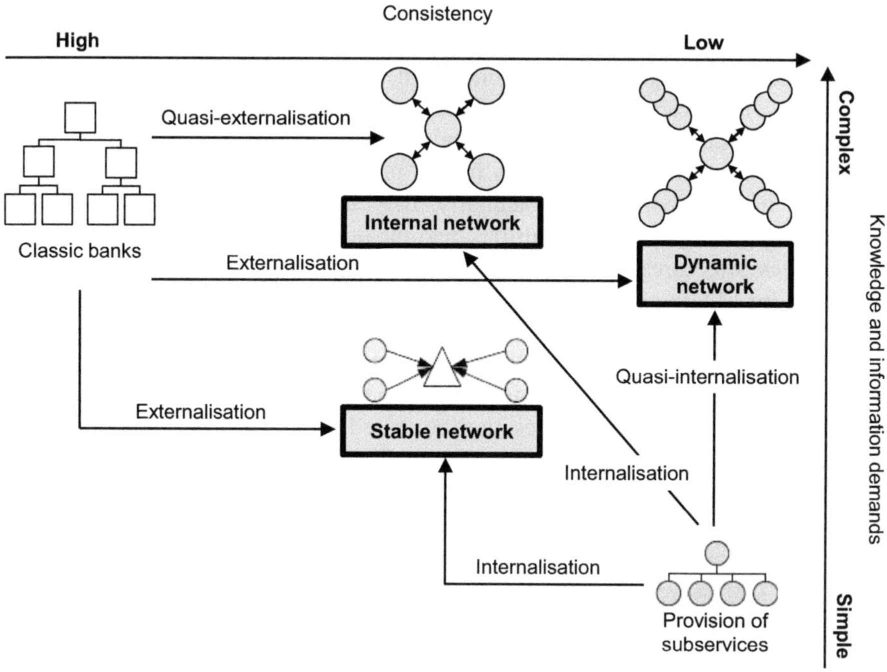

Fig. 6.3 Overview of the network organisation options (*Source* Koye 2005a, p. 187, based on Sieber 1999, p. 247)

leads to a stable network with the procurements of external products. For the smaller providers, participation in a stable network—while maintaining independence—or in an internal network—with a surrender of independence—leads to an internalisation, as their own decision-making competence is surrendered to a large degree to the focal company. Participation in a dynamic network is a quasi-internalisation—while maintaining independence—because it is integrated into the legally independent network (Fig. 6.3).

6.2.1.4 Importance of the Customer Interface

The customer interface has always been important, but now, in the digital age, it has a disruptive role. Previously, customers maintained one, or at most a few relationships with banks, who provided their services in an aggregated manner. Today, thanks to the technological possibilities, customers are able to use a number of service providers in parallel, and even to coordinate them to an ever greater extent as focal partners.

The layout of the customer interface by the banks can be described with four elements: the information status of the customer, the relationship dynamic between customers and providers, the type of product delivery including support, and the fees structure.

The greater the customers' level of information about the possibilities of procuring information and their willingness to use it actively, the more likely it is that they themselves will act as focal network partners. Depending on their needs and preferences they can compile individual components of the value chain—for example the independent selection of optimal investment solutions in the form of securities; the purchase of securities from a provider, and the management of the securities in a deposit bank. Potentially, they use three partners: the advisory platform, the provider of the securities, and the deposit bank.

The fees structures are transparent to a different degree, depending on the network form. Margins decline depending on the network structure and the degree to which the customer is informed and active. With internal networks, the fees remain completely within the bank, as it provides the whole value creation. In the case of stable networks, the focal network partner can claim the largest share of the fees. In dynamic networks, the fees must be shared with at least one partner equally, who has also contributed a key value creation. The fees structure is most transparent when the customer himself is the focal network partner. He knows the contributions of all involved parts and can choose in each case the "best-in-class source".

6.2.2 Business Models for the Transformation of Banks

6.2.2.1 Fundamentals

Banking business model options can be described in terms of network positioning, key processes and value discipline. The key processes of banking are the advisory function, product development and provision, and basic and implementation transactions. The value disciplines in banking are customer interface management, product leadership and cost leadership in processing. The models are:

- The previous classic models (see Sect. 6.1)
- The product specialist
- The transaction specialist
- The agora

6.2.2.2 Analysis of the Classic Models

The major banks, retail banks and private banking providers have concentrated on all three value disciplines simultaneously. Only the independent asset managers have concentrated solely on managing the customer interface. There were once providers that concentrated only on the product level or transaction level. Frequently they were the internal service providers of certain banking groups—for example Swisscanto in Switzerland as a funds provider for all cantonal banks or, in Germany, various different internal transaction processors for the cooperative banks—these include, for example, Fiducia with its competence in data centre operation or in software development—or savings banks. In addition, there have always been specialist providers of products, such as Fidelity or DWS in the funds area (Fig. 6.4).

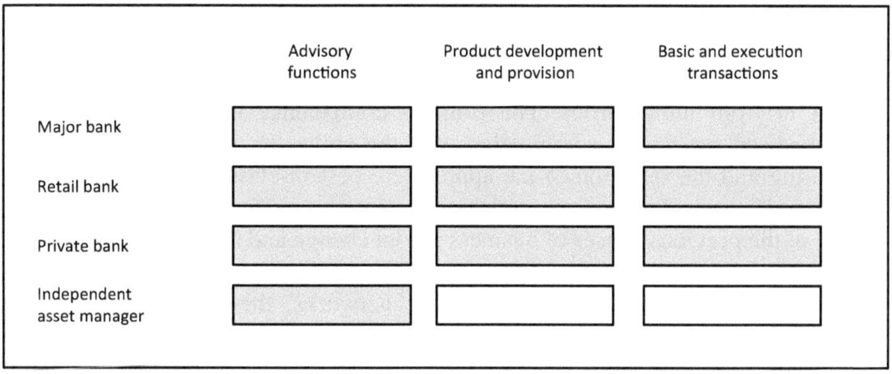

Fig. 6.4 Classic business models (*Source* Own illustration)

6.2.2.3 Current Situation

For the most part, many major, retail and private banks are holding on to previous models. The prevailing attitude is that there is sufficient development due to gradual industrialisation and in some cases the outsourcing of certain areas. Synergies and economies of scale are achieved in transaction processing by means of insourcing. In production, a best-in-class positioning of one's own products is targeted, in order to achieve greater volume with high profitability. The aim is to be positioned as a focal company. Interfaces exist both with customer and with internal network partners (B2C and B2B). The major banks can use the opportunities of mass customisation.

With regard to virtualisation and positioning in emerging networks, in recent years the major banks have driven forward the process of quasi-externalising individual units by means of service-level agreements (SLA). They focus on all three value disciplines and aim to form stable networks and assume the role of the focal company wherever the supplementation of their product or transaction process portfolio appears to make sense. In the course of developments towards open architecture, the banks' own products are made available to other providers. The cooperation corresponds with the form of stable networks.

Retail banks are focussed primarily on the customer interface. Constant monitoring of the value creation processes and the implementation of efficiency potential are crucial for long-term competitive success. Initial approaches to forming value creating networks through cooperation in the areas of transaction processing and product creation can be detected. The retailer is in a difficult position, as it is hard to reach critical mass with many products or in the area of transactions. The process of quasi-externalising individual units by means of service level agreements is underway. The core competences of asset management are not held equally by all providers. The use of technology is employed professionally by all providers, so that the information transfer is also safeguarded. However with regard to the image focus and the implementation of an enhanced customer care and loyalty concept there are clear differences in experience to those providers who concentrate on the customer interface in asset management. Among private banking providers, the option to form value creation networks is exploited more actively than in the models outlined in the previous section. Products and transaction services are bought in from third parties. The primary competence is customer care with individualised service, in combination with the ability to perform complex asset structuring and the selection of the appropriate best-in-class products and service providers. The use of technology and the information transfer are safeguarded in the course of the previous phases of business model change and the core competence of image positioning meets the different customer expectations. With regard to virtualisation and positioning in emerging networks, these providers strive to form stable networks and to assume the role of the focal company in customer interface management. Some selected products with a high degree of value creation will continue to be produced independently as a secondary value discipline, which distinguishes this business model from that of the independent asset manager. In the course of the developments towards open architecture, the in-house products or transaction systems are also made available to other customer interface providers. A quasi-internalisation takes place where the role of the focal unit is assumed by another customer interface provider.

For providers with standardised products, direct banks have presented a strong challenge in the German-speaking region in recent years. They offer the same services as the classic providers—but without a branch network and with round-the-clock availability. This development is an initial reaction to the digital opportunities, but which distinguishes them from the classic providers only in terms of the feature "channel management".

Furthermore, there are an increasing number of specialised product providers and transaction specialists who operate independently of bank groups and process the aggregated services of many banks on their own systems, thus allowing economies of scale. In Switzerland the market for process outsourcing is occupied by only a few providers—for example, the Incore Bank, Swisscom IT Services or B-Source. The Zurich Cantonal Bank, for instance, has outsourced its processing to the Incore Bank, an independent, publicly listed transaction bank that in turn evolved from a private banking parent company. Germany has Fiducia and Finanz Informatik, the IT service providers for the Sparkassen.

Some providers combine the product and processing competence—for example Hypotheken Management GmbH in Germany or Hypotheken Servicing Schweiz, who both allow banks to outsource the production and processing of their mortgage offer either in whole or in part—in the sense of overcapacity management.

Furthermore, some providers have built up strong positions in other value disciplines, alongside their primary value disciplines. UBS was able to take this approach with many banks with their "Bank for Banks"—Migros Bank, for example, processes its stock market transactions via the UBS systems, notably at much better conditions. In addition, both Migros Bank and PostFinance procure their mortgages as "white-label" products from UBS. In Switzerland the first reference example was the cooperation between the Linth and Wegelin banks, in which Linth remained the independent interface to the customer, while the asset management systems were managed completely by Wegelin: margin sharing among equals, with each using their own competences (Koye 2005b). Other examples include the cooperation of the VALIANT Group with the Geneva-based private bank LODH (Lombard Odier Darier Hentsch) in the area of product offerings and the equity stake-supported cooperation between the Vontobel banks and the Raiffeisen (Schweiz) Group in the area of product sales (Auge-Dickhut and Koye 2012).

Purely sales banks also emerge in this phase as a result—such as the aforementioned Linth bank[3]. The only value discipline is the customer interface. Neither the bank's own products nor its own processing capacities are developed. In the medium term, this model will be able to offer a more competitive pricing in the segment of affluent clients and for standard services than full providers. Economies of scale and scope can be achieved with the rigorous outsourcing of non-focus value disciplines. Customers often have a number of bank relationships and expect optimum coordination. In this role, product procurement and transaction processing can be distributed among many providers and conditions can be optimised. The added value towards the customer lies on the one hand in the efficient execution of this coordination and negotiating function, and on the other hand in the selection of best-in-class producers. With regard to virtualisation, the role of the focal company in a stable network is aspired to in order to control the customer interface. The internalisation or quasi-internalisation of other partners is conceivable, as long as a stable network can occur. Due to the technological developments of the information age, the product and transaction specialist are also a specialisation option. Neither of these two type will position themselves as a focal company.

What they all have in common is that the interface with the customer continues to be occupied or cultivated by one provider. Furthermore, the digital age already allows the customer today to identify the best offers on comparison portals, and also to contact the providers directly via these portals. Portals are usually located upstream of previous customer interfaces, even though the direct contact does then usually take place between the customer and the original provider.

In the past, customers were less willing or able to switch providers due to technological, time-related and other hindrances. If we look at the insurance industry we can see that customers with good negotiating positions/risks know their negotiating power and therefore in some case switch providers annually and accept only short-term contracts. Should these developments intensify in the banking sector, we can assume that customers in future will switch providers much faster, and the price/performance ratio will be more closely questioned and also sanctioned (Fig. 6.5).

The product specialist focuses on product development and production and distinguishes himself through his independence and by striving for a best-in-class positioning for his product. Sales to end customers are outsourced to network partners with a customer interface. Contact with network partners is made primarily over modern communications and processing channels. This business model works

[3] This has now been integrated into the LLB corporate group.

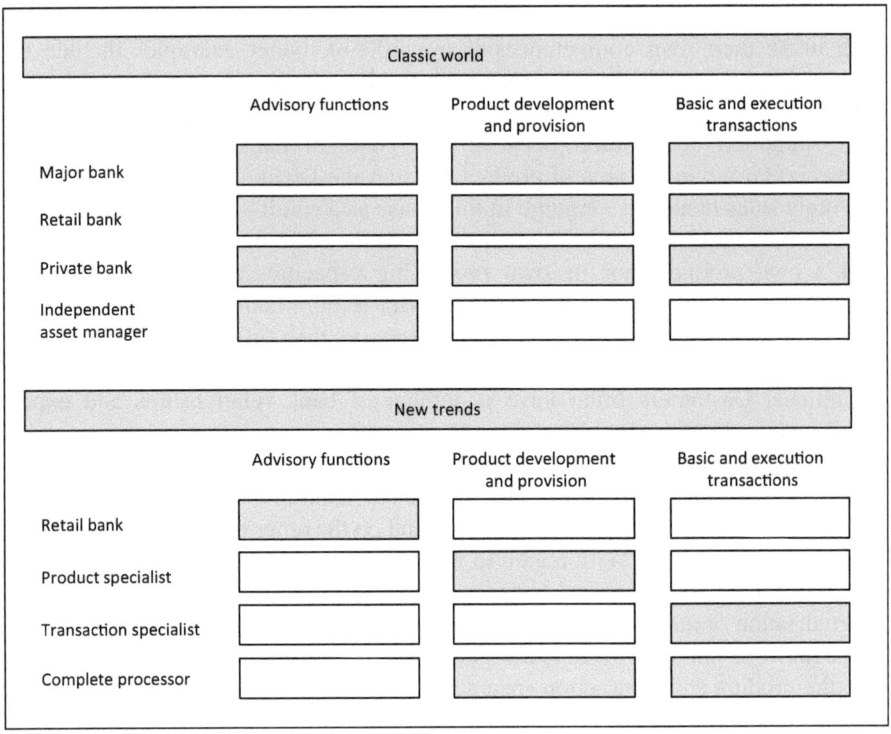

Fig. 6.5 Business models today (*Source* Own illustration)

with hardly any physical asset values, but has a lot of know-how and a brand name. By switching off all non-core activities, micro-industries are developed that are based on specialised knowledge as a core competence. This specialisation allows the rapid and profound further development of the knowledge basis, which secures expertise and reputation. The networking capability of the products is a necessary prerequisite for this strategy. The product specialist participates in internal, stable or dynamic networks. Depending on the positioning at the start of the digital age, quasi- or real externalisation, or quasi- or real internalisation takes place.

The transaction specialist concentrates on cost leadership in the processing of transactions. This business model achieves economies of scale and scope by taking on and executing the relevant process component from asset managers who are oriented towards the customer interface, and these effects can be passed onto the customer in terms of pricing. The use of technology and image maintenance towards network partners are the core competences that are need in the value-creating networks. Using modern technology facilitates membership in networks and a good image attracts many partners, thus leading to economies of scale and scope. This type is aimed at internal, stable or also dynamic network partnerships with providers of customer interfaces and/or product specialists.

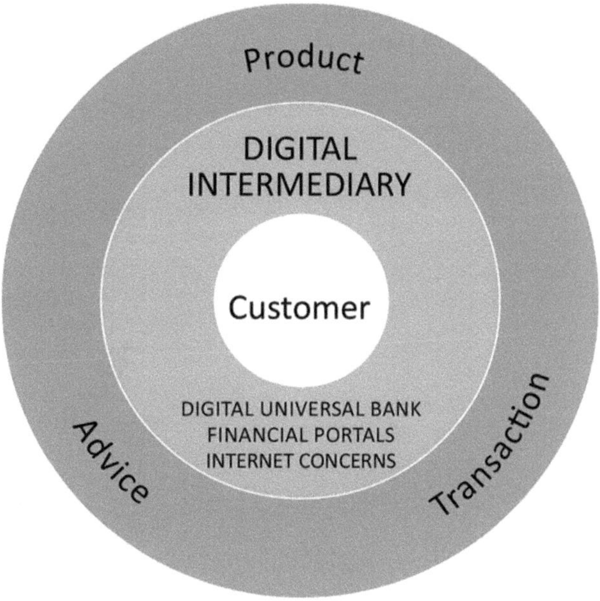

Fig. 6.6 Digital intermediaries (*Source* Own illustration)

6.2.2.4 The Future

Various different future scenarios are conceivable, for which the approaches are already visible in principle, due to digital realities (Fig. 6.6).

Customers can procure the financial services they require via a digital intermediary. This can take different forms:

- Digital universal banks
- Financial platforms
- Internet concerns

Digital universal banks usually cover the same standard service portfolios as direct banks. In addition, they act as platforms for the direct interaction between customers. For example, the FIDOR Bank acts as an intermediary for peer-to-peer loans.

Financial platforms can compile all the necessary information, products and possible transaction processing. Customers can choose their individual service portfolio, almost as if from a menu. They are not in contact with the service providers behind the products. This can be done explicitly—as suggested by the name "platform"—or implicitly– like the bank Simple, which is effectively no longer a bank, but instead offers an app interface in order to offer mobile banking and to ease the aggregation of different providers.

The internet concerns have understood the digital conception from the very outset and are in the process of analysing the user behaviour of all users via Big Data, in order to then combine perfectly tailored offers. A distinction should be

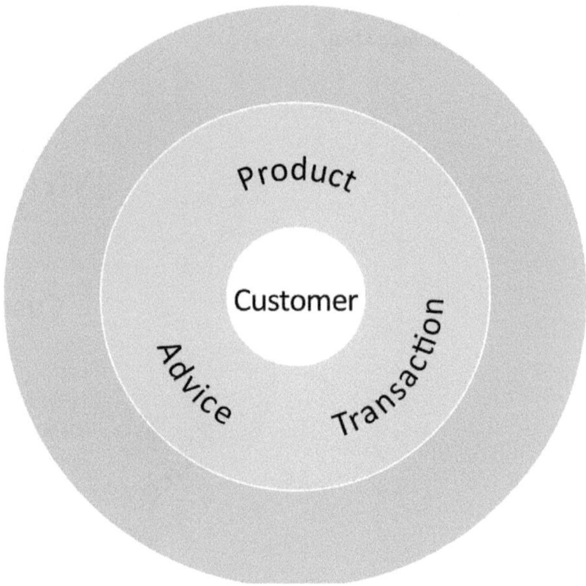

Fig. 6.7 Self-consultation by customers (*Source* Own illustration)

made here between internet payment systems like PayPal and conventional internet concerns such as Google and Yahoo. The former can analyse the payment flows of customers and derive perfectly tailored offers from this analysis, while the latter can take the interest structures of user behaviour and search requests as a basis for designing offers, without any knowledge of the financial flows. They can use this information themselves or sell it on to financial concerns. Google has already acquired a banking license in Europe and is working vehemently on the development of a new core competence: perfectly tailored advice for customers via an online platform. What payment transaction providers and internet concerns have in common is that they can probably act quite quickly as a form of financial intermediary, which—in contrast to digital universal banks and financial platforms—can generate perfectly tailored offers with risk-adequate pricing, by utilising their existing data pool (Fig. 6.7).

The customer advises himself using the available online and offline channels, selects what he believes are the best product and service providers, and allows everything to be processed by the best transaction processor. In this model, the customer takes "architectural responsibility" for his personal model with regard to customer/advice interface, production and processing.

The concept of forming a network platform integrates products and providers—and thus gradually invalidates the previous logic of the business models of banks. It represents a dynamic network without a focal company. The customer himself becomes his own "independent asset manager", he chooses the providers of the individual elements of the value chain himself using an electronic platform that allows the integration of the data of different network partners. The agora represents the realisation of a dynamic network that is compiled by the customer.

For the respective partner this means an externalisation or a quasi-internalisation, depending on their original positioning, and a completely new distribution of value creation.

The possible use options of the agora include the selection, aggregation and structuring of the overall offer of all market participants. In-house products, in the sense of a combination of other external products, are also conceivable. The benefit for the customer lies in the possibility to procure the required parts of the value chain, choosing freely among the specialist best-in-class providers for each element (Cocca et al. 2001). If such a portal manages to gain the trust of a critical number of customers, it will threaten the position of established providers as a focal company, and thus their control of the customer interface.

Dynamic networks are a consequence of this. They are formed, situation-dependent, from a number of different partners, in order to utilise current market opportunities, and they are characterised by great speed of change and complex knowledge and information requirements. The individual parts of the value chain are put together modularly as required—and the alliances with the best form of service design prevail. What is decisive about these dynamic networks is that the customer actively selects the individual service packages. Approaches can already be seen today, where payment transactions are processed on the internet by the provider PayPal, mobile payment transactions will be conducted in future via the respective telecommunications provider, and securities will be purchased from a different provider than the one who holds them in safekeeping. This trend of buying partial services separately will intensify, and will only be moderated when financial service providers come up with convincing overall concepts. Intelligent complete solutions, like those offered by the automobile industry for new-car purchases (mobility guarantee, leasing rates and insurance from one source), could be a model for similar offers in the financial services sector, starting from the personal financial management system, for example (Auge-Dickhut and Koye 2012).

The banking landscape will have changed radically with progressing digitalisation. One possible scenario: the large customer pressure on margins will lead to the formation of advisory banks and product or transaction providers. The advisory banks, in competence centres with specialists, offer qualified advice for a fee to customer groups that are not yet fully self-guided. For the provider banks (who, after all, produce the bank products) infrastructure-sharing is necessary because of the large investments. But the advisory banks are also feeling the burden of high rents in good locations, and are therefore developing a smartphone-oriented branch structure policy (Ernst & Young and University of St. Gallen 2012).

> ▶ **Outlook** Structural gains in efficiency through industrialisation might improve the price/performance configuration in the existing paradigm, and thus extend the established success position even further. Nevertheless, awareness is growing that another challenge is appearing on the horizon in the medium term, which is already beginning to display itself clearly in the behaviour of Generation

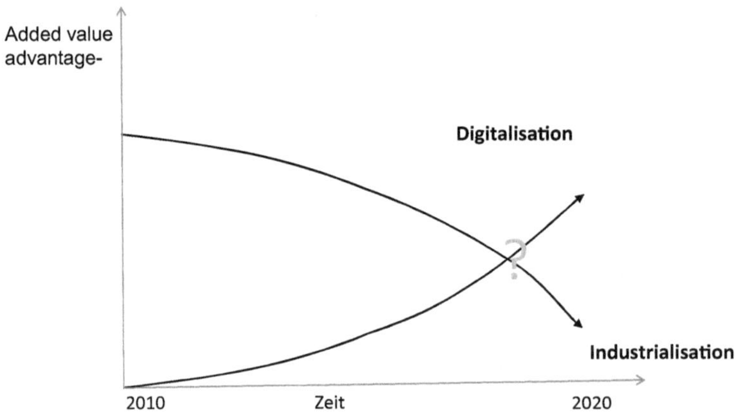

Fig. 6.8 Industrialisation and digitalisation (*Source* Own illustration)

> Y. Business models like Google have shown how digitalisation is eroding existing success positions. Upon reaching a critical mass of users, Google has now also begun to be a significant, and by now the central player in online marketing. AdWord optimisation is familiar to every marketing professional today, earning millions in turnover for Google in an anonymised market. And this logic can also be expected in the banking sector. The mere industrialisation of a bank's own business model is therefore only the admission ticket for the actually decisive competition in the next 5 years—the true digitalisation of business models at all levels of the business model (Fig. 6.8).

The challenge is to tackle the creeping-radical change in business models—strategically, structurally and culturally. Compared to other industries that have had to face radical phases of change the challenge is a double one, as the erosion process is slow but steady. The existing models should be maintained for a certain period, yet the mistakes made by many successful companies and banks in failing to address the new success potential and performance configurations due to a lack of innovative strength, must be avoided. As the Google model shows, the time will come when both curves will meet—and then the market will be too full for the new and indeed no longer very innovative business models. Therefore it is necessary for banks to firmly address the innovation and redesign of their business models now, and to live in both worlds in parallel—only those who manage this will still have a success position or simply a right to exist in 10 years' time.

As could be demonstrated in Chaps. 4 and 5, the competitors from the digital world are already very active. PayPal might already have a banking license, but at present it is earning a turnover of "only" double-digit billions in payment transactions, and it is not seen as a large competitor—but as soon as customers grow accustomed to this functionality and develop trust, the necessary critical mass will be reached and it will be possible to extend the activities in the agora age to include other functionalities of financial intermediation. These long-term revolutionary change processes form the framework for the medium- and short-term developments that should not be ignored in the industrialisation of business models. Purely structural industrialisation will not take account of the actual chances and dangers of ongoing digitalisation—buzzwords Web 2.0 and Web 3.0—as a relevant design parameter: a deadly mistake that can soon have very negative consequences. The "digital natives" are already up to 35 years old—in future they will continue to "soak up" the technological possibilities that are still in their infancy at present, and will only pay for the services they need.

That is the real challenge for the banks of today. In the next 5 years the perfect balance must be achieved between the industrialisation of present-day business models—to catch breath—and at the same time the strategic, structural and cultural digitalisation—whereby, incidentally, nobody knows how the end stages of the former business models will look. Precisely here is the challenge: in a meeting between CEO, CIO and IT consultants, all three parties will look at each other and expect from the other that he knows exactly how to shape the future. Gradual effective digitalisation and co-creation mean more than just slimmer processes, incremental process improvement and industrialised services at low margins.

The only way to maintain existing business models and at the same time to meet the prerequisites required to face creeping, yet exponentially increasing change, is an effective customer focussing. Banks must succeed in orienting themselves constantly towards the customer needs of the individual customer groups, thus strategically, structurally and culturally safeguarding the balance between preservation and renewal. Just as Samsung—in contrast to Nokia or Blackberry—managed to keep up with the iPhone, many different providers (e.g., Fidor Bank, Bank Simple) have managed to take the step into the world of the digital natives. Existing providers will manage this only if they can square the circle while at the same time implementing radical renewal and evolutionary continuation in their business models.

When individual specialised providers become a serious threat to traditional banks, the banks can then buy up their technologies. The same also applies to the direct banks, which are either developed from within or acquired in addition. In contrast, it is not yet clear which role digital intermediaries will have in the future, and how customers will handle the option of self-consultation. Among the internet concerns the options of imitation or acquisition will no longer work—and this is the real threat to today's banks, well beyond the necessity for industrialisation. A forward-looking, networked internal culture of change is required in the banks, which not only reviews the status quo from time to time, but which constantly develops its business models further from the inside in a permanent prototype mode. "Run" and "change" melt into "evolve". This has strategic, structural and cultural consequences, which will be explained in the following sections, and it will also be decisive—alongside the behaviour of the internet concerns—in the sense of "to be or not to be" in the coming decade.

6.3 Wrap Up: Business Models of Banks

Until now, the classic business models of the banks—with the exception of the independent asset manager—have concentrated on all elements of the value chain, as it has always been interesting and also possible in terms of margins. Now it is no longer possible due to the effects of the digital age, which is forcing a focussed discussion of banks' own value contributions in the various areas of the value chain. As well as the previous model types, what is now new is also the concentration on market leadership in one value discipline—for example as a product provider or a transaction specialist. Gradually, the "best-in-class" and superstar effects are coming to the fore. But the new technological possibilities are also putting providers in the position to offer a personal and cross-channel service to all segments.

Increasingly, customers can even put these service configurations together themselves via network platforms. The model of the self-determining agora is becoming ever more possible—technological and regulators barriers are falling. And precisely here is the starting point for the strategic importance of this book and the now urgent reorientation of business models, if a bank wishes to transform a position of success in the future. A prerequisite for long-term success is the ability to identify and further develop stable and mutually advantageous partnerships, and an openness towards further developments, some of which are as yet difficult to estimate. The key is to orient the service configurations towards the effective customer needs—customer focus alone will create added value in the face of the agora. Google is working on the agora—it is only a matter of time.

The need for effective and solution-oriented financial services will remain—however the business models and the possible price/performance configurations will have to change radically in coming years, with the customer in mind. The rigorous industrialisation of the business models of banks is only the admission ticket for the future developments on the horizon. Customers of the future will once again expect different price/performance configurations, and in part they will be able to assemble these themselves on the market. Just as in other industries, where radical change produces clear winners and clear losers, this will also be the case in the banking sector.

The crucial competence in coming years will be to understand the balance between renewal and retention at the level of management. Only then will it be possible to set the strategic, structural and cultural agenda within the present-day banks. Some will achieve this metamorphosis from the inside out, while others won't. A key success factor is the precise and constant observation of customer needs, and the ability to immediately introduce the changes identified into the continuous change process of one's own bank. The "industrialised workbench", with clear and agile processes, is only one necessary prerequisite in managing to contribute actively to development.

It is down to the banks to develop this understanding among all stakeholders in the coming years. Although radical deconstruction and reorientation from a customer's perspective might be painful initially, it must be grasped as an opportunity, designed from the inside with in-house top performers.

References

Auge-Dickhut, S., & Koye, B. (2012). Service Design & Netzwerkfähigkeit: Schlüsselfaktoren zukunftsfähiger Geschäftsmodelle. *Die Bank—Zeitschrift für Bankpolitik und Praxis, 2012*(2), 24–28.

Bernet, B. (2000). Universalbank ade? *Die Bank, 2*, 16.

Cocca, T., Linner, F., Podlewski, M., & Stapfer, P. (2001). Finanzportale—Die neuen Konkurrenten der klassischen Universalbanken? *Österreichisches Bankarchiv (ÖBA), 03*, 229–234.

Ernst & Young, Universität St. Gallen. (2012). *Retail banking 2020*. Retrieved September 29, 2013, from www2.eycom.ch/publications/items/banking/2012_retail_banking_2020/2012_EY_Retail_Banking_2020_d.pdf

Gabler, W. (2013). *Virtuelle organisation*. Retrieved September 18, 2013, from http://wirtschaftslexikon.gabler.de/Definition/virtuelle-organisation.html

Hamel, G. (2000). *Leading the revolution*. Boston: Harvard Business School.

Keller, M. (2000). *Virtual private banking—Vision oder illusion*. Thesis at the Swiss Banking School, Bern.

Koye, B. (2005a). *Private Banking im Informationszeitalter*. Bern: Paul Haupt.

Koye, B. (2005b). *Vernetzung ist Trumpf*. Retrieved July 18, 2013, from http://www.koye-partner.ch/pdf/Schweizer_Bank_Vernet-zung.pdf

Mertens, P., & Faisst, W. (1995). *Virtuelle Unternehmen: Idee, Informationsverarbeitung, Illusion*. Lecture at the 18th Saarbrücker Arbeitstagung für Industrie, Dienstleistung und Verwaltung, Heidelberg.

Sieber, P. (1999). Virtualität als Kernkompetenz. *Die Unternehmung, 04*, 243–266.

Tapscott, D., Ticoll, D., & Lowy, A. (2000). *Digital capital: Harnessing the power of business webs*. Boston: Harvard Business Review Press.

Treacy, M., & Wiersma, F. (1995). *The discipline of market leaders*. Boston: Harvard Business Print.

Wüthrich, H., & Philipp, A. (1998). Virtuelle Unternehmensnetzwerke—Agilität als Alternative zur Unternehmensgrösse? *io management, 11*, 38–42.

7 The New Mechanics of Success: Win-Win Cycles and Client Value Generation

7.1 Development of the Customer-Bank Relationship Prior to the Digital Age

Customer focus and creating value from customers requires a radical shift in attitude towards bank services. In an age of increasing transparency and autonomy, customers expect to interact with their bank as equals. Therefore, in the following section the connection between customer success, bank success and shareholder value will be presented in the context of the win-win cycle. Then the influence of satisfied and loyal customers on bank success will be demonstrated. Starting from these findings it is then possible to understand the influence of the characteristics of financial services on customer success.

In the second half of the nineteenth century, two types of bank groups emerged in the German-speaking region: on the one hand the savings banks and cantonal banks in Switzerland, and the Raiffeisen and cooperative banks in Germany, which were founded traditionally to provide credit to craftsmen and/or farmers; on the other hand the major banks, which financed large-scale industry. Markets and industries were of manageable size, it was possible to build a reputation on word of mouth, and the principle of the "honourable businessman" was at the forefront of the business relationships between banks and their customers (on the concept of the honourable businessman, see Der Ehrbare Kaufmann 2013).

From the mid-to-late twentieth century, this relationship tilted gradually. Product innovations such as options and futures at first allowed the diversification of risks, which also made sense from a business viewpoint, something that had been possible in the raw materials markets for centuries. In the next phase of product innovations, structured products emerged that promised much greater profitability than classic financial investments, due to their possible leverage effect. This was equally attractive to customers and banks in good economic phases—a supposed win-win in the sense of joint yield enhancement. However it should be noted that the principle of the honourable businessman was gradually neglected by the banks, as many customers were completely unaware that increasing yields also meant increasing risks. Banks

S. Auge-Dickhut et al., *Customer Value Generation in Banking*, Management for Professionals, DOI 10.1007/978-3-319-19938-2_7

were not always consistent in informing their customers of this fact. Therefore in phases of falling price developments of "underlying assets", massive losses became the reality in some cases. Furthermore, the idea of the optimisation of shareholder value from the beginning of the 1990s encouraged an increasingly "product sales-oriented" consultation culture. This situation was particularly intensified at the beginning of this millennium, as banks began—in the course of the next product innovation, securitisation (Meyer and Primozic 2011)[1]—to remove from their balances the financing they had provided. This led to a further problem, quite apart from the question of fees or yields for the extra products sold. The primary focus of the (major) banks was no longer on checking the intrinsic value of the loans granted, as they now passed on the loan default risk to the buyers of the securities, which allowed them to expand lending volume considerably. This was one of the decisive factors for the occurrence and extent of the sub-prime crisis (Gabler Wirtschaftslexikon 2013) from 2007, which triggered the necessity for states to rescue banks, including many European banks. All of these developments meant that the provision of situation-adequate and needs-oriented customer advice gradually retreated ever further into the background in the course of the yield orientation of the banks.

As shown in the previous chapters, customers today are in a much better position to inform themselves, to select the best providers—which nowadays are easy to find on the internet, as services are now globally comparable—to suit their needs, and to integrate these into their own solution architecture. Increasingly, they have come to understand that yields involve risks, and are ever less willing to accept purely sales-oriented customer advice.

The following quote, attributed to Henry Ford, could once again gain currency: "It is well enough that people of the nation do not understand our banking and monetary system, for if they did, I believe there would be a revolution before tomorrow morning" (Börsenweisheiten 2013).

Therefore, the future-oriented business models of banks will have to place effective customer needs at the centre of their business activities if they want to survive. This presents two main questions: What are the effective customer needs, and which price are customers willing to pay for the fulfilment of these needs by an intermediary in the digital age.

7.2 Customer Focus and the Win-Win Situation

Customer focus in the digital age is manifested in the creation of a win-win situation for the bank and the customer in a partnership of equals.[2] This is characterised by the fact that both parties experience success—monetary or

[1] The issue of negotiable securities on the basis of loans.

[2] When the parties involved in a negotiation agree a result by which they receive greater benefit than if there had been no agreement at all, one then speaks of a "win-win situation" (Projektmagazin 2013).

otherwise, for example where needs are met in a perfectly tailored manner—from the contractual relationship, which they would not have had if the relationship or transaction had not occurred. In addition, the success gained from the contractual relationship should be divided appropriately between both parties.[3]

Customer benefit must be emphasised more, a fair balance of interests between the customer and the bank must be secured (Walter 2012, p. 23).

The manner in which interests are balanced and thus the "appropriate way" of dividing the profit from the exchange relationship depends on the goals of the customer and the bank. Customer satisfaction or recommendation rates are suitable indicators for checking whether a win-win situation has been and will be realised for both parties.

Yet the win-win cycle does not only encompass success from the viewpoint of the customer or the bank, but also from the perspective of the shareholder. If customers perceive the exchange relationship to be successful, this also influences the success of the bank, due to the aforementioned aspects. An appropriate success for the bank, in turn, is a prerequisite for also meeting the expectations of shareholders. They make capital available (usually a scarce resource). Only when a company attains attractive yields compared to the competition can it secure its financial means. Profit can be seen as a test statistic that indicates whether the company can enable the customer to have efficient and effective success.[4] In future, banks will be measured according to whether they have created long-term value for customers and investors equally. For some time Deutsche Bank has been postulating the "fair share" principle and states that, in its view, it can only be successful in the long term if it creates benefits for customers and shareholders to an equal degree (Deutsche Bank 2013).

Along with customers there are other interest groups that are important for the survival of the company. Other stakeholders of the banks include employees, suppliers, society, regulators and also rating agencies and other financial agents. It is also the case here that the requirements of these interest groups must be considered in order to survive in the long term. Ideally, banks should manage to put together an attractive offer for all shareholders and stakeholders, which will create value for all interest groups (Capellmann et al. 2012).

The starting point of the win-win cycle shown in Fig. 7.1, therefore, is the success of the customer. However, in the next sections the win cycle of the bank will first be presented, as this is the traditional business perspective and it forms the basis for fundamental findings about the connection between reputation, trust, customer satisfaction and customer loyalty. Then we shall leave this "traditional" perspective and take an innovative look at customer needs and the success that

---

[3] The president of the Santander Bank Brazil described win-win (with regard to bank relationships with companies) as follows: "*The company received products and services according to its requirements, thus improved its image and increased its competitive strength. At the same time that had advantages for society and the environment. And we were able to make more turnover and strengthen our relationship with our customers*" (Capellmann et al. 2012, p. 244).

[4] It cannot be the task of the company to create isolated values for the shareholder, profit or options for management (Malik 2005, p. 26 ff.).

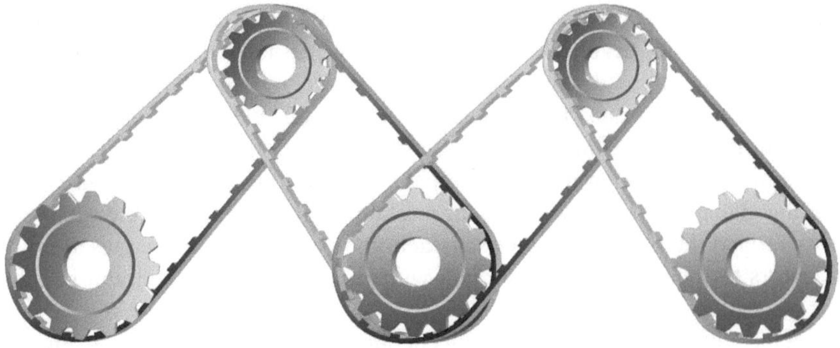

Fig. 7.1 Win-win cycles—mechanics of success (*Source* Own illustration)

customers might have gained from a bank relationship. Only this radical change in perspective allows us to recognise the facets of customer needs in the digital age, to create a win-win situation, and this to develop marketable digital business models.

7.3 Elements of the Win Cycle of a Bank

7.3.1 Overview

A win-situation for banks in the digital age means that customer satisfaction is optimised under consideration of other framework parameters, as this has a positive influence on the company's success. In a customer-centred bank architecture, the customer is at the centre of value creation.

They form the starting point of service provision: the impulse for a certain product or service comes from them or is created with a view to their needs at the customer interface. At the end of the value chain, the product or service is made available to them. At the same time there is an intensive exchange during the provision of the service—the contact with customers is used permanently in order to find out their level of satisfaction and to test their needs development (Fig. 7.2).

From a bank's perspective, it must be a declared goal to provide customers with products or services that will delight them. Only this will make satisfied customers out of customers, who will remain loyal to "their" bank in the long term and ideally act as ambassadors for "their" bank. This in turn contributes to forming the reputation of the bank.[5]

[5] Reputation can be interpreted as one of the immaterial resources of a company. Reputation plays an important role in the attainment, improvement and defence of the competitive position and in increasing company value. Surveys of managers have shown that reputation is the most important immaterial resource (Hall 1992).

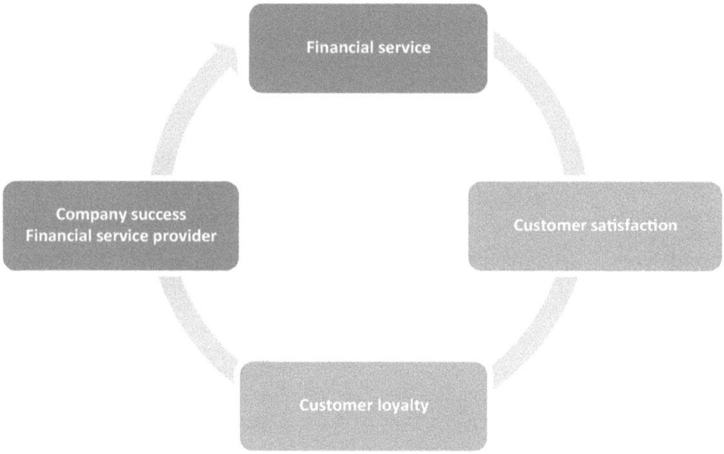

Fig. 7.2 Win cycle of the bank (*Source* Own illustration, based on Huber et al. (2006, p. 68)

Ultimately, success for a bank is measured in key financial figures. However, it is important to note which influencing factors—including soft ones—have led to this success: How it is possible to measure adequately the proportion of recommending customers, their involvement in product development or the possible higher fault tolerance in a long-term customer relationship? Classic financial control parameters are being supplemented by such new factors as Net Promotor Score (NSP) (Capellmann et al. 2012). The NSP is derived from customer surveys and states the degree to which customers who recommend the company exceed dissatisfied customers (Net Promoter System 2013).

In the following sections the individual elements of banks' win cycles and their context will be explained.

7.3.2 Customer Satisfaction as a Key Element

7.3.2.1 The Concept of Customer Satisfaction

Customer satisfaction occurs when customers compare their current experience in using a product or service (actual performance) with their expectations (target performance). If actual performance corresponds with the target performance, the result is a confirmation of expectations. This can lead to satisfaction among customers. If actual performance exceeds the target performance (positive disconfirmation), it can lead to a particularly large degree of satisfaction among customers (enthusiasm). The opposite case, when actual performance is beneath the target performance, is known as negative disconfirmation (Nerdinger and Neumann 2007, p. 128 f.). Satisfaction therefore occurs in the event of confirmation or positive

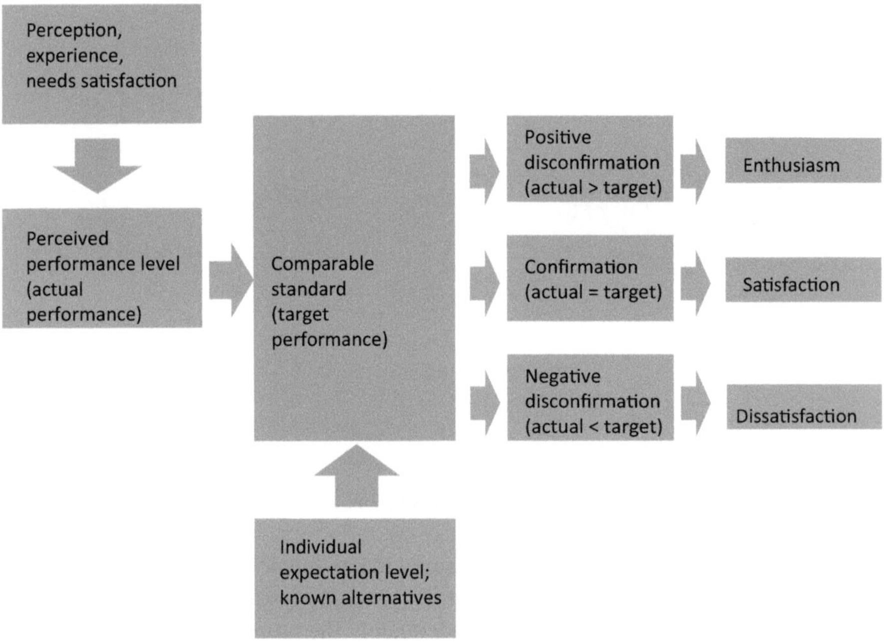

Fig. 7.3 The origin of customer satisfaction (*Source* Own illustration, based on Nerdinger and Neumann 2007, p. 129)

disconfirmation.[6] The boundary between satisfaction and dissatisfaction is often interpreted as the tolerance zone and not as a point value (Fig. 7.3).

Actual performance is the level of performance as perceived subjectively by the customer. This actual performance is the standard against which the customer's expectations are compared. It can be interpreted as the individual level of expectation of the customer, which is fed by experience, the promises of the company, or recommendations from others.[7]

When customers are dissatisfied, they are likely to break off the relationship with the bank, unless they are prevented from doing so by other restrictions such as long-term mortgages, complacency. If they are satisfied, the bank then has a chance of providing further services to the customer and of being recommended. But this does not rule out the possibility that competing banks will also be considered as potential

[6] Some authors also assume that satisfaction only occurs with positive disconfirmation (Hill 1986).

[7] The disconfirmation paradigm can be refined in some aspects of the model by a series of psychological theories. These include the assimilation contract theory, which explains how customers change in hindsight their chosen benchmarks or the perceived performance. Furthermore, the attribution theory and the two-factor theory attempt to explain the connections between expectation-fulfilment and the degree of customer satisfaction (For an overview see Nerdinger and Neumann 2007, p. 131 ff.).

service providers. However, if a bank manages to enthuse its customers, then it has reached its goal and can expect a certain degree of customer loyalty.

Analysing customer groups is part of the strategic positioning of the bank. Yet the bank cannot influence the customer's individual level of expectation in a negative sense (leading to the reduction in customers' expectations). If customers' expectations are not met, they are likely to switch to another provider, who they assume will meet their expectations. However, banks can define the customer groups whose level of expectation converge with their level of service.

7.3.2.2 Influencing Factors for Customer Satisfaction

The satisfaction of the customer depends primarily on how they define the expected target performance. The performance provided can differ from that perceived by the customer. Banks can steer this difference to an extent with expectation management—for example with their positioning on the market and the implied association of the performance promise with the brand in question.

Customer satisfaction is multidimensional. The demands placed by customers on a product, a service or a certain technology can be divided into basic, performance and enthusiasm demands. Their fulfilment has a different effect on customer satisfaction (see Fig. 7.4 and Huber et al. 2006).

- In this context, basic factors are service attributes, the lack of which leads to dissatisfaction. They can be seen as must-attributes and are comparable with the hygiene factors. Customers demand that these service attributes or characteristics are present.

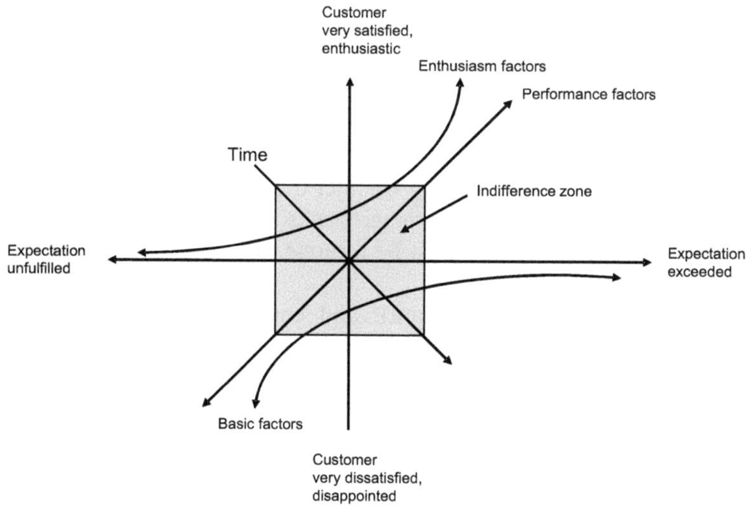

Fig. 7.4 Kano model of customer satisfaction (*Source* Kano 1984 cited from Matzerl et al. 2006, p. 20)

- With performance factors, customer satisfaction increases in proportion with the fulfilment of these factors. The greater the extent of the performance fulfilment, the more likely it is that the customer will be satisfied. These factors are usually actively demanded and communicated by customers.
- Enthusiasm factors are characteristics of services that the customer did not expect. If they are present, they increase the perceived benefit of a key service, causing enthusiasm.

To increase customer satisfaction, the basic and performance factors must be provided at all costs, but that is not enough. In addition, an increase in the perceived benefit of the key service—and thus the enthusiasm factor—is also necessary. This can be achieved by tailoring key services to certain customer groups or by offering additional unexpected and benefit-increasing services. For banks this means that the classification of customer needs in line with these three categories provides indicators for the design of the services and the prioritisation of individual service elements.[8]

In the long term, enthusiasm factors automatically become basic factors. Whereas only a few years ago electronic banking tended to be an enthusiasm factor, it is now a basic factor. This reflects the typical problem for first movers with new technological developments. They soon become technological standards, thus turning from an enthusiasm factor to a basic one. Account must be taken of this effect when developing new technologies and it should be discussed critically whether and/or how the first mover advantage can be protected. It might be worthwhile to distribute the development expense among a number of companies.

By analysing competitors banks can identify the fields in which they differ from their competitors and display greater competence in terms of enthusiasm factors. These areas provide the opportunity for differentiation based on enthusiasm factors. It should be checked beforehand, however, whether the cost of the identified enthusiasm factor can actually be covered. A typical consideration for a possible enthusiasm factor, for example, would be to offer mortgages not only domestically, but also worldwide to wealthy private customers who might wish to finance their geographically widespread real estate ownership. Yet if there is a lack of international know-how, it is worth checking whether this service could be provided with network cooperations with local mortgage banks. Alternatively, the realisation of this identified enthusiasm factor must be forgone, reverting to offering mortgages on the domestic market only.

This concept of basic, performance and enthusiasm factors also provides pointers for service development that go beyond the existing offer. If it is not possible to develop all of the desired characteristics of a desired service for cost

[8] Thus it is not recommendable, for example, to strive for an almost complete fulfilment of basic demands with comprehensive measures, if it means overlooking the satisfaction of possible performance and enthusiasm factors (Huber et al. 2006).

reasons, then those solutions that are most important for customer satisfaction should be implemented or developed.

7.3.2.3 Measuring Customer Satisfaction

Customer satisfaction can be measured using objective and subjective methods. With objective methods, customer satisfaction is measured on observable behaviour—such as turnover or market share. With subjective methods, on the other hand, the perception of the customer is key.

There are three types of subjective measurement:

- **Event-oriented methods** are aimed at the satisfaction of the customer with an experience at the customer interface.
- **Feature-oriented methods** examine certain features of the service or product.
- **Problem-oriented methods** attempt to determine the difficulties or causes of errors that are crucial to satisfaction. This can be done, for example, by analysing complaints (Fig. 7.5).

When existing customers are satisfied, they develop trust in the bank. The bank can exert influence on customer satisfaction via all aspects of financial services as perceived by the customer. These include the transparency of fees structures as well as the quality (characteristics), price and innovative character of the existing financial services. Improvements to product and service quality can also lead to

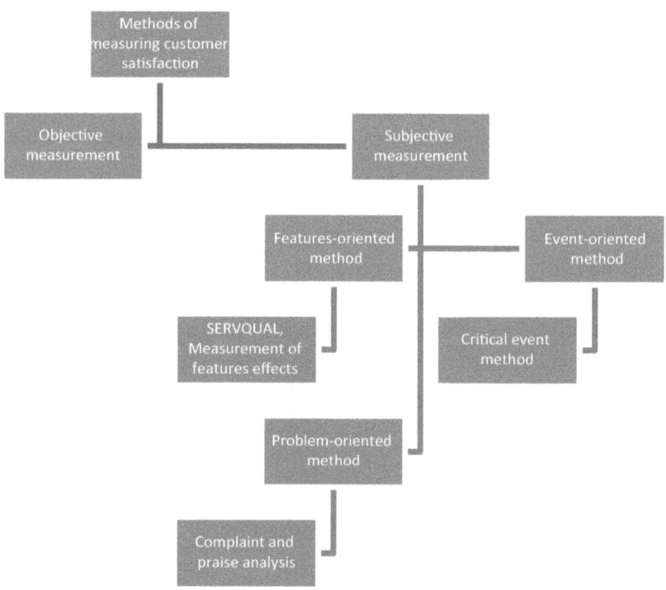

Fig. 7.5 Methods of measuring customer satisfaction (*Source* Bruhn 2006 cited from Nerdinger and Neumann 2007, p. 136)

an increase in customer satisfaction (Fornell et al. 1996). As a result, a reputation can also be gained by means of recommendations.

7.3.3 Reputation

Reputation is a decisive asset in securing future-viable profitability (Pohl and Zaby 2008, p. 4). Reputation is a potential core competence of a bank. When customers first contact a bank, they cannot yet judge its services, or at least not without high information costs. The reputation that the bank has previously earned on the market from existing customers, and which causes those customers to recommend "their" bank, can therefore be a decisive factor for new customers when selecting a certain bank. Reputation is therefore important when the quality of a service cannot be completely observed.

Reputation is defined as the public standing resulting from the perceptions of stakeholders with regard to competence, integrity and trustworthiness (Schierenbeck et al. 2004). It is composed of the sum of the perceptions of all stakeholders affected by the actions of the bank (Pohl and Zaby 2008, p. 7) and can, in this context, be understood as the esteem held by other persons—and thus, implicitly, the trust in the quality of a bank. Banks can improve their strategic competitive position by acquiring a reputation—verbally or virtually—, as it helps to bind existing customers, for example, and address new ones (Tomczak and Rudolf-Sipötz 2006).[9] The reputation of a bank can also play a role in recruiting qualified employees.

Whereas reputation was once built up within narrow local limits via word of mouth, this now takes place worldwide online. Due to the anonymity of the market participants there is a greater risk than in real markets that poor-quality products are delivered, for example, or even that the seller provides no service at all. Therefore, company reputation has an even greater significance than in physical markets. Classic examples include PowerSellers on eBay, who frequently have thousands of ratings and thus recommendations from customers (Dellarocas 2002).

An unchanged or improved reputation usually has no effect on existing customers. A decline in reputation, on the other hand, is likely to have an impact not only on potential new customers, but can also become noticeable in terms of the desertion of existing customers, even though these may not be directly affected by the reputation-damaging activities of the bank. Examples include the LIBOR manipulations and the foreign exchange speculations by the major banks, which are currently under investigation.[10]

With a view to capital lenders we can assume that a loss of reputation can lead to greater expectations with regard to risk premiums and thus to higher capital costs.

[9] Recommendations play a prominent part in credence goods such as doctor relationships or bank relationships.

[10] However, no studies exist on this matter as yet.

When applied to employees, a loss of reputation can lead to a loss in employees or difficulties in acquiring qualified staff.

The formation of the reputation of a bank depends on the actions of individual employees. The problem in this context is that staff are employed in a company for a limited time only. They might have an incentive to refrain from building up a reputation or even to destroy it towards the end of their working life or when switching employer (if past behavioural information is not transparent), as the accompanying negative consequences will no longer affect them personally.

In this context, the entire incentive structure—for example bonus discussions—should be considered for the entire bank management. The incentive with annual bonuses is to downplay long-term corporate goals when making strategic decisions.[11] In a digital world with split-second, worldwide access to information, the danger for banks is that an error as perceived by the customer becomes public immediately and reputation is destroyed.[12] The significance of the reputation of a company is reflected increasingly in the risk management of banks.[13] The topic of reputation risk management is being observed more and more in the context of the risk management of banks, although this type of risk is not (yet) subject to regulatory requirements.[14]

7.3.4 Trust

Once an exchange relationship exists between the customer and the bank, then the aspects of service provision tend to become paramount. If contractual partners enter repeated exchange relationships, it can be worthwhile for banks to refrain from exploiting an unequal distribution of information—in other words, an information advantage for the bank. This might mean selecting the best product for the customer even though it does not—at least in the short term—maximise the yields of the bank.

If customers develop the perception that they are not being exploited, they are more likely to trust their bank in the future.[15]

---

[11] Suggestions to measure bonuses for bank employees on the performance of their bank over a 10-year period should also be seen in this context (Welt 2013).

[12] This does not only apply to banks, however, but also to bank customers. Business customers in particular, who repeatedly require financing, have their own incentive, under certain circumstances (growing reputation leads to decreasing loan interest), not to invest the loans given to them in investment projects that are too risky (Diamond 1989).

[13] "Morale is a production factor," the chief communication officer of Deutsche Bank is quoted as saying (Bankrecht und Bankpraxis 2013).

[14] On the current status of reputation risk management in Swiss banks, see the study by the SIF "Reputationsrisikomanagement bei Schweizer Banken" (Auge-Dickhut et al. 2013).

[15] Even in a limited exchange relationship, in which each party actually has the incentive to behave in an opportunistic manner if the other party is also doing so, this behaviour can be overcome if there is a type of provider who has no incentive to behave opportunistically in the short term. The opportunistic providers then have an incentive to imitate the behaviour of the other type of provider. For the first game-theoretical aspects see Kreps and Wilson (1982) and Kreps et al. (1982).

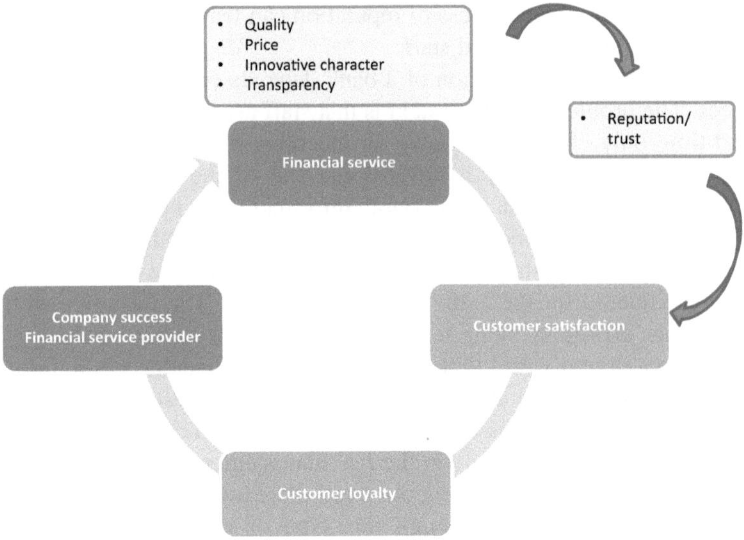

Fig. 7.6 Relevant characteristics of a bank service and a bank as an organisation for creating customer satisfaction (*Source* Own illustration)

A decisive factor in developing a win-win situation between the bank and the customer, therefore, is the building of trust. Trust can be defined as the willingness of customers to engage with a company or corresponding partner without ordering or making any further checks on his future behaviour (Bruhn and Georgi 2010, p. 13) (Fig. 7.6).

7.3.5 The Connection Between Customer Loyalty und Customer Satisfaction

7.3.5.1 Customer Loyalty

The concept of customer loyalty has frequently been subject to discussion, but never uniformly defined. Customers with a voluntary attachment to their company are also known as loyal customers.[16] Customer loyalty does not only describe the previous behaviour of customers, but also the customer's intended behaviour in the future. Below, customer loyalty is understood as a positive feeling on the part of the customer with regard to his relationship with the bank.

The essential psychological aspect is that customers want to be satisfied. They are willing to and interested in justifying in hindsight their initial decision in favour of a bank by perceiving only the positive aspects of the relationship. For example,

[16] Cf. on other concept of customer loyalty such as the reduction of perceived risks by means of the repeated purchase of a product, or also learning theory experiences (Nerdinger and Neumann 2007, p. 134 f.).

after developing an attachment to a bank and in the event of insecurity about the quality of the financial services provided, they tend to search for information that confirms their previous decision in favour of the present bank and not to check the offers made by other banks. Such information might include the positive view of friends towards the selected bank. This tendency to justify a decision in retrospect reinforces the chosen behaviour and can lead to an even stronger bond between a customer and his bank.[17]

The consequences of the "critical mass" effect could play a role in this context. In the digital age a new product or service develops a breakthrough market success when it reaches a critical mass of users—one often speaks of 13 % of the user basis—which then triggers an exponential development due to the network effects. Until this "juncture of diffusion development" is reached, products find it difficult, but thereafter they dominate the market. Conversely, however, it also means that a negative downward spiral can occur. Applied to customer trust, this means that customers remain loyal for a long time, but in the digital age a critical mass of dissatisfied customers can endanger existence. This mechanism can be dangerous for banks (Koye 2005).

The measurement of customer loyalty is still in its infancy, compared to the measurement of customer satisfaction. Either the actual behaviour shown can be measured ex-post, or the behavioural intention ex-ante. Ex-post methods include measuring a company's share of turnover or market. However this reveals nothing about the relation of new and existing customers. Ex-ante, indications can be found on the behavioural intentions of existing customers by means of questionnaires on complaints satisfaction or the intention to repurchase (Nerdinger und Neumann 2007, p. 141).

7.3.5.2 The Connection Between Customer Satisfaction and Customer Loyalty

By now the connection between customer satisfaction and customer loyalty is undisputed. Customer satisfaction is the psychological cause of the attachment of a customer to his bank and is therefore the key factor in customer loyalty (for an overview see Nerdinger and Neumann 2007, for a detailed analysis of customer loyalty from a psychological perspective see Meyer and Oevermann 1995). Satisfied customers are in a state of psychological balance. To preserve this balance, they act loyally and repeated opt for the service in question. Satisfaction can act as a positive behaviour reinforce and increase the likelihood that an exchange relationship will be sought repeatedly with a certain company. The more frequently a customer experiences this positive reinforcement of his behaviour, the closer he

[17] People attempt to attain a balance in their cognitive system and to dismantle dissonances (cognitive dissonance theory). The cognitive system is composed of various individual cognitions (opinions, knowledge). Relationships can be harmonious or dissonant. A dissonant feeling is unpleasant, people try to avoid or minimise it. This can be done by adding new consonant cognitions, which change the dissonant cognition or behaviour (Nerdinger and Neumann 2007, p. 134 f.).

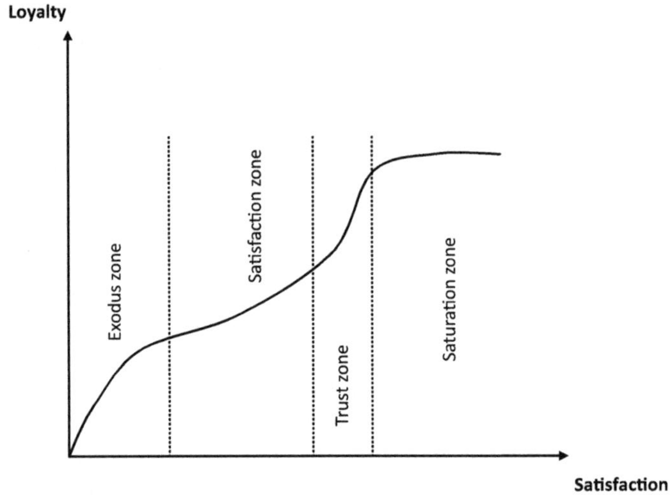

Fig. 7.7 The connection between customer satisfaction and loyalty (The illustration was developed on the basis of an American customer satisfaction barometer. *Source*: Huber et al. 2006, p. 74)

attaches himself to the respective provider (Bruhn and Georgi 2010, p. 16) (Fig. 7.7).

However, there does not appear to be a linear connection between customer satisfaction and loyalty.[18] With negative customer satisfaction values—in the migration phase—an increase in customer satisfaction has a large impact on customer loyalty. With average customer satisfaction values—in the satisfaction phase—an increase leads to only slight growth in customer loyalty. In contrast, an increase in customer satisfaction where there are already high values—in the trust phase—leads in turn to a clear increase in customer loyalty. Where there are very high customer satisfaction values—in the saturation phase—an increase in satisfaction is once again accompanied by only a marginal change in customer loyalty. It is therefore important to be aware of the current satisfaction level of the customer. Most sectors are in the satisfaction zone with their customers—an increase in customer satisfaction does not lead to a growth in customer loyalty. This explains the often marginal effect of customer satisfaction programmes (Huber et al. 2006).

7.3.5.3 Bank-Specific Drivers of Customer Loyalty

The first studies have now been conducted that analyse in detail which factors of customer satisfaction have an effect on the customer loyalty of private and retail banks, and to what extent. Below we present the study by Bruhn and Georgi (2010). The authors identified the factors that are prerequisite for establishing successful customer loyalty. There are three main areas that can be analysed individually as

[18] This seems to be the case at least in intensely competitive industries (Anderson et al. 1997).

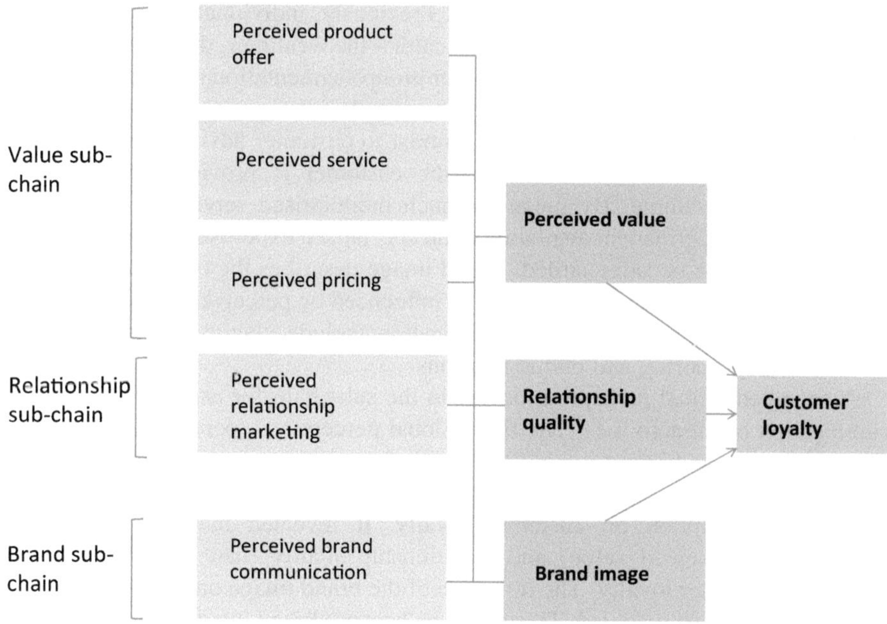

Fig. 7.8 Possible drivers of customer loyalty in private and retail banks (*Source* Own illustration based on Bruhn and Georgi 2010, p. 412)

sub-chains and which allow the integrative optimisation of customer loyalty management (Bruhn and Georgi 2010, p. 410) (Fig. 7.8). The perceived value of a service or product is influenced by the perceived product offer, the perceived service, and the perceived price. The perceived product offer refers to the various aspects of product quality. In banks this could mean product transparency or the quality of the products—for example in terms of historical performance. With perceived service, customers evaluate the service based on the sales channels offered, for example. With price perception, a distinction can be made between cognitive features (such as price knowledge) and affective features (such as price attractiveness or fairness).

The relationship quality is determined by the perceived relationship marketing. It indicates how the relationship with the bank meets customers' expectations.

A high relationship quality means that customers perceive their relationship to the bank to be strong. The relationship behaviour of the company is characterised, for example, by the type of individualisation of communication or by proactive advisor contacts—which are connected with openness and honesty towards the customer and precise knowledge of the customer's situation (for an analysis of the communication quality in customer interactions based on empirical findings in private banking, see Bruhn und Georgi 2010, p. 3 ff.). Relationship quality depends heavily on the perception and needs of the customer. Therefore it is not necessary for a customer advisor to provide the same degree of intensity in individual customer care for every single customer. Previously, individual customer service was always associated with the level of wealth—the wealthier, the more individual the service. In the digital age this customer group segmentation needs to be broken up. In matters of payment transactions, for example, all customers have access to a hotline, which is always available, in contrast to customer advisors. For products with a greater need for consultation, the customer is provided with product specialists, for example. By means of such modularised service structures, the balance between permanent availability and specialised expertise and needs-related advice quality can be safeguarded. Brand image describes the customer's perception of a brand. The brand or the image is influenced by perceived brand communication. Typical tools of brand communication include classic advertising, sales promotions, sponsoring and public relations.

A so-called global perception occurs in the sub-chain for each sub-chain, as a combination of all activities. The three global perceptions (perceived value, relationship quality and brand image) lead to the expression of customer loyalty. An empirical customer survey studied the influence of the individual sub-chains and the global perception on customer loyalty. It revealed that the two global perceptions "perceived value" and "relationship quality" had a similarly strong impact on customer loyalty. The influence of the brand image on customer loyalty, on the other hand, is disputed. This might be because brand image tends to be more of a strong driver in the initial choice of provider, and over the course of the relationship the perceived value and the relationship quality take on greater significance for customers.

Of all the factors of the three sub-chains, the perceived relationship marketing seems to have the greatest significance for customer loyalty. Therefore, an intensive relationship management would appear to be even more important for the success of customer loyalty than the perceived price or service (Fig. 7.9) (for a detailed analysis of the influence of individual drivers on global perception, see Bruhn and Georgi 2010, p. 427).

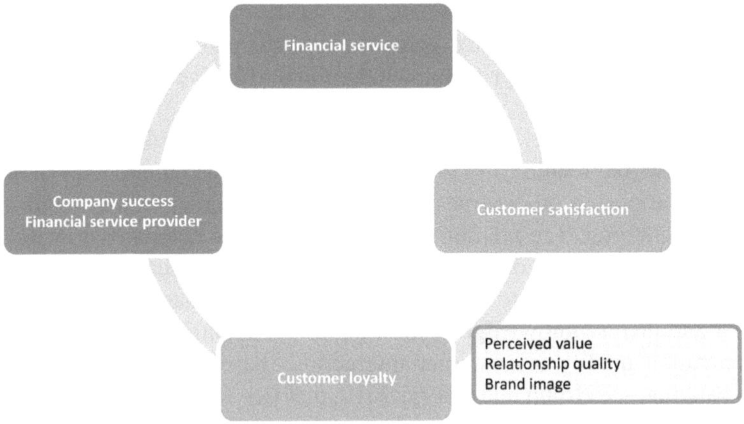

Fig. 7.9 Possible drivers of customer loyalty (*Source* Own illustration)

Banks can therefore control customer loyalty by means of the three areas perceived by the customer, the "perceived value" of the financial service, the "relationship quality" and the "brand image". This control is optimised by means of the three identified sub-chains. Other bank-specific analyses revel further drivers of customer loyalty. For example, the quantity of services availed of seems to exert an influence on customer loyalty (Homburg and Schäfer 2000).

7.3.5.4 Customer Classifications: Of Mercenaries and Terrorists

Customer loyalty and customer satisfaction are therefore not connected linearly. But even when customer loyalty is controlled optimally, it is no guarantee that satisfied customers will stay or that dissatisfied customers will switch to other banks.

That is why, against this background, the analysis of customers is an important element in order to truly derive perfectly tailored customer loyalty activities.

Huber et al. (2006) describe four customer groups. "Loyal customers" are satisfied with the service provided by their bank and do not intend to switch. "Terrorists" are dissatisfied customers who wish to change providers. At the same time they tend to inform other market participants of their bad experiences. "Mercenaries" are satisfied with the product, but often wish to switch brands (see Huber et al. 2006). This customer group is probably relatively small in banking, as the image of a bank cannot be presented externally by consumers to the same extent as an automobile brand, for example. "Prisoners" are permanently dissatisfied, but due to high barriers they cannot switch banks easily. It is likely that the not inconsiderable costs of switching banks—at least in the past—go some way to explaining the existence of such "prisoners". A key factor for the previously high costs of switching was the time involved in changing banks. In an age where less effort is required to switch banks, the effect has been seen less and less. Banks now even offer support for moving a bank account. Globalance Bank offers this service with a "change butler" online tool (Globalance 2013a, b).

Calling dissatisfied customers "terrorists" is not very appropriate in the digital age. Other authors use the terms "demanding satisfieds", "stable satisfieds", "resigned satisfieds" and "stable and demanding satisfieds" (Stauss and Neuhaus 2006).

In order to optimally control these elements of customer loyalty, it is of fundamental importance to gain information about the needs of the customers and to use this information as a true determinant. This means rejecting the previously dominant communications logic: turning away from the pure communication of information and towards two-way communication and the evaluation of existing information about the customer. This is usually comprehensively available online, and can be gleaned in great detail by analysing social networks.[19]

[19] Social networks can be used as indicators to evaluate in real time the most valuable capital of a bank—the customer basis (Capellmann et al. 2012).

7.3.6 Bank Success

So what is the effective added value in controlling customer satisfaction and customer loyalty? Customer satisfaction and loyalty have long been decisive for company success, well before the digital age (Anderson et al. 1994; Homburg and Rudolph 1997). The added value can be defined from the perspective of the customer and of the bank—the basis for a relationship between equals.

From the customers' perspective, their behaviour—if they are satisfied—changes in various different aspects. Satisfied customers—who at the same time are loyal customers—repeatedly purchase the same product, or a different product from the same provider (Anderson and Sullivan 1993).[20] They have low price sensitivity (Reichheld 1996), a higher fault tolerance, and contribute to product development (Braunstein 2001).

Successful customer loyalty is also reflected in the communication behaviour of the customer. Satisfied customers are more willing to communicate the advantages of the product to other interested parties. If the recommendation quota of loyal customers increases, this makes acquiring new customers easier. For their part, new customers who have been acquired via recommendations tend to display a more loyal behaviour than those acquired, for example, via an advertising campaign (Huber et al. 2006) (Fig. 7.10).

The behaviour of satisfied customers has various positive effects on bank success. The turnover of the bank increases as a result of the repeated sales of the same or different products (cross-selling) to existing customers (Huber et al. 2006). Banks can better estimate the creditworthiness of their existing customers—which

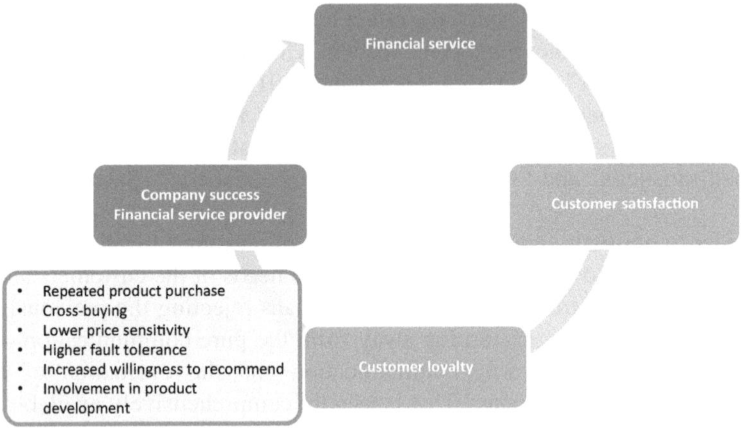

Fig. 7.10 Behaviour of satisfied bank customers (*Source* Own illustration)

[20] Numerous empirical studies show the positive effect of customer loyalty on a company's success (Bahradwaj 1996; Butz and Goodstein 1995; Kalwani and Narayandas 1995).

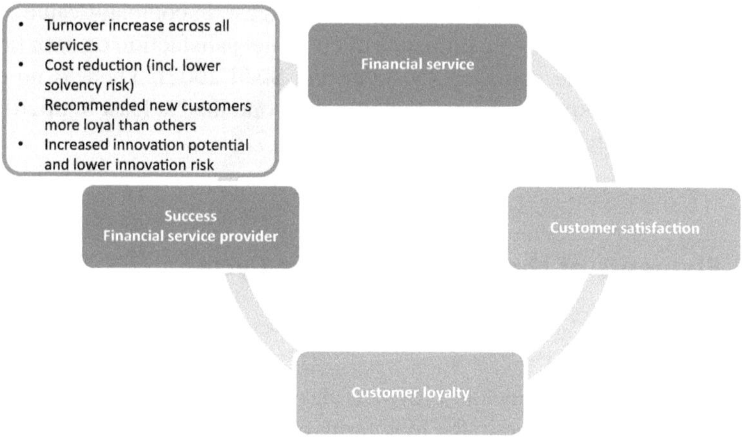

Fig. 7.11 Influence of satisfied bank customers on the bank success (*Source* Own illustration)

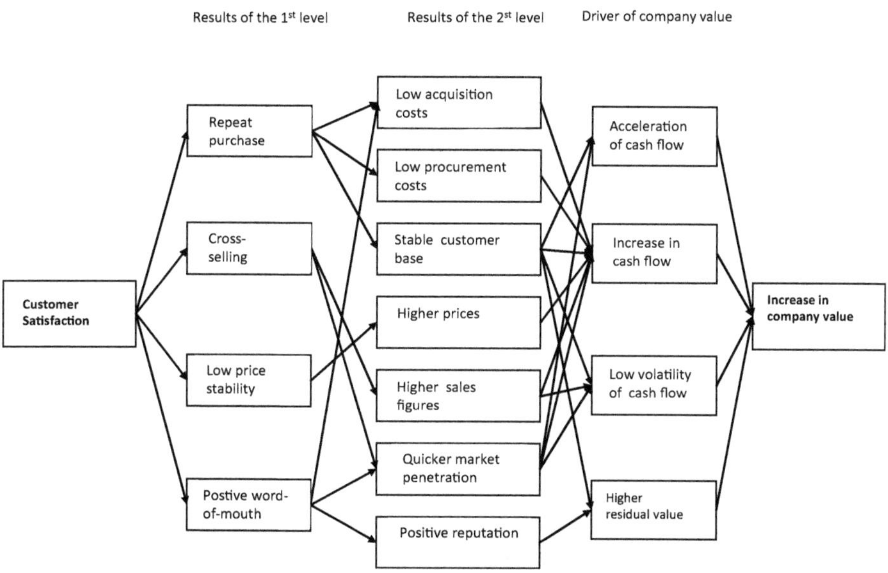

Fig. 7.12 Customer satisfaction and company value (*Source* Matzler and Stahl 2002, p. 49)

decreases risks and the information costs of providing loans. Investment recommendations can also be optimised, because there is a broader information base and investment history, compared to new customers. Due to their lower price sensitivity, existing customers are also less receptive to cheaper competing offers. Finally, innovation risk can also be minimised by involving customers in product development at an early stage, while at the same time the innovation potential is raised due to the innovative capabilities of the customers (Fig. 7.11).

Realising all of this potential can lead to an increase in company value. Matzler and Stahl presented in detail the influence of customer satisfaction on cash flow, and thus on the value of the company (Matzler and Stahl 2002). There is no explicit mention of customer loyalty as a concept, but it is contained at least implicitly in the subject of repeat purchases and cross-selling (Fig. 7.12).

7.4 Elements of the Customer's Win Cycle

7.4.1 Overview

In the win cycle of the bank the previous classic view of company success was presented. In order to survive in the long term, each bank must control its company success and at the same time satisfy customer needs with an attractive price/performance configuration. The customer needs and the benefit gained by the customer from the bank relationship have always been subject to analysis—under the premise of maximising economic utility for the bank. This premise has not changed in the digital age. However, because the classic bank products and services are increasingly becoming standard services/commodities, the previous success position of banks is being eroded. Furthermore, customers in the digital age have a very different creative and selective power—even if they are not (yet) exploiting this to the full—and their demands on banks are changing with ever greater rapidity. Therefore it is absolutely necessary to go beyond the classic perspective and to analyse what creates long-term added value for the customer. Observing the win cycle of the customer enables this analysis as a prerequisite for developing future-viable price/performance configurations.

At the customer interface customers are provided with financial products that they can compare with their needs. Whether and how customer satisfaction occurs in the process, and how this might lead to customer loyalty, was presented in the previous sections, as were the concepts of reputation and trust. Whereas the reputation of a bank plays a decisive role in the first contact when selecting a bank, trust is more important in the case of a repeated exchange relationship. Trust can be interpreted as the willingness of customers to continue to conduct further business with their bank without testing every single service in detail. This saves the customer time and money, but at the same time it makes them vulnerable, as they become dependent on the behaviour of their bank (Bruhn and Georgi 2010, p. 13).

Below, therefore, we shall address the two new aspects of customer success—the analysis of his possible needs and the success he gains from the exchange relationship with the bank. Aggregated with the previous aspects, this represent the win cycle of the customer (Fig. 7.13).

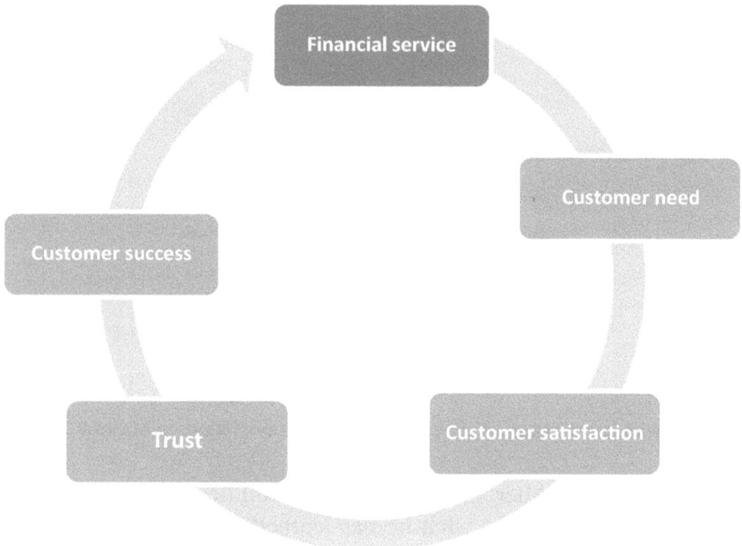

Fig. 7.13 Win cycle of the customer (*Source* Own illustration)

7.4.2 Financial Needs Pyramid: The Needs of Digital Customers

There are a number of different systematisation approaches to the topics of the needs and needs hierarchies. One of the best-known approaches, which is not undisputed, but substantially very convincing, comes from Maslow (see SDI-Research 2013). People's expectations grow with each increasing level of needs satisfaction. A distinction can be made between different needs levels: from the satisfaction of basic physiological needs, the need for security, social needs, individual needs, to self-actualisation (Fig. 7.14).

This approach can be transferred in part to the banking sector. Traditional bank product fulfil, to a certain extent, "basic needs". Like the consumption of food to maintain basic physical functions, basic needs such as payment transactions or holding a bank account are covered. In addition, needs from the needs level of "security" are fulfilled—for example the investment of financial resources or the financing of property. Increasingly, however, customers also place expectations on financial products with regard to the fulfilment of needs at the three upper levels.

The needs level of social integration is expressed in the desire for networked communication and participation, which can be fulfilled with the exchange between customers or by involvement in the development of solutions or new products.

The level of "individual needs" is expressed in the aspiration to receive largely individualised and perfectly tailored solutions, possibly in a chosen design and via a personalised sales channel mix (convenience). Such a layout of products and sales channels includes the entire area of e-banking, for example, but also the individual design of credit cards by customer. The level of "self-actualisation" concerns the

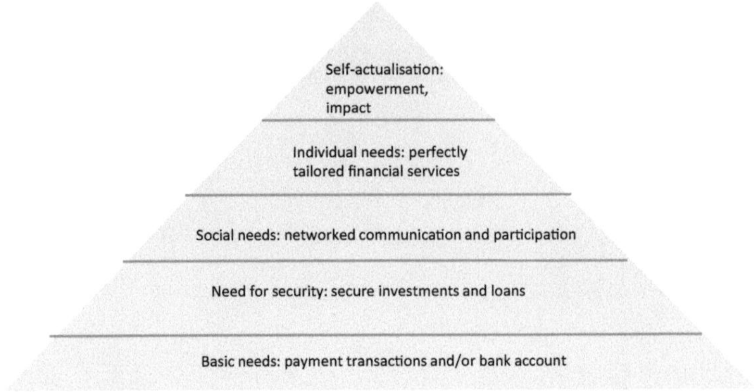

Fig. 7.14 Financial needs pyramid (*Source* Own illustration, based on Maslow 2013)

customer's desire to further develop his own abilities and thus his autonomy (empowerment), and to apply what he has learned. Banks can satisfy this needs by providing customers with the opportunity—naturally, only when required—to acquire their own financial knowledge and also to use it. This is encouraged especially by innovative banks such as Fidor Bank and others, with the establishment of forums in which bank customers can help each other if they have any questions. This presents the opportunity to mix empowerment and participation.

Another desire that could equally be positioned at the highest level of the needs pyramid is surely the topic of impact. Customers can have an interest in what influence a bank product or service, and its production, have on the environment. Investing financial resources has a social and economic effects. By choosing future-viable funds, the investor can exert a targeted influence by deeming that his financial resources should not be invested in the arms or tobacco industries, for example.[21]

Considering the needs of bank customers—especially at the highest levels of the needs pyramid—is an essential design factor for the future business models of banks. Customers will notice the added value only if their needs are addressed in a level-appropriate manner.[22] Even if not every customer will strive for the highest level of self-actualisation in the future by trading in financial products, at least the majority of customers, at the level of "individual needs", desire the optimum availability of financial services as well as permanent and cross-channel communication.

In the next 10 years, the level of self-actualisation, which is currently important to only a small and exclusive customer group, will gradually become a commodity.

[21] On the customer needs of Swiss banks with regard to sustainable investments and the lack of satisfaction from Swiss banks, see Auge-Dickhut et al. (2012).

[22] Globalance allows its customers to create an ecological footprint of their portfolio (Globalance 2013a).

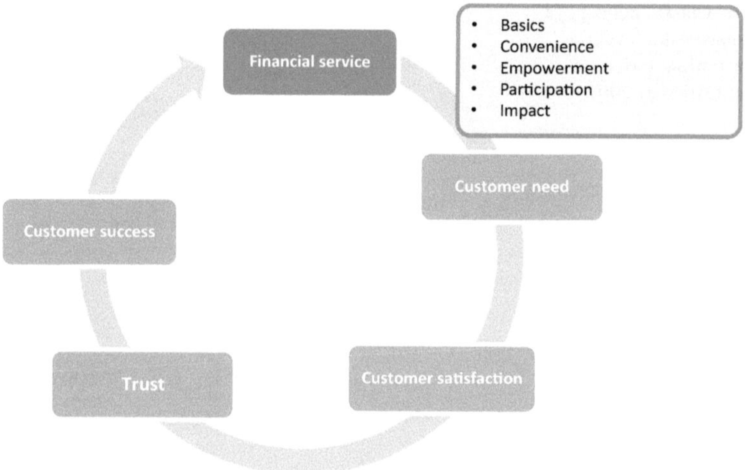

Fig. 7.15 Possible facets of customer needs (*Source* Own illustration)

For digital natives can procure all the necessary information themselves and do not require professional advice (standard needs). They expect, therefore, the provision of understandable, self-explanatory product information and support via certain tools.

Against the background of the needs pyramid, the aspect of a customer's desire for trust gains further in significance. In this context, trust means that customers enter into a performance relationship with their bank without testing, every single time, all of the aspects of the desired service provision by the bank, where possible. On the one hand this saves them time and money, but on the other hand it makes them vulnerable to the behaviour of the opposite side. Ultimately, therefore, trust is based on the positive expectation with regard to the intention or the behaviour of the bank (Capellmann et al. 2012). If banks do not manage to satisfy or uphold customers' security need for trust, then customers will realise their increasing social, individual and self-actualisation needs with other providers (Fig. 7.15).

7.4.3 Client Value Generation: Customer Success

So how can the success experienced by customers with their bank relationship in the digital age be measured and controlled? The term "customer value" has been used frequently in the literature (Pechtl 2005; Kotler and Bliemel 2007). It can have two different meanings, as it can be understood from the perspective of the bank or from that of the customer.

From the perspective of the bank, the value of the customer is seen as his contribution to achieving the monetary and non-monetary goals of a bank (Fig. 7.16). The amount of customer value from the viewpoint of the customer

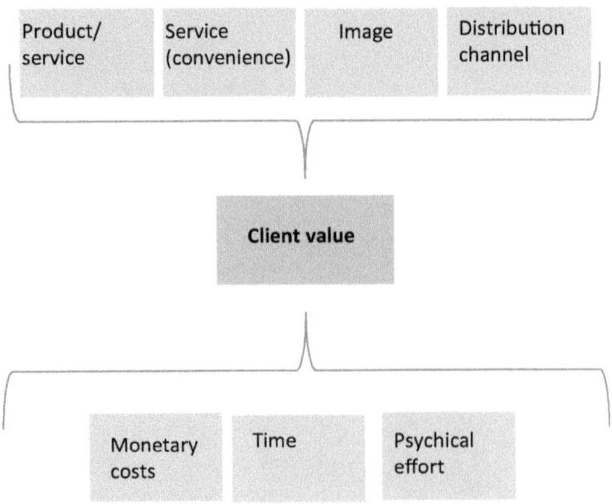

Fig. 7.16 Classic concept of the customer value (*Source* Own illustration, based on Kotler and Bliemel 2007, p. 58)

indicates whether it is worthwhile for the customer to commence or to maintain a relationship with a bank (Fig. 7.17).

The factors that influence customer value are well known. Measuring customer value, or the individual factors, is a controversial topic in the literature.[23] What all treatments of customer value have in common is that they are based on a construct such as the concept of benefit. Benefit is composed of the consumption of the good, the associated service provided, the image of the bank and the available distribution channels. The price expected to be paid and additional possible expenses for consuming the product or service are compared with the benefit from the service. The expenses frequently incurred by the customer in addition to the sales price can be termed additional costs. According to Pechtl (2005, p. 1) they are differentiated in the industrial context as follows:

- Follow-up costs (such as switching, operational, repair and maintenance costs)
- Divergence costs (such as transport costs, time required for transport)
- Transaction costs (such as search, agreement, control and implementation costs)

In the context of financial services, follow-up costs might include switching banks, divergence costs could represent the time spent in visiting a customer advisor in a branch, and transaction costs include, for example, the cost of examining account balances.

The difference between the benefit and the sum of expenses is then known as the customer value. Synonyms include net benefit or value gain. Until now, the main focus has been on how banks can exert influence on the aforementioned aspects of

[23] For instance, how much a customer is willing to pay for a service is analysed. This transformation from benefit from a service into the price that he is willing to pay is complex; it is also unclear how additional costs should be treated (Adler 2003; Balderjahn 2003).

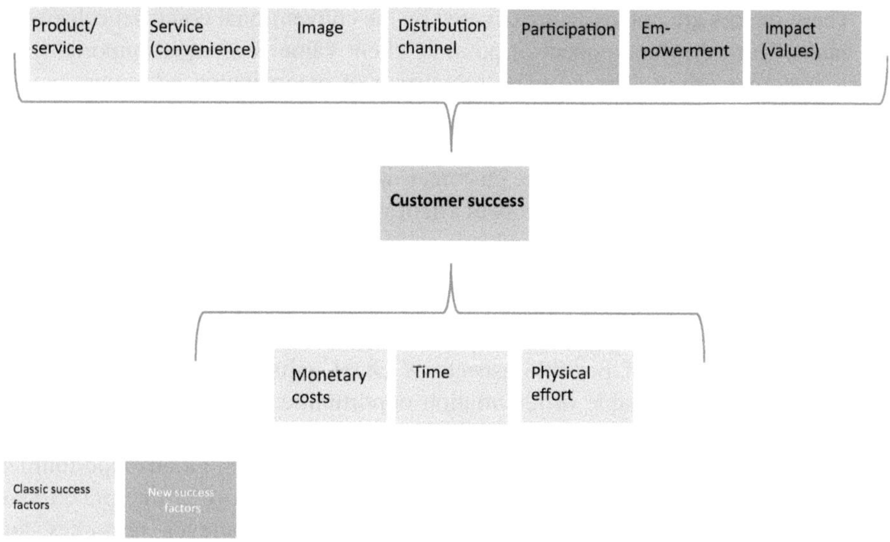

Fig. 7.17 Client value in the digital age (*Source* Own illustration, based on Kotler and Bliemel 2007, p. 58)

customer value by means of classic marketing channels, and thus maximise their success.

The previous discussion has now shown that new needs arise. Now, customers are no longer being satisfied at all needs levels. Differentiation features exist at the higher needs levels (see Fig. 7.14). The key question is which components influence the "success" derived by the customer from exchange relationships—hereafter referred to as "customer success" or "client value" (Fig. 7.17).

In contrast to customer value, the term "client value" refers to all positive and negative experiences had by the customer when consuming bank services. These include the previous classic factors of customer value. These factors operate at the level of basic physiological or security needs, as they essential comprise the classic bank services for customers. Gradually, the three highest needs levels will become ever more relevant for all customer groups (see Fig. 7.14).

The elements of client value must therefore be supplemented with the following needs to be satisfied:

- Empowerment: Learning about the financial product or the financial market in general in the context of the service relationship.
- Participation: Active involvement in the provision of the service or the development of the product.
- Impact: Satisfaction by procuring services with a positive social influence—such as future-viable investment products.

These factors are not yet being covered by the conventional control mechanisms of banks. Not every component of possible client value is of equal importance to each customer group. The growing proportion of emancipated customers means that the "new" and previously unfulfilled needs—from the classic banking perspective—will become increasingly significant. Therefore, the future-oriented control of client value integrates all of the customer needs presented.

Prior to the digital age the factors of client value were stable over a long period. The new understanding of client value is a sensible initial rough categorisation for the challenges of the digital age. In future, the development of the needs of digital natives must be observed very closely in order to refine or, where necessary to adapt this rough categorisation. In that respect, the graphic shown above is merely a momentary snapshot of possible aspects of client value. Changes to needs will produce not inconsiderable differentiation opportunities, as customer experience the difference between actual offers and their needs as a "pain". Those who succeed in evaluating these "pain points" can exploit these differentiation opportunities (Osterwalder et al. 2011). The resulting client value can also be interpreted as a standard for the performance capability of banks. Wherever resources are transformed into success from the customer perspective, added value will be created (Mairhofer 2009). It remains unclear, however, for which aspects of client value customers are willing to pay banks in future, and which needs they can cover without the help of banks.

7.5 Wrap Up: Win-Win Cycles and Client Value Generation

In the digital age, customers are in the driver's seat and are increasing choosing the business models that will provide them effectively and subjectively with added value. What is characteristic for a win-win situation in the customer-bank relationship is that there is an exchange relationship among equals, and an appropriate distribution of the success derived from this exchange relationship, for both the customer and the bank. How is the bank success from an exchange relationship with the customer structured when the customer is satisfied and "bound", in a positive sense, to his bank? Which aspects influence client value—customer success in the digital age? And what influence do satisfied customers have on bank success? These are the key questions of the Client Value Generation.

The win-win cycles show how customer success influences the success of the bank and also that of other shareholders and stakeholders. The aspects of how the customer relationship influences bank success have already been analysed in detail in the literature, at least in a cross-sector manner. Thus, where there is an unequal distribution of information, reputation plays an important role in acquiring new customers. As soon as customers enter into a bank relationship, they can gain personal experience from the services provided by "their" bank. They build up trust in the form that they do not need to test the service provided by their bank each and every time, for example, by comparing it with the services of other banks. So what factors determine customer satisfaction?

Here, the components of the individual banks services can be divided into basic factors, performance factors and enthusiasm factors. Banks can use these to optimise their existing performance portfolio or to improve customer satisfaction in the area of new investments. While basic factors are simply a must-have, and a basic level must be fulfilled here, customer satisfaction can be increased with performance and enthusiasm factors. With regard to technological innovations, it should be examined where the technology can be deployed for the aforementioned factors, and how long, for example, advantages in the enthusiasm factor can be exploited before they mutate into a state-of-the-art technology, such as online banking, thereafter becoming merely a must-have.

Customer satisfaction can lead to customer loyalty, although there does not appear to be a linear correlation. Customer loyalty refers to the future behaviour of the customer, i.e., his intention to remain with the existing provider. There are areas in which an increase in customer satisfaction does not lead to additional customer loyalty. From a financial viewpoint, therefore, it is not attractive for a bank to expend more effort. In the banking sector the perceived value of a performance (offer, service, price) and the relationship quality seem to have a greater influence on customer loyalty than the brand image of a bank. But also the quantity of services availed of can influence customer loyalty.

What success can a bank gain from having satisfied, and therefor loyal customers? They will repeatedly buy the same product, or a different product from the same provider, they have lower price sensitivity and a higher fault tolerance, and may even contribute to product development. This leads to an increase in turnover, a reduction in costs—for example with solvency risks, as the customers are known—, an increase in innovation potential, a decrease in innovation risk, and more loyal new customers if these have been acquired via recommendations. In an age of saturated markets and cutthroat competition, banks must have a vital interest in cultivating the existing group of customers.

The following customer success factors were considered previously from a classic business perspective: product, service, image and the manner of service provision. As customers in the digital age have a greater creative and selection power, and because their expectations of banks are changing ever more rapidly, it is absolutely necessary to go beyond the conventional viewpoint and to analyse what provides future-viable added value to the customer. Customers have demands that are placed on different levels of the financial needs pyramid. The better educated or informed a customer is, the more such new or previously ignored needs appear to play a role in the context of financial products. As well as the purely basic needs such as payment transactions or bank accounts, banks have also previously satisfied the need for security (safe investments or loan provision). Now, however, the authors believe that customers have increasing needs at a higher level of expectation. These include the need for participation and social exchange. This can be provided by involving customers in the development of financial products or in the exchange and enabling of advice from customer to customer in forums established by the bank (see the offers of the digital universal banks). The individual needs of the customer can be addressed by offering perfectly tailored financial services. This is likely to occur already with wealthy private customers, but this wish can also be fulfilled in retail banking, by means of individual mass customisation. The desire for self-actualisation can be realised by giving customers the opportunity to educate themselves further and to deal (mostly) autonomously with financial products. The customer's wish to know which economic, social and ecological impact the chosen financial product will have is also positioned on the highest level of the financial needs pyramid.

This lists of needs is certainly not rigid, but rather changes over time. For the analysis of customer needs it is essential to change perspective radically and to include the customer function, for which a number of different techniques can be used, such as customer journey. Then it is certainly worth discussing which needs of the respective customer groups can be fulfilled optimally by the respective bank at an appropriate price/performance ratio. First, however, it is more relevant to pursue this radical change in perspective and to place the customer at the centre of the analysis, instead of regarding him merely as a means towards profit optimisation. Increasingly, in an age of sinking information procurement costs, this behaviour can also be adopted by customers. This could then lead to economic disadvantages, as the described advantages of a long-term exchange relationship (from low solvency risks to low investment risks) can no longer be realised by banks. But for customers, too, permanently comparing services is also associated with costs and effort.

References

Adler, J. (2003). *Methoden zur Messung der Zahlungsbereitschaft von Nachfragern* (Arbeitsbericht). Duisburg.

Anderson, E. W., & Sullivan, M. (1993). The antecedents and consequences of customer satisfaction for firms. *Marketing Science, 12*(2), 124–143.

Anderson, W., Fornell, C., & Lehmann, D. R. (1994). Customer satisfaction, market share and profitability: Findings from Sweden. *Journal of Marketing, 58*(3), 53–66 (Cited from Huber et al. Der Zusammenhang zwischen Produktqualität, Kundenzufriedenheit und Unternehmenserfolg. In H. Hinterhuber & K. Matzler (Eds.), *Kundenorientierte Unternehmensführung: Kundenorientierung—Kundenzufriedenheit—Kundenbindung* (pp. 67–83). Wiesbaden.).

Anderson, W., Fornell, C., & Rust, R. (1997). Customer satisfaction, productivity and profitability, differences between goods and services. *Marketing Science, 12*, 129–145 (Cited from Huber et al. Der Zusammenhang zwischen Produktqualität, Kundenzufriedenheit und Unternehmenserfolg. In H. Hinterhuber & K. Matzler (Eds.), *Kundenorientierte Unternehmensführung: Kundenorientierung—Kundenzufriedenheit—Kundenbindung* (pp. 67–83). Wiesbaden.).

Auge-Dickhut, S., Baumast, A., Fichter, C., & Koye, B. (2012). *Nachhaltigkeit bei Bankgeschäften in der Schweiz*. Retrieved September 29, 2013, from www.koye-partner.ch/pdf/Nachhaltigkeit_SIF.pdf

Auge-Dickhut, S., Düblin, R., Hemmo, M., & Koye, B. (2013). *Reputationsrisikomanagement bei Schweizer Banken*. Zürich: Compendio Bildung.

Bahradwaj, S. G. (1996). The risk implications of a customer retention strategy in the manufacturing industry. In: *Research Convergence Proceedings: Contemporary Knowledge of Relationship Marketing*, Emory University, Atlanta (Cited from Huber et al. Der Zusammenhang zwischen Produktqualität, Kundenzufriedenheit und Unternehmenserfolg. In

H. Hinterhuber & K. Matzler (Eds.), *Kundenorientierte Unternehmensführung: Kundenorientierung—Kundenzufriedenheit—Kundenbindung* (pp. 67–83). Wiesbaden.)

Balderjahn, I. (2003). Erfassung der Preisbereitschaft. In H. Diller & A. Hermann (Eds.), *Handbuch Preispolitik: Strategien—Planung—Organisation—Umsetzung* (pp. 387–404). Wiesbaden: Gabler.

BankrechtundBankpraxis. (2013). *Reputationsrisiko: DievernachlässigteRisikokategorie*. Retrieved September 29, 2013, from http://www.bank-recht-und-bankpraxis.de/index.php?id=931&tx_ttnews[pS]=1235862000&tx_ttnews[pL]=2674799&tx_ttnews[arc]=1&tx_ttnews[tt_news]=95&tx_ttnews[backPid]=988&cHash=38f65df6d

Börsenweisheiten. (2013). *Zitate und Weisheiten*. Retrieved January 31, 2013, from http://boersenweisheiten.c11.de/henry-ford/es-ist-gut-dass-die-menschen-des-landes-unser-banken-und-geldsystem

Braunstein, C. (2001). *Einstellungsforschung und Kundenbindung: Zur Erklärung des Treueverhaltens von Konsumenten*. Wiesbaden: Deutscher Universitätsverlag.

Bruhn, M. (2006). *Qualitätsmanagement für Dienstleistungen. Grundlagen, Konzepte, Methoden*. Berlin: Springer.

Bruhn, M., & Georgi, D. (2010). Eine integrative Analyse der Treiber der Kundenbindung bei Banken—Systematisierung und empirische Befunde. *KREDIT und KAPITAL* Heft 3, 407–436

Butz, H. E., & Goodstein, L. D. (1995). Measuring customer value: Gaining the strategic advantage. *Organizational Dynamics, 24*, 63–77 (Cited from Huber et al. Der Zusammenhang zwischen Produktqualität, Kundenzufriedenheit und Unternehmenserfolg. In H. Hinterhuber & K. Matzler (Eds.), *Kundenorientierte Unternehmensführung: Kundenorientierung—Kundenzufriedenheit—Kundenbindung* (pp. 67–83). Wiesbaden.).

Capellmann, W., Peverelli, R., & de Feniks, R. (2012). *Wie sich die Finanzbranche neu erfindet—Was Kunden von Finanzdienstleistern wirklich erwarten*. Munich: FinanzBuch.

Dellarocas, C. (2002). *The digitization of word-of-mouth: Promise and challenges of online reputation mechanism* (Working paper MIT) (Cited from Schwalbach, J. (2004). *Reputation*. Retrieved May 1, 2013, from http://www2.wiwi.hu-berlin.de/institute/im/publikdl/2004-2.pdf)

Der Ehrbare Kaufmann. (2013). *Leitbild des ehrbaren Kaufmanns*. Retrieved September 23, 2013, from http://www.der-ehrbare-kaufmann.de/zum-leitbild-des-ehrbaren-kaufmanns/

Deutsche Bank. (2013). *Bank der Zukunft*. Retrieved August 12, 2013, from https://www.deutsche-bank.de/medien/de/downloads/2013-02-26_Rede_RN_Bank_der_Zukunft.pdf

Diamond, D. (1989). Reputation acquisition in debt markets. *Journal of Political Economy, 97*, 828–862.

Fornell, C., Johnson, M. D., Anderson, E. W., Cha, J., & Everitt, B. (1996). The American customer satisfaction index: Nature, purpose and findings. *Journal of Marketing, 60*, 7–18.

Gabler Wirtschaftslexikon. (2013). *Subprime Krise*. Retrieved January 14, 2014, from http://wirtschaftslexikon.gabler.de/Definition/subprime-krise.html

Globalance. (2013a). *Vermögensverwaltung—Investments mit Doppelter Rendite*. Retrieved August 24, 2013, from http://www.globalance-bank.com/leistungen-fuer-sie/vermoegensverwaltung.html

Globalance. (2013b). *Sinnvestieren Sie auch—oder legen Sie immer noch an?* Retrieved November 18, 2013, from http://www.globalance-bank.com/

Hall, R. (1992). The strategic analysis of intangible resources. *Strategic Management Journal, 13*, 135–144.

Hill, D. J. (1986). Satisfaction and consumer services. *Advances in Consumer Research, 13*, 311–315 (Cited from Nerdinger, F., & Neumann, C. (2007). Kundenzufriedenheit und Kundenbindung. In K. Moser (Ed.), *Wirtschaftspsychologie* (pp. 127–146). Heidelberg 2006.).

Homburg, C., & Rudolph, B. (1997). *Customer satisfaction in industrial markets: Dimensional and multiple role issues*. Vallendar: Wissenschaftliche Schriftenreihe ZMU.

Homburg, C., & Schäfer, H. (2000). Cross-selling. Aus der Kundenbeziehung mehr herausholen. *Harvard Business Manager, 6*, 35–44.

Huber, F., Herrmann, A., & Braunstein, C. (2006). Der Zusammenhang zwischen Produktqualität, Kundenzufriedenheit und Unternehmenserfolg. In H. Hinterhuber & K. Matzler (Eds.), *Kundenorientierte Unternehmensführung: Kundenorientierung—Kundenzufriedenheit—Kundenbindung* (pp. 67–83). Wiesbaden: Gabler.

Kalwani, M. U., & Narayandas, N. (1995). Long-term manufacture-supplier relationships: Do they pay off for supplier firms? *Journal of Marketing, 20*, 1–16 (Cited from Huber et al. (2006). Der Zusammenhang zwischen Produktqualität, Kundenzufriedenheit und Unternehmenserfolg. In H. Hinterhuber & K. Matzler (Eds.) (pp. 67–83). Wiesbaden.).

Kotler, P., & Bliemel, F. (2007). *Marketing-management*. Stuttgart: Schäffer-Poeschel.

Koye, B. (2005). *Private Banking im Informationszeitalter*. Bern: Haupt.

Kreps, D. M., & Wilson, R. (1982). Reputation and imperfect information. *Journal of Economic Theory, 27*, 253–279.

Kreps, D. M., Milgrom, P., Roberts, J., & Wilson, R. (1982). Rational cooperation in the finitely repeated prisoner's dilemma. *Journal of Economic Theory, 27*, 245–252.

Mairhofer, E. (2009). *Customer Value Management. Wie findet man die richtige Balance zwischen Kunden- und Gewinnlogik?* (Working Paper). Retrieved September 29, 2013, from http://www.campus02.at/uploads/Arbeitspapier_CustomerValueManagement_2825_DE.pdf

Malik, F. (2005). *Management*. Frankfurt a. M: Frankfurter Allgemeine Buch.

Maslow, A. (2013). *Needs pyramid*. Retrieved November 22, 2013, from http://www.abraham-maslow.de/beduerfnispyramide.shtml

Matzler, K., & Stahl, H. (2002). Was bedeutet für die Wertsteigerung für die Führung von Dienstleistungs- unternehmen. In H. Hinterhuber & H. Stahl (Eds.), *Erfolg durch Dienen—Beiträge zur wertsteigernden Führung von Dienstleitungsunternehmen* (pp. 46–62). Renningen: Expert.

Matzerl, K., Stahl, K., & Hinterhuber, H. (2006). Die Customer-based Vies der Unternehmung. In H. Hinterhuber & K. Matzler (Eds.), *Kundenoreintierte Unternehmensführung* (pp. 5–21). Wiesbaden: Gabler.

Meyer, A., & Oevermann, D. (1995). Kundenbindung. In B. Tietz, R. Köhler, & J. Zentes (Eds.), *Handwörterbuch des Marketings* (pp. 1340–1351). Stuttgart: Schäffer-Poeschel.

Meyer, H., & Primozic, F. R. (2011). *Die Verbriefungstransaktion*. Frankfurt a. M: Boorberg.

Nerdinger, F. W., & Neumann, C. (2007). Kundenzufriedenheit und Kundenbindung. In K. Moser (Ed.), *Wirtschaftspsychologie* (pp. 127–444). Heidelberg: Springer.

Net Promoter System. (2013). *Measuring your Net Promoter® score*. Retrieved August 12, 2013, from http://www.netpromotersystem.com/about/measuring-your-net-promoter-score.aspx

Osterwalder, A., Pigneur, Y., & Wegberg, J. T. A. (2011). *Business model generation: Ein Handbuch für Visionäre, Spielveränderer und Herausforderer*. Frankfurt a. M: Campus.

Pechtl, H. (2005). *Preispolitik*. Stuttgart: UTB.

Pohl, M., & Zaby, S. (2008). *Das bankbetriebliche Reputationsmanagement in dessen Umsetzung*. Retrieved July 24, 2013, from http://www.unibas.ch/fileadmin/wwz/redaktion/Forum/Forschungsberichte/2008/01_08.pdf

Projektmagazin. (2013). *Win-win situation*. Retrieved January 26, 2013, from http://www.projektmagazin.de/glossarterm/Win-win-situation

Reichheld, F. F. (1996). Learning form customer defections. *Harvard Business Review, 56*, 56–59.

Schierenbeck, H., Grüter, M. D., & Kunz, M. J. (2004). *Management von Reputationsrisiken in Banken* (WWZ Forschungsbericht 03/04). Basel

SDI Research. (2013). *Bedürfnishierarchie*. Retrieved November 18, 2013, from http://www.sdi-research.at/lexikon/beduerfnishierarchie.html

Stauss, B., & Neuhaus, P. (2006). Das Qualitative Zufriedenheitsmodell. In H. Hinterhuber & K. Matzler (Eds.), *Kundenorientierte Unternehmensführung: Kundenorientierung—Kundenzufriedenheit—Kundenbindung* (pp. 85–100). Wiesbaden.

Tomczak, T., & Rudolf-Sipötz, E. (2006). Bestimmungsfaktoren des Kundenwertes: Ergebnisse einer branchenübergreifenden Studie. In B. Günter & S. Helm (Eds.), *Kundenwert* (pp. 125–155). Wiesbaden: Gabler.

Walter, H. (2012). Gelingt der Neuanfang? In W. Capellmann, R. Peverelli, & R. de Feniks (Eds.), *Wie sich die Finanzbranche neu erfindet—Was Kunden von Finanzdienstleistern wirklich erwarten* (pp. 22–23). Munich: FinanzBuch.

Welt. (2013). *Banken sollten Boni-Auszahlung über 10 Jahre strecken—Haldane*. Retrieved September 28, 2013, from http://www.welt.de/newsticker/bloomberg/article113034485/Banken-sollten-Boni-Auszahlung-ueber-10-Jahre-strecken-Haldane.html

Part III

Change: The Path to a Future-Viable Bank Architecture (With a Significant Contribution by Charlotte Götz)

8 Successful Reorganisation (I): Systemic Change Frameworks

8.1 Change Frameworks

In the previous chapters we described who the customers are and what they expect from their bank in the future. Naturally, the question now arises: How can banks meet these external demands internally? Convincing large organisations to change is always a difficult subject. By now change management has become a specialist field in itself, and countless books are concerned with its theoretical and practical aspects.

This chapter will provide an insight into the different levels of change, which will enable a basic understanding for the key levers and stumbling blocks associated with a successful future-viable transformation. These levers, consisting of strategy, structure and culture, represent the external framework of the Zurich model, and processing and integrating these within the organisation should produce the result that the internal attitude of the organisation is oriented towards the external needs of the market. Neither transformation nor customer orientation can be decreed. Therefore we shall describe here from the practical change perspective how such a process of radical change can lead to more customer orientation, by thinking from the customer's perspective and making a collective contribution that finds expression in the form of a network-like cooperation. We shall describe how such a change process is prepared and implemented, which topics of power and group dynamic will be encountered, and how change can be introduced across the whole employee spectrum.

Change does not happen overnight, unless one has the opportunity to start afresh on a green field site. Whoever does not have this option must embark on the process-related path to change. This does not involve a management process, but rather a change or development process, because it is not possible to suddenly tell those people with whom you wish to shape the future that everything they have done so far was completely wrong. And yet now we demand that these people change from one day to the next. Luckily they do not do so, otherwise chaos might have reigned in light of the countless and somewhat short-sighted attempts at

S. Auge-Dickhut et al., *Customer Value Generation in Banking*, Management for Professionals, DOI 10.1007/978-3-319-19938-2_8

change in the last decade. Nevertheless, banks need to start preparing for the future now. We are not talking about renovation or optimisation, but rather preparing to take permanent account of the constantly changing market conditions.

We have almost become accustomed to the repeated financial crises and dramatic fluctuations on the stock exchanges. The pressure on banks to change, however, has only apparently declined. That also applies to banks that are proud of their good customer loyalty. "Luckily customers have not yet grasped how badly and inconveniently we actually serve them," said one savings bank employee in Germany. It is not that bank employees are unwilling to take care of the needs of their customers fairly. However, the increasingly flexible customer behaviour is now clashing with the still immovable inner structures of banks. Added to this is the sales pressure logic of "push product selling", with a simultaneous cost reduction of the shareholder value paradigm. The numbers of new customers are a good indication of future viability: even those who are doing well now suspect that if everything remains as it is, the black numbers could change into red numbers in only a few years. Banks can avoid neither industrialisation nor customer focus if they wish to secure their survival. In other words, a "future-viable industrialisation," as declared by the COO of a regional Swiss bank, "cannot merely concentrate on efficiency growth, but demands thorough changes from a bank." The diagram is based on the model of social interaction or on the interplay between actions and persons at the different levels of social life. Social interaction is always determined by the personal development process and the selective perception that builds on this.

Change takes place at different levels: at an individual, team, organisational and social level (Fig. 8.1). These levels each pursue their own logic, roles or norms, but they also influence each other. The success of social interaction depends on the ability to assume other perspectives. Thus an increase in individual measures will not make a better whole. Only changes to attitude and behaviour that are visible on a collective level can lead to future-viable changes in organisations. The pressure on banks is increasing: on the one hand, society is demanding more ethical and value-oriented action, and on the other hand the individual yearns for financial benefit and more for personal meaning at work. One often hears talk of the treadmill, inhuman waves of dismissals, pressure from above, control instead of leadership. In our consultation work in banks we have also encountered exceptions, especially among young bankers, and the first signs of solution-oriented cooperative behaviour and network structures and thinking can be detected.[1]

For a long time banks have felt secure in their position at the end of the "economic food chain". After all, even in the face of creeping disappointment, an awful lot has to happen before a long-term customer terminates his relationship

[1] In our training seminars at the Schweizerische Institut für Finanzausbildung of the Kalaidos Fachhochschule Zurich we regularly ask students to prepare a seminar paper on the willingness to change within their own working fields. The results are remarkable: the knowledge of management tools has become must better in recent years. What is often missing, however, are formats that support cross-sector dovetailing.

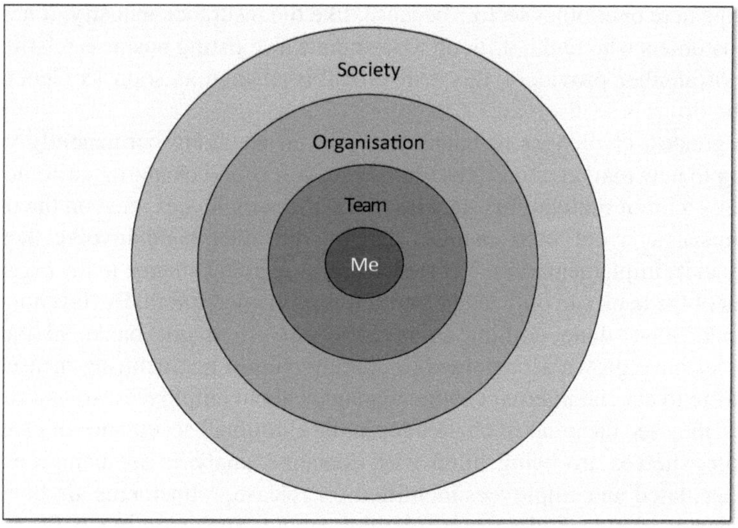

Fig. 8.1 The different levels of change (*Source* Own illustration)

with his principle bank. But not even the most loyal customers stay forever, and new ones do not simply appear of their own accord. There are loads of change concepts, but implementation is poor. Therefore, the basic mood in banks can be described as at least uneasy. It is becoming clear to ever more institutions that using short-term reactions to cost pressures as a lifebelt leads to many internal wounds, but not to new shores or, ultimately, to more customer intimacy. Too frequently, employees see much-praised increases in efficiency as nothing more than dismissal manoeuvres, after which the same work can be carried out with fewer staff. Following so many measures to increase efficiency, employees are either worn out, or at the very least disillusioned. They therefore accept impassively the PowerPoint battles over the latest structural forms, and attend countless interviews, for most of them have learned that things will continue as they always have anyway. Professor Peter Kruse describes this movement of employees nicely as a "bend and wait" strategy (Kruse 2008), where they duck down and then reappear when it's all over. What is missing is a captivating view of the future and an honest strategy that will help to find the way back to the customer. Instead it seems as if many banks during the crisis years simply withdrew further into the shell of their paralysing behavioural pattern, which is too frequently characterised by the contradiction that ultimately the survival of the bank is paramount and not the wellbeing of the customer. The lack of good leadership is worrying. Employees are simply delivering, while encountering a thicket of process constructs and control mechanisms—hardly anyone is able to shape anything anymore.

Those who now manage to develop the necessary energy for change, both argumentatively and emotionally, has a good chance of doing justice to the changed customer needs and of securing his survival. The banking industry still has an advantage here over other sectors because, like the insurance industry, it has quite a lot of customers who find it difficult to terminate an existing business relationship in favour of another provider—this will probably change as soon as Generation Y takes the driver's seat.

The greatest challenges to banks today lie in engaging permanently with and adapting to new market conditions, industrialisation, and changing customer needs. It requires a lot of motivation—in a double sense: employees must on the one hand be enthusiastic about such changes and on the other hand involve themselves actively in its implementation. Yet such a thoroughgoing change in the organisation learning of the bank can only take place if it is motivated internally. It is not the case that banks have done nothing in recent years. In major banks in particular, employees have grown accustomed to operationalised restructuring measures. Yet if one were to ask the internal change managers about employees' transformational abilities, they see the greatest challenges in the emotional acceptance of change. All the while, shelves are being filled with concepts, analyses are being conducted, FTEs calculated and employees identified for release, refinements are being made to efficiency—but nobody wants to think about implementing a fundamental, collective change in behaviour to the benefit of the customer.

Regulations or market pressure are not sufficient motivators for conveying the added value of change from the management level down to employees in a meaningful manner. The necessity for change must be built on an internal process of recognition and meaningfulness among management and staff, so that fundamental behavioural patterns and attitudes can change. How can an employee develop more professional and social competence towards the customer, if he cannot also do so internally?

Thus there is a mutual effect between a healthy customer relationship and the future viability of banks. In an empirical study by the Schweizerische Institut für Finanzausbildung, 200 bankers were asked about the transformability of their bank. It was argued that the future of banks depends on their networking abilities and why additional customer orientation leads to more transformability: "*... the transformability of a company depends on its network orientation, but the latter is dependent on customer orientation. These dependencies increase with the importance of the customer interface*" (Auge-Dickhut et al. 2014, p. 14). Customer orientation has long been seen as an element of the market orientation of a company, continued the study, along with competitive orientation and cross-departmental coordination. The path towards network organisation begins with increasing cross-departmental coordination. At the same time, this means that the customer interface will become the central unit in designing the business model, especially for service companies. Market orientation will thus become customer orientation.

In order for customer orientation to contribute to network orientation, there needs to be fundamentally more agile in-house structures and processes that respond repeatedly and flexibly to the needs of the market. To ensure that this learning process is future-viable and synchronised, it cannot be left to individuals or be based on individual stand-alone measures. These days, organisations are too complex and varied for change to be simply dictated from above, with the rest being left to the local manager to implement. If the entire organisation is to participate, and if it should reach the customer as added value (value proposition), change must be supported by a coordinated change management system that makes sense to those involved and which develops sufficient energy to have a collective impact.

Sadly, rigidly hierarchical banks are confronted with difficult contradictions. Only when the individual parts of a company are aligned to the whole can an effective and future-viable difference be made. If, for example, incentives are not adapted to new customer advice objectives, it will be difficult to implement them permanently. As long as "hunters" with little expertise are in a better implicit and explicit position in banks than "farmers", who act in the sense of customer needs, the main focus of advisors will not be on a comprehensive consultation. As long as large margins are aimed for in the product area, product departments will not be willing to take their products from the shelves. The current dilemma is nicely illustrated here: management must justify its existence in the current paradigm with higher turnover targets, but is at the same time obliged to keep costs down with a wide range of individual measures. But the growing flood of initiatives and reorganisations merely restricts employees in providing services to customers and dampens their motivation. One of the main weaknesses of many banks is their self-preserving management attitude and their control and leadership culture. Instead, what is necessary is a permanent monitoring of the effects of new trends on the business model, and accordingly increased adaptation flexibility. This can be achieved by means of an integrated orientation of strategy, structure and control.

8.2 Systemic Change

When we speak here of how a transformation to more customer orientation can be effected, this is done in the context of a systemically motivated change management system in organisations.[2] This is not an introduction to change management. But without a glance at the organisation and how more customer orientation can be implemented in practice, customer-focussed banking remains little more than a theory. The most important paradigms and levers of systemic change work will be explained here briefly, using a practical example.

Systemic change management is not so much a model that leads by means of intervention from actual state A to target state B, but rather it is an approach whose origin lies in various natural and sociological theories. It is expressed more by its systemic attitude and corresponding intervention instruments than by a logical-linear or mechanistic change of the given reality.

The key basic assumptions of systemic organisational development can be described as follows: everything revolves around how an effect can be generated

[2] See here in particular Königswieser and Hillebrand (2004) and Königswieser et al. (2012), with whom the authors developed the systemic-complementary advisory approach.

in a social (i.e., human-made), autopoietic[3] (self-referential) entity such as an organisation. Companies, as social systems, can be changed only from the inside. While the necessity for change usually results from the insufficient answer to market needs, the solution to the problem can be found only from within the company. Therefore, whoever wishes to design a change process must pay special attention to communicative and interactional patterns and systems (Simon 2004).

System theory offers many approaches to carry out change in an existing system. The human is not seen as an individual person, but rather always in the context and the movement (dynamic) of a greater cause. Thus many people are always involved in a problem, just as in its solution, all of whom shape what is happening and influence each other mutually through interaction. From the area of professional advice we are accustomed to the situation that work is carried out on a single problem (symptoms) on behalf of the hierarchical management, without involving management in the change process. It is a different matter in this case: solutions arise in joint development processes. Work is carried out on the patterns on which the visible problematic behaviour is based, in order to then develop solution-oriented alternatives in reflection phases. The different organisational levels are involved in this process (Fig. 8.2).

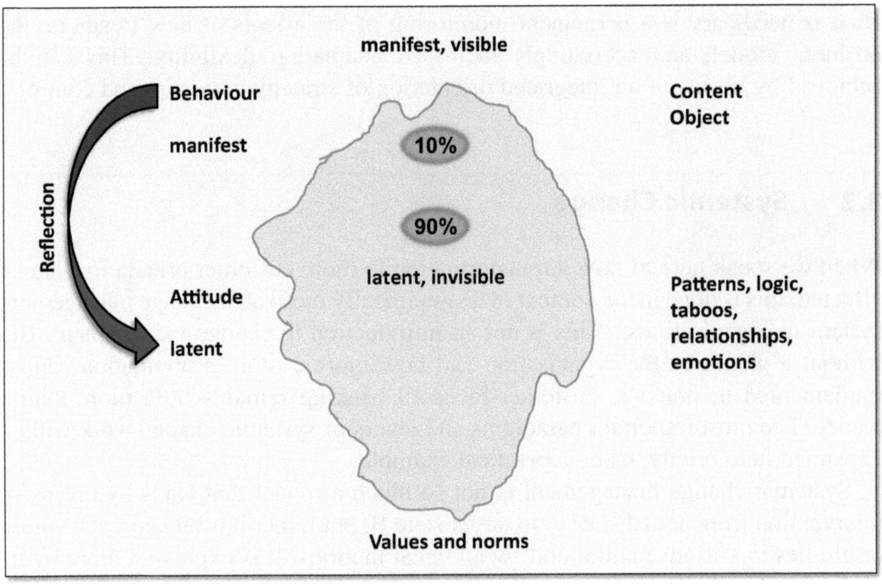

Fig. 8.2 The iceberg model (*Source* Own illustration)

[3]Autopoiesis is a key concept in the sociological system theory of Luhmann (1984): Social systems consist solely of communication and they produce and reproduce themselves continuously—like living organisms—in non-targeted processes.

The cultural iceberg model was developed by Edgar H. Schein (2003, p. 25), who used it to describe behaviour in organisations in terms of the visible, formal company culture and hidden, informal aspects such as attitudes, relationships, power or beliefs.

Nobody likes to change customary habits or processes. Especially if it involves moving in the direction of an as yet unknown future or when it concerns changing not only the other, but also oneself. That is why change processes often begin with a certain disappointment: change plans are always accompanied by the indirect accusation that one is incapable of doing one's job and now needs help from outside. Generally, those responsible feel more confident when external experts are called in. That makes it easier at first to deal with resistance, to cover oneself or to legitimise unpopular decisions. This consultants often come and go after endless PowerPoint presentations in which they outline what has to be done differently in future to those people tasked with carrying out the change. Yet change can only be permanent if is also takes account of the behavioural level.

Another basic systemic idea assumes that the knowledge is already available for change in an organisation. Managers should not be replaced by external consultants in change processes. It is easier for an organisation to implement change successfully if it has its own creative freedom, i.e., turning those affected into those involved. Only co-designers will later take responsibility for future action. That also applies to the board of management. During a change project in an automobile financing company that was focussed solely on consultation, one of the board members concluded: *"In the end I no longer even knew what I had taken responsibility for. If we had had an honest discussion in our meeting, I would have decided differently on some matters."* Successful change management is not visible in concepts, but instead in the degree of actual implementation.

Systemic support tends to be restricted to involving external knowledge only sparingly and compensatory. The main task of systemic advice is to generate enough trust in the interaction between the professional and process levels so that there is room for change in which the employees of an organisation can themselves develop new forms of cooperation in a social process. In other words, learning to learn.

Changes are incredibly time- and resource-intensive. They demand of those involved a great degree of commitment, often to the capacity limit, especially when the work to be carried out must be done in addition to the line function. Change processes often fail because they are not given enough time to be completed before another change process is set in motion. Unlike 10 or 20 years ago, companies can no longer start a change process, bring it to an end, and then work according to it in subsequent years. In a situation of constantly changing market conditions and technologies organisations must now be enabled to be permanently adaptable and to learn to live with constant transformation.

How can the radical conversion process of a "non-trivial machine"—as systemic thinkers say—be turned into a transformation process in which the reaction of the single individual involved cannot be predicted, let alone dictated? A key problem in controlling organisations is creating agreement between organisational and

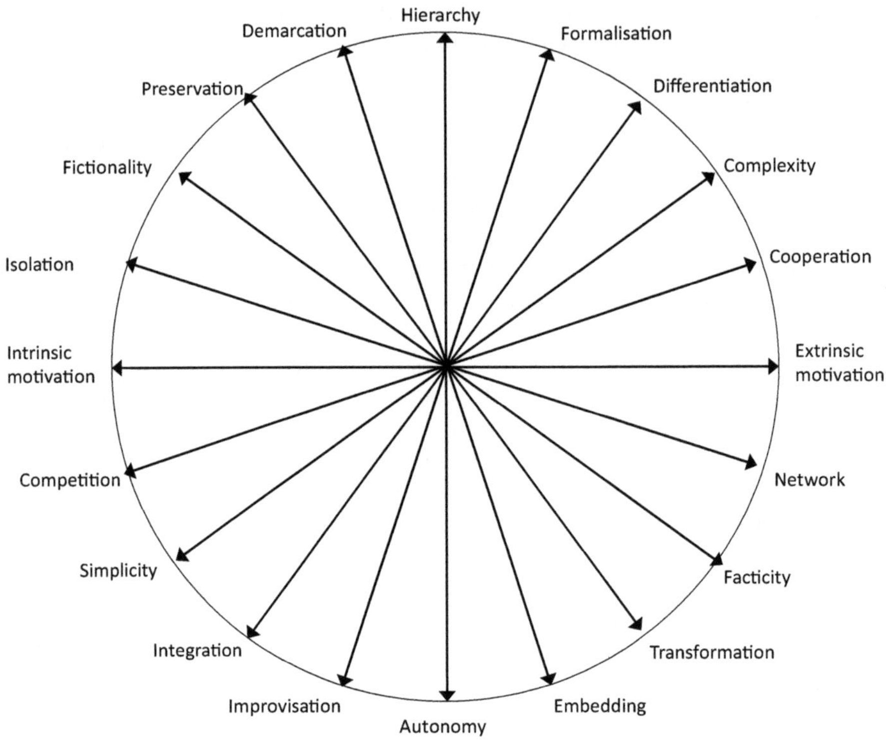

Fig. 8.3 Antagonistic control principles (*Source* Deeg et al. 2010, p. 220)

personal culture. As organisations are fusions of very different people with just as different ideas and goals, a congruent cooperation must take place to reach company objectives, by means of targeted steering and a certain degree of social control. An organisation must be able to handle contradictory control principles (Fig. 8.3). These areas of tension are especially effective, particularly in an age of transformation. However the issue is not to dissolve these areas of tension between contradictory demands, but rather to make them visible, workable, and emotionally bearable, and to use them constructively to set new forms of behaviour (Deeg et al. 2010).

Future-viable change begins with a moment of introspection and self-reflection. Despite any economic urgency, deceleration is now required and a critical self-examination. For this reason, the first intervention in an organisation generally results from a so-called system diagnosis. It serves to identify strengths and weaknesses and at the same time is the first company-wide communication initiative that heralds the change process. This is where the first dialogue exchange regarding change occurs across all hierarchical levels. Furthermore, the system diagnosis holds up a mirror to the organisation, which should facilitate a collective self-reflection of one's own situation and a moment of contemplation about this situation. This involves the first pattern change, in which an initial common

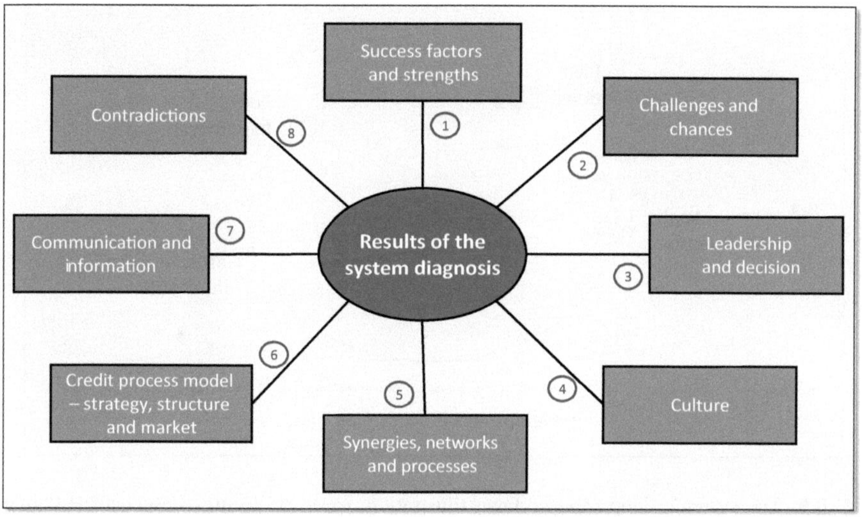

Fig. 8.4 The examined dimensions of system diagnosis reflect the most important currents in the organisation. An example (*Source* Own illustration)

commitment should be created by seeking the best arguments for the need for change and possible solutions; thereafter, the change process can be situated on a broader basis. The system diagnosis is intended to mobilise energies for the change. It is led by hypotheses and works honestly and appreciatively on the reasons why the bank finds itself in its current position (Fig. 8.4).

The systemic loop (Fig. 8.5) expresses a basic principle of systemic work on changing behavioural patterns: a solution to the problem is not sought immediately after the present-state analysis; instead the organisation should be supported in also finding the (good) reasons for an earlier, perhaps sensible behaviour. By forming hypotheses, the perception radius should expand and by examining different perspectives, suitable solutions should be found for the organisation in question. This "detour" towards finding a solution should prevent working only on the symptoms of a problem and not on the often deeper underlying cause. The systemic loop is a simple process model that encourages engagement with one's own viewpoint, motivation or the possible picture of the future, while at the same time also including different perspectives. Working with this model ultimately leads to more clarity and thus to more effective interventions.

With the system diagnosis the organisation looks at itself collectively and thus starts to change from a common standpoint. By recognising the current situation, an initial development of trust emerges for the joint view of the future. The key to this trust development is communicating the results across all hierarchical levels. All of those involved in the interviews should receive the same feedback. This is initial proof that the objections of employees will be heard. Only now does the organisation have a collective understanding for the starting point, and it can now be decided which topic should be worked on next.

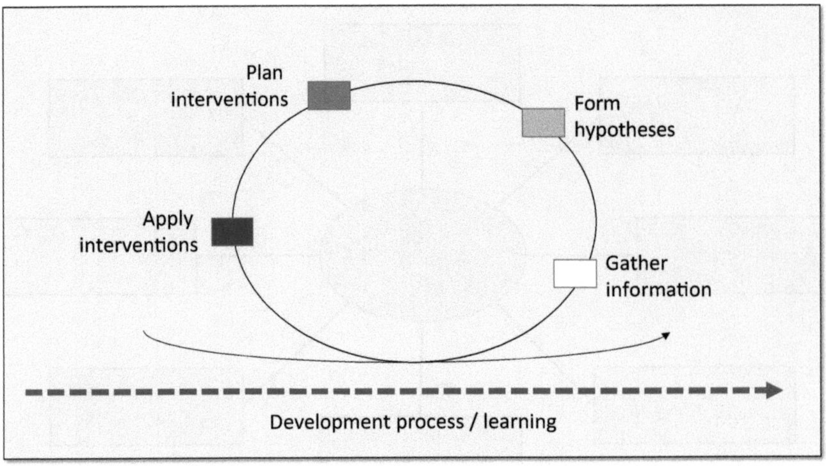

Fig. 8.5 The systemic loop (*Source* Own illustration, based on Königswieser and Hillebrand 2004, p. 46)

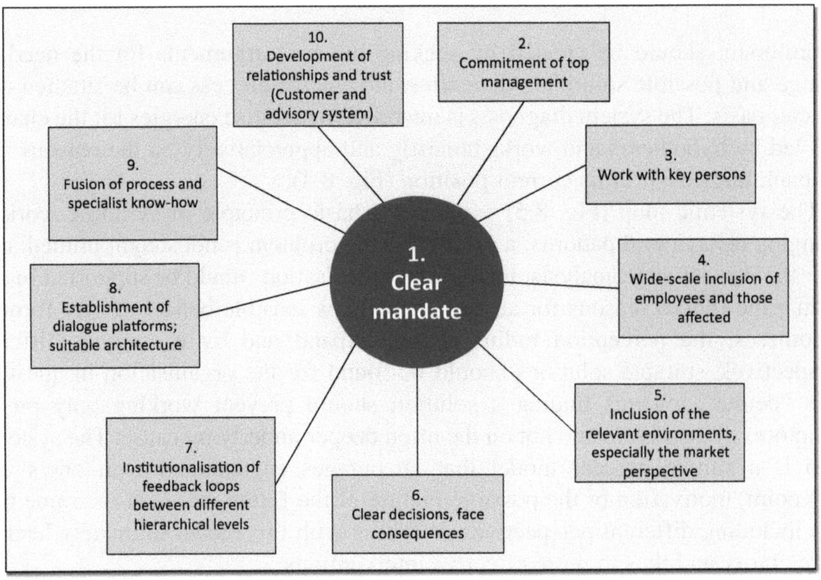

Fig. 8.6 Success factors for change (*Source* Own illustration, based on Königswieser and Hillebrand 2004, p. 44)

Simply knowing the problem certainly does not mean have the solution. We are all experts in our own problems and like to spend our time analysing them, but that doesn't change anything. In order for change to succeed, certain framework conditions are required. These are presented from the consultant's viewpoint in Fig. 8.6. But the 10 success factors are also generally applicable.

References

Auge-Dickhut, S., Del Don, C., Götz-Pagni, C., Hemmo, M., Koye, B., & Roth, T. (2014). *Wandlungsfähigkeit von Banken*. Zurich: Schweizerisches Institut für Finanzausbildung der Kalaidos Fachhochschule.

Deeg, J., Küpers, W., & Weibler, J. (2010). *Integrale Steuerung von Organisationen*. Munich: Oldenbourg.

Königswieser, R., & Hillebrand, M. (2004). *Einführung in die systemische Organisationsberatung*. Heidelberg: Carl Auer.

Königswieser, R., Burmeister, L., & Keil, M. (Eds.). (2012). *Komplementärberatung in der Praxis*. Stuttgart: Schäffer-Poeschel.

Kruse, P. (2008). *Unternehmensberater zu "8 Regeln für den totalen Stillstand in Unternehmen"*. Retrieved September 29, 2013, from www.youtube.com/watch?v=Ug83sF_3_Ec

Luhmann, N. (1984). *Soziale Systeme. Grundriss einer allgemeinen Theorie*. Berlin: Suhrkamp.

Schein, E. H. (2003). *Organisationskultur*. Bergisch Gladbach: EHP.

Simon, F. B. (2004). *Gemeinsam sind wir blöd!? Die Intelligenz von Unternehmen. Managern und Märkten*. Heidelberg: Carl-Auer Systeme Verlag.

References

9 Successful Reorganisation (II): The Levers of Change

Once the decision has been made to change—which is always connected to the disappointment of having to admit this necessity for change to oneself and others—, a process begins that should lead from the current situation to the target situation.

Organisations have three central levers in order to shape change sustainably:

- Strategy, in which the fundamental company decisions, business policy, and objectives are determined, based on the analysis of relevant trends
- Structure, which channels and coordinates the process in business and management support processes
- and culture, which is characterised by the core competences, norms and values, concerns and interests, motivators and interaction topics. It should enable action for the general benefit of the company by means of leadership and cooperation.

Only when these three ordering principles are mobilised at the same time and with the same energy can they influence and reinforce each other mutually. Then a change process will be successful and future-viable (Fig. 9.1).

In this simplified systemic control model, this process is guided by the objective and borne by the company's values. The process model shows very clearly that an organisation can only become whole when the key change levels interlock. Such a change process is neither straightforward, nor does it work on command or follow some vision from a glossy pamphlet. *"After the fireworks it is dark,"* the chairman of a large steel concern once said. The main thing is dealing with contradictions and finding a joint path to reach the goal. The process operates in the context of the relative environments such as stakeholders, panels, customers or suppliers, all of whom also need to be integrated into the change process.

So now we move from theory to practice: the change process of a bank towards more customer orientation will be presented here using a real example, in which the board of directors decided at strategic level to initiate a fundamental and future-viable process of renewal. The bank is active in the private customer and commercial customer business and serves both affluent clients (private banking) and private

S. Auge-Dickhut et al., *Customer Value Generation in Banking*, Management for Professionals, DOI 10.1007/978-3-319-19938-2_9

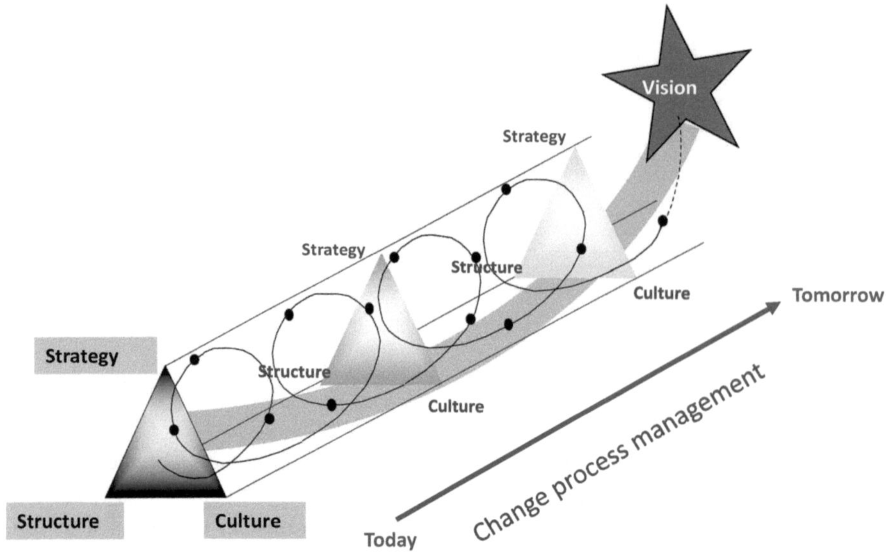

Fig. 9.1 The SIM model (Systemic Integration Management). The SIM model places the interdependent areas of culture, structure and strategy at the centre of organisational development, with the goal of combining hard and soft change factors, so that they can work together in an integrated manner for future-viable change (Königswieser et al. 2001) (*Source* Own illustration, based on Königswieser et al. 2001, S. 53)

customers with medium- and small-scale assets. A number of individual change initiative have already occurred in the last few years, especially in the area of sales. *"Actually we know everything about ourselves and our customers. We have files full of concepts on our shelves,"* says the project manager. *"We are just weak when it comes to implementation."*

Below we will show what is necessary in order to mobilise a bank from its current situation to the target situation, using the three central levers strategy, structure and culture.

How can an organisation learn another form of cooperation? Without a doubt, this work begins with the central decision-makers. The subject of power is a decisive one in systemic consulting. The impact of a change process stretches only as far as the influential reach of the client. Therefore, the same change work must be carried out at the highest management level as that done below. Anything else would be "shadowboxing", as Wimmer (2004) calls it, when a consultant takes on a contract intended to change only the employees of lower management levels. That only disturbs the dust, while the fundamental decision resources remain excluded from the process. If no alliance is created here, everything new at the juncture between above and below in the organisation will remain snagged. Thereafter it can take a long time to motivate people who have engaged in such a process to try for further change. Organisations are too complex in order to complete a transformation process at a purely technical-functional level. There are always winners and losers at every level in change processes. For this reason, the change process must be planned just as carefully within the highest leadership level, as the pressure of expectation is especially high there. As well as functional topics, cooperation or new power constellations should be considered and designed at this level. Differences that are perhaps concealed in everyday business rise to the surface in change processes, and individuals are quickly forced into the role of the promotor or inhibitor. Even if the goal of customer orientation is clearly in sight, the process to get there is not immune to uncertainty and insecurity, triggered by the complexity and inner dynamic of the organisation that has been set in motion. This process requires reflected control, flanking decisions must be made continuously. In this phase, management has a very particular role model function, which is expressed in common decision-making, new behavioural patterns, and above all in providing for those employees affected by the change.

9.1 Lever 1: Strategy

The strategic decision in favour of more customer orientation has many internal consequences. Whoever starts rigorously by asking which added value is produced by the customer's own actions will see just how thorough the change will have to be in his own company. It doesn't help to cling to the old business model, or to imitate competitors. A company must find its own tailored business model. The steps towards doing so are described in Chap. 6. Yet placing the focus on the customer does not mean ignoring the security aspects within the bank's business, or the interests of one's own employees. Customer-centred banking demands a large degree of flexibility. One of the key tasks will be to increase the speed of decision-making processes, so that customers will soon notice the new innovation strategy and structure that is oriented towards their needs.

The most important task of top management in times of change is to enable the implementation of the changed strategy. That also means that organisations must get used to addressing the subject of strategy more regularly and to always willingly face the questions that arise from the implementation. One of the greatest challenges here is to pull together. Obstacles—often disagreements within the executive committee itself—must be removed, decisions must be made in a timely manner, and resistance from the employees involved must be avoided as far as possible. This can only succeed if top management is also willing to participate personally in the change, to question itself, and to work on a group-dynamic process within the committee (Fig. 9.2).

The interaction between the change levers strategy, structure and culture is planned on a timeline in a so-called "change architecture" and generally lasts 1–2 years. The "accelerators" or reinforcers illustrated in Fig. 9.2 should be placed in this change architecture. Change is a process in which the path to the objective is not straightforward. A huge number of actions or measures are required to reach this goal, and in the best case they can influence and reinforce each other. These actions are best coordinated with a timely provision of "spaces" in which change

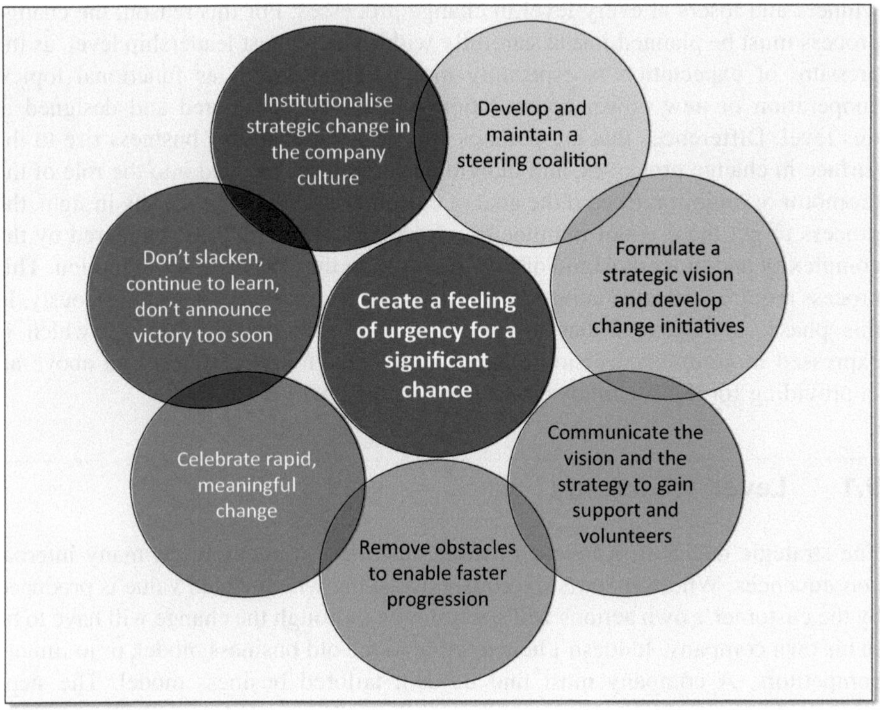

Fig. 9.2 Eight accelerators that allow a change process to gain strength (*Source* Kotter 2012, p. 32)

can occur, rather than by planning each individual step. That does not mean that the planning of change according to system principles is random. Quite the contrary: here, too, the central faulty actions will be defined, resources and people will be allocated, goals set and milestones planned. What is important is that, alongside the fixing of a cost plan and time schedule, the individual actions are constantly coordinated with each other, with a view to the goal (Fig. 9.3).

How can change be rolled out to all levels? As well as the self-committed top management of the company, another strong engine is needed, that will hold together all the strings of change initiatives and learn this new kind of network-promoting cooperation when implementing into practice. All of this happens in the steering group, the centre of the learning process of network-like cooperation. This is where it will be decided whether the change will also succeed from the bottom up. It is the heart and the head of the change, it steers the entire change process, and develops in a sense into a prototype for the functional and cultural reorientation. This is where the substantial topics in a change organisation will be worked out in lever projects and decision templates developed for management, who will then approve these for implementation along the line, ideally following a dialogue process. Things are generally quite turbulent at the beginning: there are fights and disputes, accusations and hierarchical limits must be overcome until ultimately a

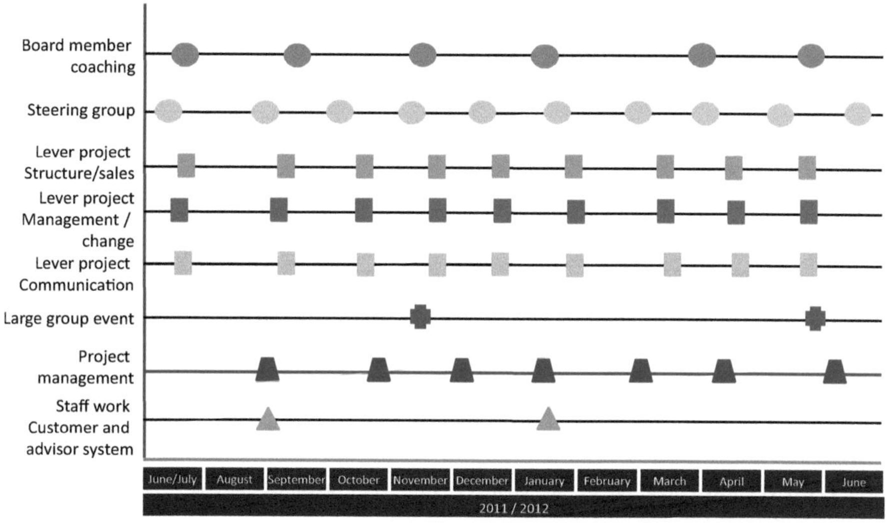

Fig. 9.3 The change architecture illustrates the interaction between the levers of the change process (*Source* Own illustration)

new working culture emerges that enables flexible, networked work in parallel with the linear structure (Fig. 9.4).

The group should be composed in such a manner that it represents a microcosm of the social structure of the organisation: it should comprise those with power, those with expertise, those affected and lateral thinkers or opinion-makers (Fig. 9.5).[1]

A new form of collegial cooperation and a different attitude to power will be learned in this social fabric, so that the steering group will become a kind of prototype for designing the network structure. As well as working on substantial functional topics, the group also receives training in group dynamics, which will make them personally resilient in the face of conflicts and projections. Emotional resilience means being able to engage with and withstand the emotions of others.[2]

In order for an organisation to learn how to adapt swiftly to changing external conditions, it must above all redefine the topic of hierarchy. Management structures are required for each market demand. Hierarchical differences are important for organising complexity in companies, but they must be based on performance and functionality, as a survival guarantee for the whole, and not on the protection of privileges or territoriality. Apart from the actual work on the technical issues, overcoming these egotisms in favour of the power of the better argument is perhaps

[1] The description of the group-dynamic processes of a steering group can be found in: Götz-Pagni and Koye (2012).

[2] The systemic support for this group is concerned with learning self-steering. Alf Däumling, the founder of German group dynamics, calls the experiences had in such training groups "therapy for normal people" (König and Schattenhofer 2011, p. 108).

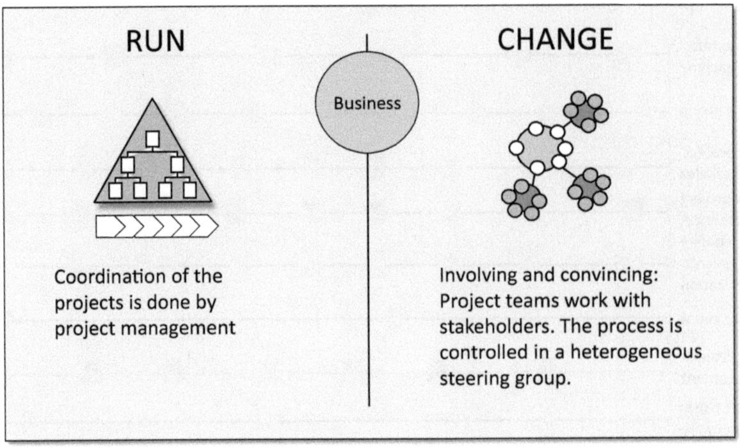

Fig. 9.4 Networked steering during change: "run" (line organisation) and "change" (project organisation) (*Source* Own illustration)

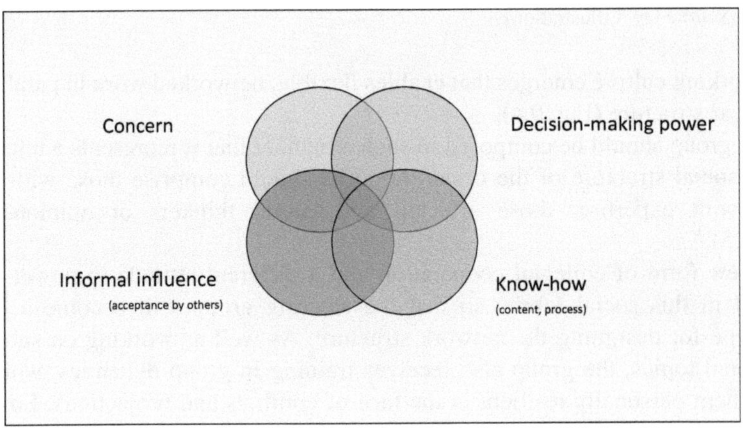

Fig. 9.5 A heterogeneous composition of teams increases the acceptance of change (*Source* Own illustration)

the most important contribution of the steering group to the formation of the new company or management culture.

Following the evaluation of the system diagnosis and its connection with other analyses (such as strengths, weaknesses, opportunities and threats) it is clear which topics need to be addressed. After feedback from the system diagnosis the development of a change architecture begins. This determines the most important subjects to be worked on most intensely. In general, certain decision-making processes or workshops are required in advance, as normally such decisions are made by the respective top management alone. In systemic consultation, new forms of participation and delegation are important from the very outset. The guidelines for these are usually set by top management, and within these the network-like decision-making becomes an element that shapes the entire change process right from the start. In the change architecture, the working groups concerned with the individual technical issues are known as lever projects. They are composed in a socially similar manner to the steering group. This is where the concrete substantial work is done, while at the same time the radius of the change wave is extended to other areas of the organisation. Each customer and each bank is different. We shall now take a look at our working hypothesis to see what is necessary for a wide-ranging change process towards more customer orientation. In our case study the topics of structure and sales, management and cooperation, as well as communication, were chosen.

9.2 Lever 2: Structure

If an organisation changes its strategy, this always requires an adjustment of the work processes and responsibilities. Where should the bank consultant apply his advanced advisory and social competence if the necessary structures have not been established? The talk was of "hybrid" consulting and transaction processes that can be designed across all sales channels. One form that promotes this objective at a structural level is the network organisation, which shapes its process and structural organisation for the benefit of the customer, which makes it more competitive. On the cultural level, forms of cooperation must be developed that enable coexistence in one's own area, while at the same time understanding one's own contribution to the overall wellbeing of the bank.

If organisations aim to structure themselves in a networked manner with interacting departments and teams working across different areas, new forms of responsibility in an ever more flexible hierarchy must be learned. At the beginning of change, the balance between changing and preserving always plays a role. It is always difficult to dismantle integrated groups, not because the people involved are unwilling to change, but because these groups represent the actual emotional collegial home system of the employees in an organisation, which initially has nothing to do with the overall objectives of the organisation. Tearing this open is a painful process that can be overcome only by communicating the why. Employees are generally much more willing to engage in necessary changes than commonly believed by management, as long as they are allowed to understand the sense and the necessity of it. The more an organisation learns to see itself as a network and to measure itself against whether its actions benefit customers, the more flexible will the people who work in it be in letting go of or modifying old processes, while at the same time preserving that which should be maintained.

These network-like structure are not intended to replace the traditional hierarchies, but rather to work in parallel with them and supplement them. In our case study, one goal was to introduce quickly noticeable changes for faster and more flexible decisions. The topic of mass customisation was implemented in the lever project structure and sales, and the cooperation between sales and back office improved significantly and rapidly: the banking process subsequent to the conclusion of a contract was designed in its basic framework and in its partial steps in such a manner that it can always operate in the same way, irrespective of the type of sales channel. The challenge here was that this process had to be flexible enough to also take account of current different and future sales characteristics. Bringing together different experts from the organisation and working together on a good solution for all immediately triggers positive resonances and leads to a good communal result. Indirectly, the working team also initiated the strategic process of engaging more quickly and intensively with the decision about future sales channels and their multi-channel capabilities.

9.3 Lever 3: Culture

9.3.1 Values as the Basis for Joint Action

Every organisation has its own culture, which is based on the product and underpinned by its own value system. This forms the basis for a coexistence based on partnership, which holds together functions and departments. Two subcultures can often be observed in banks: one formed around the lending of money, and another in the area of the investment function (Schein 2010). These must be considered whenever attempts are made in a change process to create energy for a joint reorientation.

Successful companies are able to state clearly what they believe in, what they stand for, and what goals they have. A value-based company management creates a community-oriented corporate culture that favours innovative and ethical behaviour, thus enabling future-viable growth. Companies should not formulate any fixed moral codes, but instead concentrate on the discrepancy between fundamental values and their practical implementation. The more possibilities employees have to help define company values, the more innovative and productive they will be. Values underline and determine our behaviour. Those who are aware of this have another control tool for making decisions and shaping relationships—whether with employees, teams or the board of directors.

Anyone who has ever experienced a group process on the topic of mission statements will have a clear opinion on whether simply an empty phrase or a genuine intention has been formulated. If declared values are merely trumpeted and not lived out, cynicism soon spreads in organisations. The organisation must develop a management level that is able to create values and lead by example. When designing such a role model function, self-management comes before staff management.

Mission statements can be a very sensitive topic for an organisation. Proclaimed mission statements are compared with reality and soon lose their meaning if work is not carried out on the contradictions between ideal and reality. They can be developed in cooperation and less brilliantly formulated, but rather cleared in a joint group process, when those involved truly connect with each other and with their wider environment (Senge et al. 2005). Whoever has experienced this power of joint development knows how much an individual manager can benefit from group-dynamic processes. Successful management is reflected in this collection "we" of the organisation.

When organisations grow, the need for self-organised units grows, which on the one hand must be organised in a hierarchical structure, and on the other hand require sufficient space for autonomous market processing and innovation. Global concern structures are composed of globally networked, smaller units, which develop into a group of agile partial companies. The traditional hierarchical levels are organised in a flatter and thus less controlled manner. This is a not inconsiderable hurdle, especially for the very hierarchical banking world. Network organisations needs interlocking forms of cooperation, agreement on general norms and rules, and the same standards for roles, processes and the treatment of employees, suppliers, outsourcing partner and customers.

A collectively shared and condensed value system is the foundation and orientation benchmark for an extensive cooperative environment. At the same time, value-based management is a means for the joint orientation towards company goals and a visible expression at the behavioural level. A common value basis, i.e., a fundamental conformity with regard to human qualities at the organisational level, leads at the same time to more outward flexibility on the market.

Those who feel obligated to inner values tend to be better at motivating themselves and their environment. The great responsibility of management also has a role model function here. Employees expect respect for their performance, and they want to be involved in relevant decision-making processes, so that they can encounter the ever better informed customer as an equal. The inner attachment also radiates outwardly. The current loss of trust in banks on the part of society is reflected by an internal lack of trust and a sense of meaning.

Management, which is obligated to a common value system, is measured or "rated" against everyday practice. At the same time, and ethical basis develops, which has a positive effect on the social image. Value-oriented management grants freedom for the creative potential on which the future of the organisation is based. Even if this future is unclear, values provide orientation and compensate uncertainty.

Since the 1960s the understanding of management has moved from command and control, which demanded unlimited loyalty from employees to the organisation and management, towards a much more agile, dynamic and meaningful reality. Today we know that small but diverse teams perform better than large homogenous groups. One expert alone does not have as many ideas as a creative, heterogeneous group that has signed up for a common goal. Yet teams cannot be controlled so easily by a hierarchy, as they can develop their own strong intrinsic dynamic. Organisations must adapt to these autonomous movements of teams. It is particularly noticeable in banks that this creative mobility is often restricted by hedging tendencies. Nowadays security is being increasingly replaced by control, which leads to rigidity rather than customer orientation or innovation. Under constantly changing market conditions, the attachment to an organisation is rarely generated by assuring lifelong employment, but rather by the interpersonal attractiveness conveyed by a company. In an age in which transformation has become a permanent condition, the need for loyalty to an organisation has not changed, but rather the manner in which this is lived out through the attachment of employees and customers to the company.

Greater hierarchical flexibility within organisations also corresponds with the values of junior staff. Young talented workers prefer to work for Google than for banks because the value system of the former tends to better represent their need for more creative space. In the network age the establishment of a value-based company culture and a suitable company structure are essential elements of a modern company strategy. They lead to a common understanding and a common conviction with regard to goals, the market and customers. Control is being replaced by shared meaningfulness and own initiative. The value-based company culture is oriented towards the customer, therefore satisfied customers are at the same time an expression of satisfaction within the organisation. Values not only embody the roots of a bank, collegial cooperation, trust and transformability, they are also the key success factors for modern companies.

How can one define values that will be accepted throughout the company? It is not an exclusively democratic process—after all, it is always the values of the company management that exert the greatest influence on the company culture—but much more can and should be done to ensure that they are merely installed in a top-down process.

Ultimately, long- and medium-term company goals are also based on values, as is the implementation of the strategies following market analysis or product development. If a strategy conforms to the structure and culture of a company, employees know which measures to take, because they can see the sense in them.

The greatest benefit of values lies therefore in the creation of identity and diversity (Prange 2006). Entrepreneurial success and collegiality are not contradictory. In this respect, companies are not only economic but also social entities, where we learn to take ethical responsibility for our actions when dealing with each other economically. This value-based responsibility also plays a role during difficult times, when for existential reasons tough steps need to be taken, dismissals announced or structural measures implemented, such as outsourcing services or closing branches. The people affected must be given space to deal with their emotions, and they must not be ignored (Burmeister and Hillebrand 2011). Painful steps such as job cuts must make sense both emotionally and rationally, also to those who remain in the company and observe very closely whether or not a dismissal was based on values and conducted in a humane manner.

An important factor in mobilising change energy is an idea of how the organisation will look after the change (Kotter 1996). An image of the future provides a general direction in which the journey is headed, even and indeed especially if it is not yet known which individual steps will lead there. For many managers the term future image or vision is too abstract, as one is on the one hand accustomed to being measured on the attainment of specific goals, and on the other hand it is difficult, particularly in times of upheaval and uncertainty, to imagine a different future. An image of the future, for example, goes beyond the target of customer orientation. In our banking example, the work on an image of the future was one of the central success factors in reminding participants, repeatedly and in a positive manner, why they had taken on all of the difficulties of change and how the initiated change activities were paying off. The development of a future image is closely linked to the formulation of a mission statement. The transitions between values, goals and the journey to attain these are fluent. The steering group in our case study decided in favour of a value-based mission statement process. In this process it was important to find out what the core competences are today and what the bank wishes to stand for in the future. The first indication came from the system diagnosis, and later the core competences and their underlying values were defined in large group meetings. It emerged that the topic of customer orientation was not only a matter of strategy, but also of identity. The employees wanted to be closer to customers, as they based their personal success and work satisfaction on the satisfaction of the customers. On the subject of customer orientation, the steering group defined in hindsight the core competences that would most likely give the customer the impression that he was getting something for his money. The win-win effect of customer orientation becomes clear here, at least at the emotional level. In this change process, customer orientation became the driving leitmotif.

9.3.2 Leadership in a Changing Organisation

Leadership is one of the central success factors for change processes, because management staff are at the interface between the organisation and interpersonal relationships. They manage the contradiction between company goals and employee relationships and have an important function in communicating and conveying meaning. Studies on competences in organisations show that leadership is the key factor that characterises successful companies (Boston Consulting Group 2012). Leadership is the quality feature of an organisation, and it succeeds when organisations manage to adapt continually to the given framework conditions and the changing challenges of the market, thus guaranteeing continuity. When we speak of successful change in companies, we can see that this does not occur solely due to certain organisational structures, rules, processes or role descriptions, but rather primarily due to the constant encouragement to cooperate across all departments, and due to a management that fills the structures with meaning and life. Good leadership injects energy into the company and contributes to raising the potential of the individual, promoting cooperation and the exchange of ideas, and—perhaps most importantly—enthusing employees for the company goals and encouraging personal engagement. Good leadership enables people to do their job as well as they can. "*One cannot motivate people,*" says the chairman of a German savings bank, "*but it is very easy to demotivate them.*" For this reason, change processes should always be accompanied by a programme for management, so that the contradiction between personal concern and the responsibility for process and employees can be addressed.

The subject of management or leadership is always a phenomenon of its time. It mirrors, like almost no other organisational topic, currently valid basic values, according to Königswieser (2004). Especially in phases of change, with constantly increasing complexity and uncertainty, companies need not so much a charismatic star, but rather people who radiate constancy and reliability.

Nevertheless, good management is always a very personal matter and is characterised by one this above all: authenticity. A behaviour is credible when it is seen to be congruent with the person and that which he says. Credibility is not a question of character, but rather a question of attitude, based on the respectful perception of the world, its people and oneself.

Companies expect a lot from their managers. They must be able to deal with complexity and change, to handle stress, be internationally competent, manage localities, be flexible—both spatially and intellectually—, to work in networks—also virtual ones—, to constantly want to learn, to prove social competence, to encourage their own and others' creativity, and to show willingness to develop their own personality. A new generation of managers is currently emerging that prefers working beyond hierarchical and mental boundaries. More and more managers are orienting themselves less on financial offers as remuneration for their engagement. Rather, motivation tends to involve more emotional factors, such as being able to recognise the results of one's own work, exert influence, relationships, security, possibilities for personal and professional development, and contextual drivers such as the personal experience of the organisation and the exchange with peers.[3] Furthermore, personal drivers such as values and attitude, work-life balance and health are gaining in importance.[4] The professional challenges are especially high during change phases, the level of sickness can be a mirror for workplace satisfaction. Collegial solidarity becomes particularly important in phases of uncertainty, and it is therefore important to create opportunities for exchange. High burn-out rates were found particularly where there were heavy work demands and little creative space at the workplace. Therefore the argument to turn those affected into those involved gains not only a motivational, but also a health perspective (Bauer 2004). Interestingly, the specialist literature on burn-out considers those persons to be threatened who place high performance demands on themselves, but who wish to achieve their goals alone as "lonely warriors". No one person can change an organisation alone. Therefore a change process must and can be a collection opportunity for more collegial solidarity.

What do employees expect from management? They seek orientation, they want to be led where necessary, motivated, kept up to date; they want to learn more, to cooperate in teams and understand the consequences of their actions. That is why successful companies have a shared vision, a joint management picture, which

[3] *"Money is the most expensive means for motivating people,"* says Dan Ariely, Professor of Behavioural Economics at Duke University (Ariely 2008, p. 47).

[4] Based on an AOK study from 2000, interpersonal and organisational factors have become the no. 1 illness factor today (Bauer 2004, p. 199).

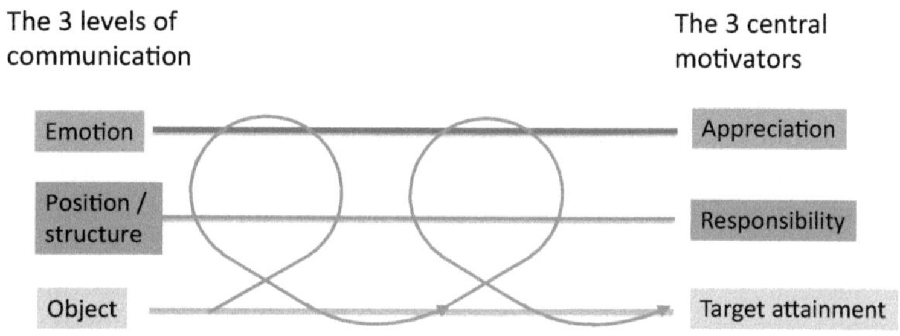

Fig. 9.6 Creation of motivation in change processes (*Source* Own illustration)

follows a common mission statement. At the same time these companies possess the structural prerequisites for overreaching cooperation. When more communication is required in change processes or difficult situations, it is less about conveying information but rather whether managers stay in touch with their surroundings and can communicate credibly that they will campaign for their team or department, even in turbulent times (Fig. 9.6).

The task of change management is to create many opportunities in which learning can take place in reflection loops. Figure 9.6 illustrates how the three communication levels—emotion, position and object—affect the central motivating factors of appreciation, responsibility and target achievement. Only when it is possible to remove so-called de-motivators, i.e., disturbances at this communication level, can a new form of cooperation emerge. This can be done if employees name these disturbances and together find joint solutions for them.

Then they will be motivated, because they will feel that their concerns have been noticed and appreciated, hierarchical barriers have been broken down in dialogue, and ultimately the success, the joint target achievement, is a collective one. Thus it is not so much the style that is important, but instead the context in which management takes place. The fast pace of the economy and the continuously changing market conditions increase the level of uncertainty that management must face. It can best confront these conditions if employees are allowed to act on their own initiative and if there is continuous encouragement for the internal interlocking of overreaching areas. Strengthening strengths and learning through exchanges of experience has the greatest positive effect on performance capability.

The two magic words on the subject of management in uncertain economic situations are therefore: responsibility and network capability. Being a leader means being responsible, maintaining the right proportion between that which must be preserved and that which must change. However, responsibility can only be learned by taking it on, being aware of the consequences of one's own actions, while at the same time not releasing others from their own responsibility (Cichy et al. 2011). Whoever is responsible for others will not try to change them, but rather to deploy them in such a manner that they can use their skills to the best of their ability. What used to be known as co-determination is now called "empowerment". People may and should take responsibility for their own creative fields;

power and influence are divided among managers and their staff. Taken to its logical consequence, however, it also means allowing these enabled colleagues to lead "from below". Management merely sets the operational frameworks and intercedes to compensate only where necessary.[5]

Today, management must be network-capable and act in the interests of the whole organisation. This requires not so much a certain method, but instead the will to encounter people as equals.

"My" success is "your" success. Departmental egotisms are transformed into a contribution to the whole, and merged with the competences of the others. Solutions are developed jointly (Götz-Pagni and Koye 2012): short-term self-interest is regulated by the orientation towards the end result. Being networked means feeling bound to the superordinate overall context of the company.

The American sociologist Sennett describes this ability as a "fundamental attitude of cooperation", as an exchange from which all benefit (Sennett 2012). This exchange can also be combined with the competition of the markets.

Simply managing by numbers no longer corresponds with the complex challenges of the constantly changing and increasingly internationalised markets. The functioning of multinational corporate organisations depends on intercultural communication and cooperation (Hofstede and Hofstede 2009). The demand for continuous transformation requires managers to remain agile and to motivate those around them to be equally flexible. That calls for dialogue above all else, which requires a lot of time. The optimum spread of working hours for a manager with responsibility for personnel therefore looks as follows: 40 % proactive management, 25 % reactive management, 15 % training and coaching, and 20 % administration (Wunderer 2006). With a regulating and controlling management we speak of management of the first order. But if the issue is to inspire for the benefit of the common good and to shape the joint learning of responsibility in interpersonal relationships, then we speak of management of the second order. Whoever wishes to anchor this in his organisation should, in the change process, think above all about new categories of measurement when assessing management work. These are primarily qualitative in nature. Activities that promote mutual trust, such as employee appraisals, team development, encouragement of cooperation and joint solution-finding must be given greater weight when evaluating managers.

This growing and learning in the organisation goes well beyond one-off or short-term economic business goals. How can one teach or learn good leadership when it is not about training specific personal characteristics? Leadership cannot be learned, as each person can lead only in his own way.

"Leading is learning," says Sprenger (2000). Many managers feel compelled to act in structures that they do not consider to be functional. The creative radius is frequently too small in order to achieve a balance between autonomy and interdependence. Learning together in change processes with moments for reflection and

[5] Compensate in the sense of the complementary approach for systemic management (Königswieser et al. 2006, p. 92 ff.).

feedback helps to develop a new understanding of management. Those who engage with others find it easier to admit mistakes and to counteract these in time. Employees have an excellent instinct for whether things are going well or not. But how can one inspire others to change if everything was impeccable before? Neither success not failure depend on one single person. Dealing constructively with mistakes or even failure can only occur if an open and honest dialogue is possible at all levels of the organisation (Götz et al. 2011). This is the only way to create room for renewal, which will not deflate into monotony at the end of the change process.

Ultimately, how is good management visible? When managers do the right thing, live their values and remind themselves of their duties. Whichever manager wishes to be a role model will only be credible by his own example. This generates trust, the basis of all leadership. When we ask for positive examples of leadership at the beginning of leadership seminars, there is less talk of outstanding successes or expertise, but instead of the ability to discover the talents of others and to encourage these in such a manner that employees feel noticed and understood. Those people are described as role models who have learned not to correct the mistakes of others, but rather to work constantly towards a joint solution. The fundamental belief that there is always more than one solution leads to an openness that generate not fear, but serious respect for the abilities of others. It frees people from resentment and disappointment and provides space for irreplaceable learning opportunities.

Role models are also often considered to be people who knew why they were doing something, and who could convey their belief in their own path, with firm values and freedom of thought. People who appear to be satisfied, because they look after their own wellbeing and are understanding of and empathic towards those who think differently. Naturally, there are numerous other qualities, such as passion, creativity, the courage to take an entrepreneurial risk or the display of civil courage in dealing with others. In the context of management and its effects, however, the main quality is the strength that allows the growth of higher values and connections between people, in order to provide a service together that would not have been possible for a sole individual.

Zen master Thich (2009) names fives resources that cause leadership to radiate strength:

1. Confidence in one's own path—this leads to clear decisions and expectations.
2. Care of oneself and one's wellbeing—this can promote one's own health and that of the organisation and its employees.
3. Focus on the present moment—that is the energy introduced to the company by one's own presence, with which the future will be shaped.
4. Concentration on the true nature of the thing, without being led astray by previous experience. That means not insisting on right or wrong, but instead focussing on the solution of the core.
5. Recognising the greater context, which allows action for the benefit of the common good. Success is not an individual matter, but instead is shaped jointly and holistically in harmony with the environment.

Complex tasks cannot be solved alone. Many people in management positions who are faced with difficult tasks realise that today's challenges demand new collective forms of action and innovation (Scharmer 2009, p. 431 ff.). Perhaps the most useful resource for good management in times of crisis and global upheaval is the virtue of letting go, in order to be able to welcome change and doubt into working life. It is not constant growth or "more of the same" that is demanded, but rather the ability to confront the given circumstances honestly and consistently, in order to change along with them. With good leadership, we can all begin to work on a more aware treatment of ourselves, with and as part of a community, in which bankers and customers, ultimately, seek the same solution.

9.3.3 Communication

Communication—it may be the last section here, yet it is everything. Sadly it often just slinks alongside change processes, more of a duty than a feat, and is only very rarely planned from the outset. Opinions differ when it comes to communication. Employees feel, at best, merely informed about where management wishes to place its emphasis, and only rarely do they really feel involved in the change. Often, the wish for more communication does not refer to more information, but a yearning for meaning. The formula is simple: the more meaningful the change is for the survival of the organisation, the less must be communicated about it. The more management enters into dialogue with employees on subjects such as uncertainty and fears for the future, the less need there is to inform them.

In all well-meaning change communication we should not forget employees' basic belief that change is generally something unpleasant, characterised by fears of loss. As well as the flood of information encountered by employees today, they now also need to face the fact that changes might have personal consequences for their workplace, without any chance for them to exert any influence on it. Many managers still believe that the concepts are worked out upstairs in the hierarchy and must be then executed unquestioningly below. In such a case not even the most refined or brilliant pep talk will suffice to convince or even to lead to behavioural change. It was best expressed by the behavioural scientist Konrad Lorenz, who refers to the relationship character of communication: "Thinking is not the same as saying/saying is not the same as hearing properly/hearing is not the same as understanding correctly/understanding is not the same as agreeing/agreeing is not the same as applying/applying is not the same as retaining." In addition, information must also break through the barriers or prior experience and previous moods before it can even reach its intended target (Fig. 9.7).

Thus communication is the main means for controlling personal sensitivities and should lead to employees feeling not only addressed, but above all motivated to participate actively. Communication creates relationships and sets the mood.

There is a lot that can be said about communication in general, company communication and change communication and their techniques. In our bank example and the targeted customer orientation, talk was also of communication,

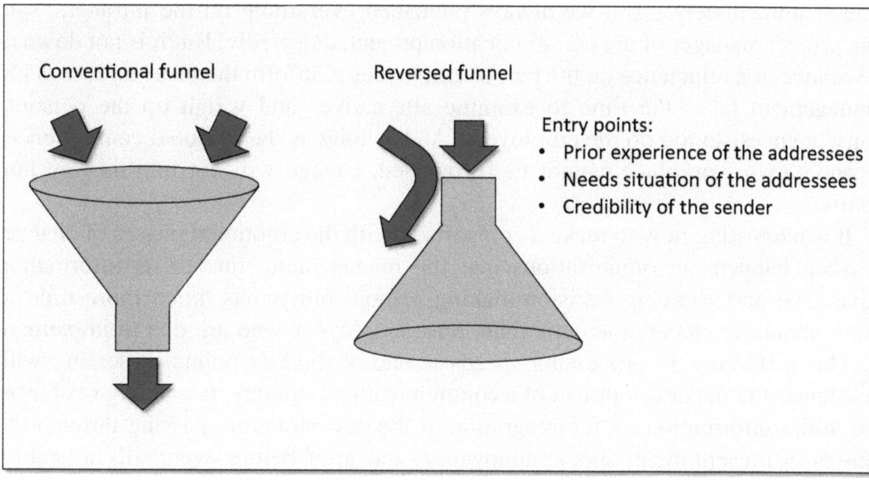

Fig. 9.7 The inlet funnel for information by Doppler (*Source* Doppler 2012, p. 84)

which a company needs to support when building up customer relationships in an age of social and mobile internet. If customers no longer come into the bank, perhaps they prefer to be advised online. What does customer loyalty look like in the call centre? A lot of consulting capacity is lying idle here. If future communication between customers and sales will increasingly take place wherever the customer is located, communication will also become a technical issue. The technical dimension of the banking business was described above. Both the expansion of consulting capabilities for customer dialogues among equals and the development of adequate communications technologies are being conducted rather shabbily.

At this point it is worth briefly explaining the specific challenges of communication that are particularly relevant in a change process. Change processes are characterised on the one hand by a great need for communication, and on the other hand by great uncertainty about the path of change. And then there is the time component: while the upper management levels have known about the need for change and the necessary consequences for a long time, very little is known at the lower levels about concrete plans. This inequality of information speed often leads to the fact that managers are surprised when the measures they have announced are not implemented immediately with great enthusiasm. At a departmental workshop in our sample bank we set up a timeline, along which the affected parties were to stand in the order in which they heard of the change process. It emerged that the managers had already been concerned with the impending change for 2 years, yet most of the employees had learned about the measures only 2 weeks previously, and then mainly indirectly. Despite this, agreement and commitment, indeed even enthusiasm was being demanded from them in the workshop. Absorbing information is conditioned by previous experience and become truly credible only with repetition. Therefore nobody can expect that everyone will jump on the change wagon immediately. "But we always published everything on the intranet," said one project manager of the communication project, dejectedly. But it is not down to resistance or a reluctance on the part of employees to inform themselves. Just as top management takes the time to examine alternatives and weigh up the personal consequences, so too do the employees. And as long as the personal consequences at one's own workplace cannot be recognised, change will not find its way into hearts.

It is interesting now to make a comparison with the emotional phases of change. It often happens in organisations that top management, due to its information advantage and strategic decision-making responsibility, has much more time to think about the change thematic than those employees who are due to implement it. This difference in processing speeds is one of the key points in dealing with resistance and the development of a communications strategy. It is a long road from the initial information to the integration of the new situation, passing through the phases of presentiment, shock, annoyance, and grief before eventually a healthy new self-confidence emerges, which can lead the new path to success (Fig. 9.8).

An accompanying change communication is therefore incredibly important, which represents both the sense and a uniform image of the measures and their timeline. At an early meeting between the steering group and the second management level, one of the departmental heads posed the truly central question as to how one can convey not only information about the proposed projects, but also enthusiasm and commitment. Emotions are hard to generate by PowerPoint, regardless of how well-formulated. Presentations without discussion are one-directional, they remain nothing more than information and not communication. Managements can

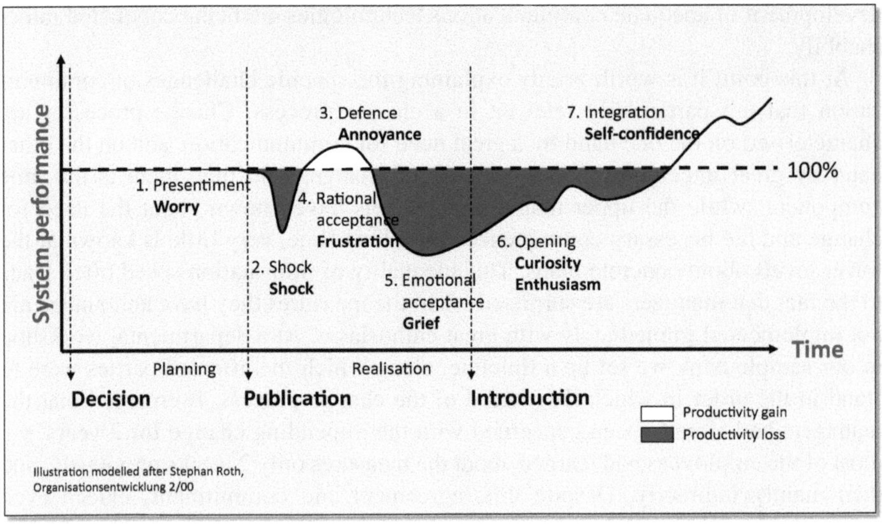

Fig. 9.8 The emotional phases of change based on S. Roth (*Source* Own illustration, based on Roth 2000, p. 14)

only show how seriously they take the project and how much they are considering the insecurities and worries of staff by communicating in two directions, i.e., in an exchange dialogue. Credibility is more important than details. Only by asking the addressees it is possible to know what the recipient has understood and whether this can produce the energy to implement. Only the interpersonal confrontation with a topic, the answering of questions that arise, and the joint wrestling for the right path will cause those affected to feel they are being taken seriously as participants. Sadly, emotions are the very things that many managers fear, as they think they cannot control them.

"Resistance is an offer to communicate,"[6] said Insoo Kim Berg. People are not resisting the change itself, but rather are resisting being changed by others. It is worth being courageous in these unsettled moments and to deal honestly with one's own insecurity, to use the energy to enter dialogue and to argue, to become visible with one's own conviction and to open up creative possibilities.

In our case study the communications project was used not only to provide clear and simply-formulated, regular information about the current status of the change process via the available information channels, but also to initiate road shows with the managers and symbolically effective events with small and large groups. Communication is hard work. In addition the project team constantly asked itself how it could encourage personal discourse, and repeatedly created occasions in which employees could engage with change bilaterally. As well as the upper management level, the members of the steering group were also important disseminators for new forms of topical discussion and inter-hierarchical dialogue. The rapidly scheduled rhythms of preparatory work by the working groups, presentation of the decision models to the decision makers, feedback and elaboration meant that a large amount of trust was built up, which made the implementation of even difficult decisions easier and quicker. It is an example for the whole organisation not just to look to the top for a decision. *"It certainly is a revolution for us to publish things that have not been developed one hundred percent,"* said one steering group member. In order to pick up speed and involve many people quickly, the 80/20 rule proved very useful, so that some uncertainties were allowed to remain. It is a fallacy to believe that perfection can be more convincing than participating in the planning, development and decision-making. It is better to go public with an 80 % fundamental decision than to potter away in splendid isolation at the perfect solution, which will only be dismantled in the subsequent discussion, since only working through an argument can lead to an understanding of it. Those who argue with details without conveying the overall picture need not be surprised at detailed questions. The main tasks of change communication should be to report repeatedly and at brief intervals about the change status and to provide many opportunities for exchange on the subject. However, this can succeed only if the topics are not detained for too long in hierarchical loops. Personal communication

---

[6] Insoo Kim Berg was a co-founder of solution-focussed work. The quote is from her seminar "Solution-focussed work" at the Iskon Institute Milan, on the topic of conflict, 2006.

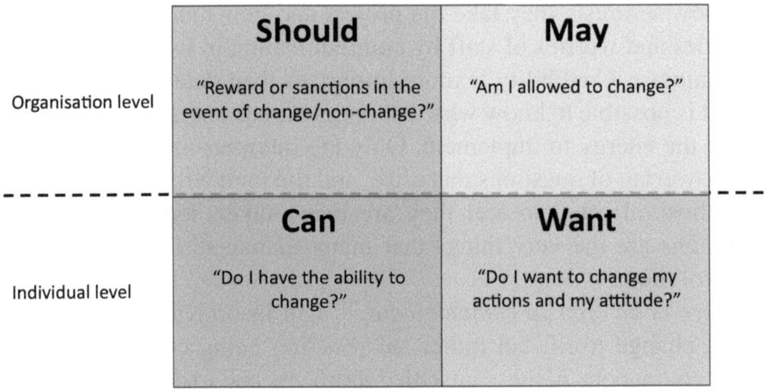

Fig. 9.9 Changes are questioned by employees at four levels; this is where the key levers lie for the motivation to support a change process (*Source* Own illustration)

is time-intensive, but a much more positive participation can be achieved by these means than by general communication or fixed timeframes at team meetings. All of that might be important, but it makes a big difference whether a PowerPoint presentation is shown or whether a member of the steering group drops by to give a brief update in person. The board members were also surprised at how willing the employees were to help carry even difficult consequences when they had the feeling that their contribution to the survival of the company was visible and honoured through personal discourse (Fig. 9.9).

In times of change, great demands are placed on managers. Figure 9.10 shows the area of tension in which they are situated: is the change really wanted or is it just lip service to ensure that everything will proceed as before? What will happen to me if I participate? To whom should I be loyal, is my immediate superior a winner or a loser? Do I even have the necessary abilities to occupy a position in the new organisation? And: do I personally agree at all with the plan? Frequently, managers do not even have a private answer to these questions, and yet it is expected of them to cascade down the change information to the basis, and to pose the same questions to them. Thus communication does not only mean the imparting of information, but is rather a process that serves to create a common perspective. That is a totally different understanding, based on very different interaction mechanisms. A common perspective cannot be generated by a one-sided opinion.

The most important success factor for the customer-oriented conversion of a bank is the generation of emotional enthusiasm for the topic and the will to design the necessary route together as a group. Even if the effect of functioning relationships cannot be measured, they are fundamental in implementing objectives (Senge et al. 2005).

Doppler and Voigt (2012, p. 84 ff.) describe communication as applied mood management, for which figures, data and facts provide a framework for measurement. What is decisive for the implementation process, however, is to what extent a mood can be generated that will lead to the desired action. Some explanations:

The future to come

Primacy of the whole			Primacy of the parts
	Presencing • Common creativity • Silence • The other = authentic self • Being able to see oneself as part of the future whole	**Dialogue** • Exploration reflection • I can change my point of view • The other = you • Seeing oneself as part of the whole now	
	Downloading • Polite phrases • Polite, careful • Not saying what I think • Observing rules and norms	**Debate** • Talking tough; confrontation • I am my standpoint • Saying what I think • The other = counterpart	

The past

Fig. 9.10 The four fields of communicative action (*Source* Scharmer 2009, p. 272)

- Emotions form the actual core of the communications process.
- Warning against emotions and demanding objectivity are based on the fear of emotion held by managers.
- Focussing on the tools is based strongly in the belief and hope of being able to control communication perfectly.
- Whoever wishes to influence behaviour must shake up emotions.

The idea is to arrive at a collective "communicative action" (Scharmer 2009) which then leads to groups recognising the patterns that they produce together, assessing their effect and changing them if they are not strengthening or beneficial. Whoever wishes to change behavioural patterns must create opportunities and framework conditions in which an exchange dialogue is possible. Dialogue should be understood here as defined by Schein: it is a form of conversation in which the people involved can relax enough to begin addressing the presentiments underlying their own thought processes (Schein 2010, p. 391). In group coaching processes this communicative action can lead to a point where, following a momentary pause, something new appears in a completely new quality in joint process of creation.[7] Now it is no longer about who contributes what, but rather all have the feeling that they have participated in a common creative process. Such a quality of conversation arises as soon as the old is jettisoned and the space is expanded in order to be cognisant of the whole. Such special moments can also be part of a change process, the expression of interpersonal attachment, triggering joyful surprise at what a group can do when the barriers between dialogue partners have been removed.

[7] The Co [13] Gruppe für systemische Beratung is currently conducting a research project on this spiritual phenomenon of the group dynamic.

Scharmer (2009) describes this process in his dialogue model which, in line with the team development process, begins first with ritual polite phrases before moving via debate and then dialogue to a creative design of the new (Fig. 9.10).

The creative moments in which individuals regard themselves as part of a whole occur more frequently in the world of work than might sometimes appear. If we understand organisations as human communities and allow a deeper understanding of our action there, it opens up new paths for designing a common future. Ultimately, the idea of networking is based on the breaking up not only of organisational, but also and above all interpersonal boundaries.

9.4 Wrap Up: Change

This chapter provides a brief insight into the course of a change process from a practical viewpoint: What levers are available to a bank in order to design a future-viable development process that will ensure a long-term future for the entire organisation across its whole breadth; what are the internally motivate answers to the external change in customer behaviour? How can sufficient energy be summoned for change, so that it is not simply dictated from above but also carried and accepted below? To answer these questions, the key elements of a change process are briefly outlined and the central change mechanisms are presented, based on the systemic approach.

Even if there is a great need for change, the figures don't add up and time is pressing, the path to a future-viable banking structure begins by pausing and diagnosing the current situation together. There needs to be a serious build-up of trust in the initial phase of further development, in which as many employees as possible are listened to at the different hierarchical levels and their needs understood. With the widespread publication of the system diagnosis, the employees get an overall view of the strengths and weaknesses of their organisation. Building on this, a change architecture is developed, which connects the three most important levers of change: strategy, structure and culture. Theoretically the systemic change work is oriented on the SIM model and the systemic loop; practically, the change process is driven and controlled by a steering group. This steering group undergoes all of the behavioural patterns to be changed and will later become the prototypes of the new coexistence of the bank. This is where the first power and group dynamics will clash, they can be addressed and thus solved in a protected framework, the new coexistence starts to have an impact in the form of networked cooperation, and knowledge is gained about the development of solutions with a view of the whole. This group is the core of the change, the effect of which will be expanded outwardly through the lever projects applied—in this example, structure and sales, leadership and communication. This project organisation enables the organisation to learn both substantially and culturally, and with the vision of customer orientation as its guiding light it has the objective to promote a new, cross-departmental interweaving, and to integrate internal top performers into ever more forms of cooperation. The change initiatives constantly pose the question whether their implementation work serves this vision, and what changes in personal patterns are required. This process is undergone by the commissioning board member to the same degree as those on the second management level or the employees at the basis. Achieving future-viable change is hard and intensive work in which communication plays a central role. Turning those affected into those involved is possible only in dialogue, in which the wellbeing of the customer sets the tone and is at the centre of all activities. Thus a new management culture will emerge, which will lead to problems being addressed and solved where they arise, in networked cooperation, and thinking from the customer's perspective will be understood as the responsible entrepreneurial contribution to a financial service.

References

Ariely, D. (2008). *Denken hilft zwar, nützt aber nichts. Warum wir immer wieder unvernünftige Entscheidungen treffen*. Munich: Droemer HC.

Bauer, J. (2004). *Das Gedächtnis des Körpers. Wie Beziehungen und Lebensstile unsere Gene steuern*. Munich: Piper Taschenbuch.

Boston Consulting Group. (2012). *Organizational capabilities matter*. Retrieved September 29, 2013, from www.jma.or.jp/keikakusin/pdf/english_report.pdf

Burmeister, L., & Hillebrand, H. (2011). Die dunkle Seite des Managements. Wie man in Personalabbauprozessen aus der Hilf- und Sprachlosigkeit findet. *OrganisationsEntwicklung, Zeitschrift für Unternehmensentwicklung und Change Manag, 3*, 13–20.

Cichy, U., Matul, C., & Rochow, M. (2011). *Vertrauen gewinnt. Die bessere Art in Unternehmen zu führen*. Stuttgart: Schäffer-Poeschel.

Doppler, K., & Voigt, B. (2012). *Feel the change. Wie erfolgreiche Manager Emotionen steuern*. Frankfurt a. M: Campus.

Götz, C., Vorberg, S., & Schel, B. (2011). Scheitern in Organisationen und in der Beratung von Organisationen. In L. Burmeister & L. Steinhilper (Eds.), *Gescheiter Scheitern. Eine Anleitung für Führungskräfte und Berater*. Heidelberg: Carl Auer.

Götz-Pagni, C., & Koye, B. (2012). Fachkompetenz, Der Schlüssel zur vernetzten Organisation. In U. Königswieser, L. Burmeister, & M. Keil (Eds.), *Komplementärberatung in der Praxis* (pp. 70–77). Stuttgart: Schäffer-Poeschel.

Hofstede, G., & Hofstede, G. J. (2009). *Lokales Denken, globales Handeln. Interkulturelle Zusammenarbeit und globales Management*. Munich: Dt. Taschenbuch-Verlag.

König, O., & Schattenhofer, K. (2011). *Einführung in die Gruppendynamik*. Heidelberg: Carl Auer.

Königswieser, R. (2004). *Phänomen leadership*. Retrieved September 30, 2013, from www.koenigswieser.net/uploads/media/Phaenomen_Leadership.pdf

Königswieser, R., Cichy, U., & Jochum, G. (2001). *Simsalabim. Veränderung ist keine Zauberei. Systemisches IntegrationsManagement*. Stuttgart: Schäffer-Poeschel.

Königswieser, R., Sonuc, E., & Gebhardt, J. (Eds.). (2006). *Komplementärberatung. Das Zusammenspiel von Fach- und Prozess-Know-how*. Stuttgart: Klett-Cotta.

Kotter, J. P. (1996). *Leading change*. Boston: Harvard Business.

Kotter, J. P. (2012). Die Kraft der zwei Systeme. *Harvard Business Manager, 12*, 22–38.

Prange, P. (2006). *Werte von Plato bis Pop. Alles was uns verbindet*. Munich: Droemer HC.

Roth, S. (2000). Emotionen im Visier. Neue Wege des Change Managements. *Organisations Entwicklung. Z. Unternehmensentwicklung Change Manag, 2*, 14–21.

Scharmer, C. O. (2009). *Theorie U. Von der Zukunft her führen*. Heidelberg: Carl-Auer-Systeme.

Schein, E. H. (2010). *Organizational culture and leadership*. San Francisco: Jossey-Bass.

Senge, P., Scharmer, C. O., Jaworski, J., & Flowers, B. S. (2005). *Presence. Exploring profound change in people, organizations and society*. London: Nicholas Brealey.

Sennett, R. (2012). *Zusammenarbeit—Was unsere Gesellschaft zusammen halt*. Berlin: Hanser.

Sprenger, R. K. (2000). *Aufstand des Individuums. Warum wir Führung komplett neu denken müssen*. Frankfurt a. M: Campus.

Thich, N. H. (2009). *The art of power*. New York: HarperCollins.

Wimmer, R. (2004). *Organisation und Beratung. Systemtheoretische Perspektiven für die Praxis*. Heidelberg: Carl-Auer-Systeme.

Wunderer, R. (2006). *Führung und Zusammenarbeit. Eine unternehmerische Führungslehre*. Munich: Hermann Luchterhand.

Part IV

Guidelines for Future-Viable Business Models

The Zurich Model of Customer-Centricity 10

The Zurich Model provides the economic orientation framework for the further development of the business models of banks. It is the analytical framework for deriving the perfectly tailored consequences of the influencing factors outlined in this book, for every single bank. In the digital age, the fundamentals of successful banking business models have changed drastically, as the knowledge advantage of the banks over customers has eroded and the entry barriers for new market participants are sinking. The informed customer is putting pressure on margins. In addition, the regulatory pressure on the banks as a result of the global financial and debt crisis and growing global transparency is intensifying the situation and increasing the pressure to change. The danger is that banks might wish to shape the future using their existing thought patterns, and thus fall into thought traps. And there is the further danger of being undermined by companies whose business models are based on new thought patterns.

The paradigmatic change from a buyer's to a seller's market in banking is almost complete. If business models are to be viable in the future, then future customer behaviour and customer preferences must be anticipated as precisely as possible and used rigorously as guidelines for implementation. This is possible when the thought traps that arise from merely continuing previous thought and explanation patterns are recognised:

- Customers are not only rational and informed. They decide on the basis of heuristics, in order to reduce complexity.
- Understanding their needs in the here and now is not the sole basis for developing future-viable service configurations.
- In future, customers will use bank branches much less.
- They interact on all available communication channels in parallel.
- They use the latest available devices and technologies and expect this also of their customer advisors. The banks' internal IT can at best merely (co-) design the consulting environment in parts.

S. Auge-Dickhut et al., *Customer Value Generation in Banking*, Management for Professionals, DOI 10.1007/978-3-319-19938-2_10

Classic banks are also under competitive threat from newcomers with and without banking licenses. The fact with regard to newcomers with a banking license is that established direct banks are already displaying a much higher level of customer satisfaction than classic banks. It is likely that the customer basis of the established providers will be hollowed out by a pull effect, and therefore the profit margins of established business forms will continue to sink further. Future threats, on the other hand, include the options provided to customers by digital universal banks. Some are already positioning themselves with their consistent use of modern forms of communication and in part a "retreat" into being purely platform providers for different financial transactions, on which customers can advise themselves and processes investments and loans directly. In addition, the "big data" strategy of the likes of Google or PayPal seems to be incredibly threatening, for these providers also possess banking licenses and can create perfectly tailored offers for customers' individual financial needs in the coming years by rigorously exploiting customer information and the payment, search and information behaviour of customers.

With regard to newcomers without a banking license, who cover only part of the value chain of classic banks, it can be observed already that the complete sales process is possible medially, without the involvement of any personal contact with customer advisors. In consultation situations, in which standardisable products form the core of the solution, customers advise themselves. In addition, they can conclude the transaction online without the involvement of a bank as advisor. In the event of problems, help can be provided on online forums or by private tips from peers.

There are two possible future scenarios as to how the development pattern of the business models in the banking sector might look with regard to competitors without a banking license. One hypothesis is that existing providers will integrate the USPs of those providers without a full banking license into their own value chains as soon as the critical mass has been reached in terms of demand from the existing customers of the banks. This pattern has often been observed in the past. Integration is carried out either by buying up smaller competitors or by reproducing the relevant technologies. The alternative hypothesis is that those competitors who are strong in their subservices cause an erosion of the value chain of bank services and customers, using the technological possibilities, integrate the providers' subservices in a quasi "plug and play" manner.

The consequence of this fundamental change is that customers are placed at the centre of this review of the business model and the individual elements of service provision (customer focus), and a win-win situation must be realised for both the customer and the bank.

The bad news is that there are no prefabricated solutions on this path. In this context too—and not only at the customer level— tailoring services is both a chance and a necessity for banks. The good news is that there are strategic, structural and cultural guidelines for the business models of banks in the digital age. Deriving the individual strategic consequences and developing a feasible service offer with adequate sales channels is the responsibility of each individual

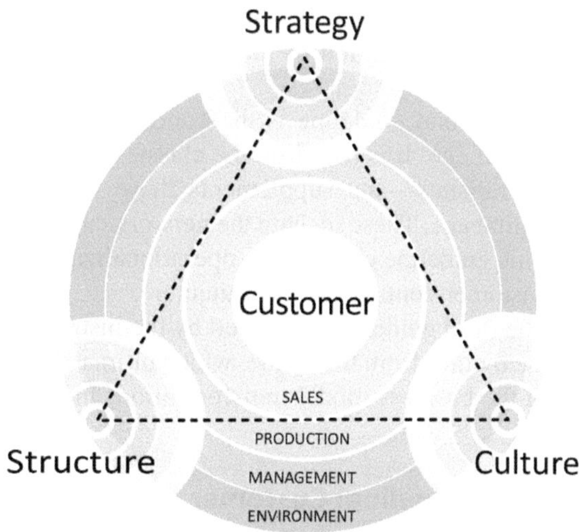

Fig. 10.1 The Zurich Model of customer-centred bank architecture (*Source* Own illustration)

provider. Rigorous differentiation is not only possible, but existentially necessary (Fig. 10.1).

In the future, the price/performance configurations on offer must be considered from the customer's perspective and the business models, which continue to be composed of the fusion of strategic analyses with the structural positioning taken along the network-based value chain, must be redesigned under this premise, both sequentially and consistently.

A decisive factor for the successful transformation will be the question of whether the existing corporate culture can be made networkable at the collective and individual level of the employees. The same also applies to the control patterns of the banks. They must enable—at the level of both "hard" and "soft" facts—the measurement of individual success contributions and the value contribution of the individual organisational unit on the basis of the key success factors for networkable business models. The same premise applies to the core processes—subsumed here under sales and production. The orientation towards the central consequences of the digital age must be done substantially, incentivised by the control model, and accompanied by an appropriate resource allocation.

10.1 The Guidelines of the Zurich Model

10.1.1 Overview

Taking the St. Gallen Management Model as a reference model, the Zurich Model of a customer-centred bank architecture differs, in summary, in three main aspects, which represent the guidelines of the model.

- The first guideline is consistent customer orientation. It is manifested by a rigorous orientation of all strategic, structural and cultural dimensions on the customer.
- The second guideline is the conceptual framework of business models in the digital age. It is based on the classic business models—or more precisely, their instruments—and supplements these with the success-relevant factors in the digital age. These include the network capability and the virtuality of companies. This guideline enables the operationalization of the business economic tools of customer-centred bank architecture.
- The third guideline is defined by the instrument for the truly effective change of the models from the inside, which ultimately will decide on the success or failure of the business model transformations in the coming years.

10.1.2 Guideline: Customer Focus

In the digital age, customers are in the "driver's seat" and are increasingly choosing the business models that provided them with the desired added value effectively and subjectively. For this reason, business models must be conceived and designed from the customer's viewpoint. In the digital age, added value means to the customer that they consider this added value to be appropriate and valuable at an objective level, after examining the offer on all information channels.

The starting point for the dissatisfaction of customers with their bank is, to a great extent, their changed expectations. With regard to offers and advice, bank customers today stand for the basic values of communication, transparency and participation. Web 2.0 makes it much easier to procure detailed information about banks and their offers. In addition, this information can be shared with other people on social media and similar applications, pretty much in real time and with unlimited reach. These "new" customers, with their transformed information systems (ROPO: Research Online, Purchase Offline) and values expect a counterpart who will offer them authentic, uniform and individualised advice on all touchpoints, on an equal footing and in real time. The solutions discussed must allow a win-win for both contractual parties from the customer's perspective.

It is characteristic for a win-win situation in the customer–bank relationship that there is an exchange between equals and an appropriate sharing of the success arising from the exchange relationship between the customer and the bank. How is the bank success arising from the exchange relationship with the customer shaped, when customers are satisfied and "attached" to their bank in a positive sense? Which aspects influence the client value—customer success in the digital age? And what influence do satisfied customers have on bank success? These are the key questions of the Client Value Generation.

The win-win cycles show how customer success influences the success of the bank and that of other shareholders and stakeholders. The aspects of how the customer relationship influences a company's success have already been analysed in detail, across all sectors, in the literature. Reputation plays an important role in acquiring new customers where there is an unequal distribution of information—in practice, the "knowledge advantage" held by banks is relevant here. As soon as customers find themselves in a bank relationship, they can glean personal experience from the services provided from "their" bank. They build up trust to the extent that they do not test the services provided by their bank each and every time, for example by making comparisons with the services of other banks.

Customer satisfaction can lead to customer loyalty, however there does not appear to be a linear correlation between the two. Customer loyalty refers to the future behaviour of customers, i.e., their intention to remain with the existing provider. What success can a bank derive from having satisfied and thus loyal customers? They will repeatedly buy the same products, or other products from the same provider, they have a lower price sensitivity and a higher fault tolerance, and may even contribute to product development. This leads to an increase in turnover, cost reductions—because, for example, the solvency risks of the customer are known—, an increase in the innovation potential, a reduction in innovation costs, and more loyal new customers, where these have been acquired on personal recommendation. In times of saturated markets and cutthroat competition banks must have a vital interest in cultivating the existing group of customers.

The following customer success factors were considered previously from a classic business perspective: product, service, image and the manner of service provision. As customers in the digital age have a greater creative and selection power, and because their expectations of banks are changing ever more rapidly, it is absolutely necessary to go beyond the conventional viewpoint and to analyse what provides future-viable added value to the customer. The better educated or informed a customer is, the more such new or previously ignored needs appear to play a role in the context of financial products.

Now, however, the authors believe that customers have increasing needs at a higher level of expectation. These include the need for participation and social exchange. This can be provided by involving customers in the development of financial products or in the exchange and enabling of advice from customer to customer in forums established by the bank (see the offers of the digital universal banks). The individual needs of the customer can be addressed by offering perfectly tailored financial services. This is likely to occur already with wealthy private customers, but this wish can also be fulfilled in retail banking, by means of individual mass customisation. The desire for self-actualisation can be realised by giving customers the opportunity to educate themselves further and to deal (mostly) autonomously with financial products. The customer's wish to know which economic, social and ecological impact the chosen financial product will have can also play a role.

This list of needs is certainly not rigid, but rather changes over time. For the analysis of customer needs it is essential to change perspective radically and to include the customer function, for which a number of different techniques can be used, such as customer journey. Then it is certainly worth discussing which needs of the respective customer groups can be fulfilled optimally by the respective bank at an appropriate price/performance ratio.

The more informed and economically experienced the customers are, the more likely they are to formulate their expectations and demand that these be taken seriously and met adequately. Naturally, banks could concentrate on fulfilling the permanently increasing regulatory requirements, on reducing costs in the context of industrialisation processes and focussing more on the somewhat (in terms of switching) immobile and non-internet-using customers. This strategy might secure profitability for a couple of years. But those who fail to react to the growing number of enlightened and self-confident customers, who can generally be equated with "digital natives", undermine the business fields of the future.

Business models can already be observed today where consistent industrialisation and customer-focus approaches are being combined digitally by banks. In Europe, Scandinavian banks in particular, and some German (special) banks have industrialised their service provision stringently. This is also reflected in the financial figures of these banks (zeb 2013). In some cases, hybrid forms of these approaches (stringent industrialisation combined with customer-focus approaches) can already be observed. The trend can be detected among different forms of provider—from purely credit providers[1] to private banks.[2] Fulfilling the needs of customers at any price in the sense of a manufactory—as can be seen frequently in private banking—cannot represent the primacy of future customer focus, against the background of sinking margins. Rather, the skill lies in combining the maximum possible individualisation and needs satisfaction with the maximum possible standardisation of service provision. For banks, fulfilling the needs of customers means a renunciation of the frequently margin-driven sale of certain products, and instead focussing on supporting "their" customers in solving their problems.[3]

Customer focus therefore goes hand in hand with a precise customer segmentation. In a first step, banks must derive from their strategy which customer segments should be addressed. The framework parameters of the service spectrum must be determined for these customers, and adjusted and refined constantly over time, as a consequence of changed customer needs and wishes. Customer focus does not automatically mean that complete, advice-intensive solutions must be offered, but rather that the services offered must be oriented towards the needs of the customer.

---

[1] See for example the instalment credit provider easycredit, which has stringently industrialised the loan provision process. At the same time, sales are conducted via the Raiffeisen and cooperative banks as well as its own branches. The customers are integrated into the company's own branches. They can submit their credit data, calculate the desired loan and it conditions in a stand-alone manner, and then decide whether the data should be sent as a loan application to the credit provider. At the same time the transparency and fairness of the products are advertised.

[2] The Jyske Bank points out that it traditionally places value on the balance between the interests of all stakeholders such as customers, employees and shareholders. No bonuses are paid, and there is transparency about salary figures, from lower-level staff to the head of the concern. No shareholder may own more than 10 % of shares without the consent of the bank, and all costs of asset management are also disclosed openly to the customer. There are no retrocessions at all (Marschall 2013).

[3] This approach also entails that the banks are competitive. They can only be competitive if they are better than others in fulfilling that for which the customer pays.

"Self-sufficient" customers, for example in the framework of a standardised mortgage loan or in the prolongation of existing mortgages, can get a building loan via the internet, where the focus is clearly on cheaper interest and highly standardised performance.

Other customers, in the context of this typical "once in a lifetime" decision, have the need for comprehensive advice and problem-solving. Therefore one possibility of customer focus can be to support or to take on the entire process that the customer must undertake to satisfy his needs. Here the focus could be on complete, lifecycle-oriented financial advice. There is a growing number of examples for this integrated approach in the practice. One of the first sectors to have taken this route, in terms of the lending aspect, was the automobile industry. On request, manufacturers offer their customers a mobility package that integrates not only the producer, but also the respective automobile banks, associated insurance companies and dealers. The customer's need for mobility is covered by a total package comprising car purchase, loan, insurance and ongoing maintenance or repair in the event of accidents. A possible approach for banks, for example, would be to provide a total package for houses purchases: brokerage, loan, insurance, and relocation service, i.e., furniture removal and registering at all the relevant places, from utility suppliers to schools, etc.

The key question, therefore, is which customer needs or solutions can banks fulfil. Customers have no needs with regard to making bank transfers or owning credit cards; what is relevant to them when purchasing goods is to be able to make the necessary payments without any effort. Switching the focus from individual products to the customer's entire living situation or to certain problems can lead to the discovery of new product packages. Does the bank wish to sell foreign currencies or facilitate a comfortable holiday for customers? An integrated service might be to analyse the customer's data to see if any travel expenses, for example flight bookings, have been incurred. On the bank's initiative, the customer could be offered the necessary payment means, perhaps with added insurance cover.

It should be noted that direct touchpoint management is essential for the quality of service provided by the bank as perceived by the customer. Each of these interfaces must be integrated in the context of a customer-centred bank architecture. Another essential factor at this interface is the transparent handling of information, both by the customer (willingness to disclose financial conditions and needs) and the bank (product features, conditions, etc.). The overriding needs across all of the subjects mentioned is simplicity. Products and services should be clearly structured and understandable, and the same applies to the language with which they are presented and which is used to communicate with the customer. Customers might not need to understand every technical detail of a financial product, but they should at least be in a position to understand the yield-risk profile. The aspect of simplicity in financial solutions can be broken down into six dimensions: comprehensibility, accessibility, clarity, time, effort and flexibility (Capellmann et al. 2012).

In order to best control these elements of customer loyalty, there is one prerequisite: attaining information about the needs of the customers and the willingness to truly use this information as a determinant. This means renouncing the previously dominant communication direction—away from the mere provision of information towards two-way communication, together with the evaluation of exisiting information about the customer. This is usually widely available on the internet and can be gathered in detail by analysing social media, for example.[4]

Banks should remember, when analysing their win cycle, that they will not be able to acquire new customers or customer segments "on a green field site". There is an existing portfolio that has grown historically. In an age of overbanking, growth—gaining new/other customer segments—is a challenging task.[5] The focus of customer segmentation, therefore, should be placed on existing customer segments.

10.1.3 Guideline: Business Models That Are Equipped for Digitalisation

10.1.3.1 Introduction

The long-term success positions of banks are not (yet) known, but the already scientifically proven success factors of the digital age can be used to trigger a gradual transformation of business models from the inside on a strategic, structural and cultural level. Industrialisation only creates breathing space for banks for the next 2–3 years—it is necessary, but not sufficient for a transformation that will be successful in the medium term. Competitors of the classic banks have already integrated the thought traps of the digital age into their business models, with growing success as prototypes of the business models of tomorrow. Practically, existing banks cannot be founded anew on a green field site. Therefore the previously used business model concept will be developed gradually in the direction of a customer-centred bank architecture, in which customer needs (must) form the centre—effectively, and not only in the strategy papers.

The future success of the world's banks will be inexorably linked to the ways and means they service their customers. Products will mean little in a world where competitors can copy product innovation in hours, technology will be imperceptible to customers who live with constant technology change, traditional advertising methods will be relegated to core brandings only, and the only thing that will matter is what we know about our customers and how that makes us a better bank for him, her or them (King 2010, p. 264).

Understanding how to adjust banks' previous business models will allow the foundations to be set for a tailored redesign of the business models. One can speak figuratively of the DNA of a customer-centred banking offer. The DNA[6] of living

[4] Social networks can be used as a thermometer in order to evaluate in real time the most valuable capital of a bank: its customer base (Capellmann et al. 2012).

[5] The topic of offshore banking seems to be an alternative in avoiding overbanking domestically. However, it is frequently difficult to deal with the large number of state interests affected.

[6] More precise sections of DNA are the so-called genes.

beings determines the structure and organisation of an organism, and can be described as a kind of "modular kit" of life. In a figurative sense, organisations such as banks also have a DNA. The key components of the architecture, in the sense of success factors or "adjusting screws", are formed by the bank's DNA, which enables a rigorous customer-centred orientation and the structure of the bank architecture. The DNA can be divided into the components of the structure of a bank and for the process of service provision. The structural components are strategy, structure and culture. The components for service provision are sales, production and control.

10.1.3.2 Structure

A networked perspective has developed with regard to the components of structure. Today the combination of strategy, structure and culture is seen as a triangle in which the individual aspects are connected to each other—this is the illustration of the finding that adjusting one of the three levels always influences the other two levels. This finding has prevailed more and more in the last 15 years—it is the systemic view of business models.

Strategically, the permanent analysis of environmental developments is essential in order to detect changes to the existing business model or the emergence of new influencing factors and the significance these might have. Then the questions of "what" and "how" must be clarified. A clear analysis of the future trends, expectations and activities of the stakeholders, as well as of market developments, is a necessary factor for survival. Therefore the development of customer needs to be observed permanently, new prototypes and offers must be created using design methods such as service design, and further development and perfecting must be driven together with customers, in the sense of co-creation. This new manner of developing success positions requires a fundamentally different company culture in banks, in which the different "faces" of innovation development can come into effect.

10.1.3.3 Process

With regard to process, the DNA of a customer-centred bank is characterised by the orientation of the entire architecture and value chain on the primacy of equal benefit for the bank and the customer. The partners in the network provide added-value performances that are calculated transparently and which give each network partner a sensible income and also cover the needs of the customer effectively, at a fair market price. Search and information costs have decreased radically in the digital age, buying in individual subservices from the market has become much more attractive for service provision, and at the same time it is necessary in order to maintain an attractive price/performance configuration for the critical customer.

Present-day banks can be compared with the industrial firms of the 1980s in terms of functional organisation with a lack of customer- and process-orientation (Disselbeck 2007). The universal bank concepts, which still dominate, display significant parallels with the wide diversification of industrial firms prior to globalisation. Back then such industrial companies were usually large concerns without any clear orientation or core competences, coupled with high production depth.

Transformation is necessary. Industrialisation is a necessary answer to the key trends of the digital age for every bank—economies of scale and an improvement to the price/performance configurations are merely the admission ticket to the further metamorphosis of banks' business models. Future-viable success positions depend on the competence not only to recognise effective customer needs in an open dialogue, but also to translate these into modern solution packages with attractive price/performance configurations. At all touchpoints of the bank the customer experiences just how strongly the DNA of a bank is anchored in customer focus. The value creating processes downstream from sales, such as production and control also contribute indirectly to the experience of customers at the touchpoints, irrespective of whether these have been produced in-house or externally.

Coordinating these is a decisive competitive factor; the perfectly tailored combination of the configuration is a potential differentiation feature. This requires a shifting of the previous, often purely vertical view of the organisational structure to a primarily horizontal (process-focussed) perspective and an interlocking of both by means of role and job profiles. This process-oriented view also allows the analysis of the question as to which competences should be provided in-house and which should be procured externally. There are three key process steps in banking: providing customer advice, allocating products to fulfil customer needs, and transaction processing. In principle, banking does not differ here from any other sector, so that the analysis of the price/performance configuration can also be conducted in every banks according to the usual standards, and this lead to better competitiveness.

Every area that contributes to satisfying customers' needs—whether from within or outside today's banking business models—, constantly faces a test of efficiency and effectiveness. Therefore each cell must question its own contribution permanently and independently, and orient itself strategically, structurally and culturally as a "mini business model" on the constantly changing demands and possibilities. Here, each area is "its own company" and therefore obliged to permanently observe the best practice developments in its own business field, and where possible to utilise these immediately for the value chain network of which they are a member. In some circumstances this may be accompanied by painful consequences such as outsourcing, de-investment or mergers and acquisitions, as the pressure on margins will always remain in the transformation process. But only if new potential can be created alongside the exisiting success positions, which are gradually declining, will long-lasting success be possible in this digital landscape.

By creating an agile process structure, the process costs can also be optimised consistently. The existing services of banks can be offered more efficiently through network-like price/performance configurations, new services become possible, and the economies of scale will increase in the area of processing. Organisational and functional boundaries will shift gradually and become more permeable, or are even dispersed. The organisational form of the future is based on the clear understanding of responsibilities along all of the steps of the performance configuration, which are increasingly taking place within networks, with the concentration of each member on his own core abilities.

10.1.4 Business Models

The concept of the business model arises as a fusion of an external and internal strategic analysis and the derivation of suitable structures. In the digital age the classic concept is supplemented by the dimensions of the cooperation partner network and adequate channel management.

The classic business models of the banks—with the exception of the independent asset manager—have concentrated on all elements of the value chain, as it has always been interesting and also possible in terms of margins. The effects of the digital age are forcing a focussed discussion of banks' own value contributions in the various areas of the value chain. As well as the previous model types, what is now new is also the concentration on market leadership in one value discipline—for example as a product provider or a transaction specialist. Gradually, the "best-in-class" and superstar effects are coming to the fore.

Successful business models will be "critical mass systems", in which a large number of users will be reached. Structures must become more network-like in character in order to reach the necessary flexibility and speed of reaction and continue to enable attractive price/performance configurations. It will become less and less possible for a bank to produce all of the components of the value chain in-house. The change will take place gradually, as individuals take up new models at different speeds—the ability to maintain a gradual balance between preserving what is of value to conservative customers and implementing rigorous change for those customers willing to change will be the decisive core competence for redesigning the business models of the banks.

10.1.5 Guideline: Transformation Competence

The conventional world view of many managers is that the analytical penetration of new challenges is the only necessary component for the future success of companies. This assumption has proven to be a fallacy in recent years—the implementation of up to 75 % of important change projects failed either completely or partially (Boston Consulting Group 2009). This is a key finding of recent years from a shareholder's perspective, as it has led to the destruction of much shareholder value. This catastrophe in relation to the ROI of change projects necessitates a deeper analysis of the true success factors of change processes.

The competence to sustainably implement the defined success factors is therefore a decisive guideline and a key differentiation factor for banks. Only the integrated view of the triangle strategy/structure/culture, an integrated approach involving the formal and informal decision makers, and a decision-making culture that is based on the effective illumination and weighting of the different arguments of the various stakeholders by a core team will allow effective implementation (Königswieser and Hillebrand 2004, p. 19 ff. on the systemic perspective). The fundamental form of implementation is the interlocking exchange between those who bear responsibility, which is considered to be motivating and meaningful.

Even if there is a great need for change, the figures do not add up and time is pressing, the path to a future-viable banking structure begins by pausing and diagnosing the current situation together. There needs to be a serious build-up of trust in the initial phase of further development, in which as many employees as possible are listened to at the different hierarchical levels and their needs understood. With the widespread publication of the system diagnosis, the employees get an overall view of the strengths and weaknesses of their organisation. Building on this, a change architecture is developed, which connects the three most important levers of change: strategy, structure and culture. Theoretically the systemic change work is oriented on the SIM model and the systemic loop; practically, the change process is driven and controlled by a steering group.

This steering group undergoes all of the behavioural patterns to be changed and will later become the prototypes of the new coexistence of the bank. This is where the first power and group dynamics will clash, they can be addressed and thus solved in a protected framework, the new coexistence starts to have an impact in the form of networked cooperation, and knowledge is gained about the development of solutions with a view of the whole. This group is the core of the change, the effect of which will be expanded outwardly through the lever projects applied. This project organisation enables the organisation to learn both substantially and culturally. With the vision of customer orientation as its guiding light it has the objective to promote a new, cross-departmental interweaving, and to integrate internal top performers into ever more forms of cooperation.

Achieving future-viable change is hard and intensive work in which communication plays a central role. Turning those affected into those involved is possible only in dialogue, in which the wellbeing of the customer sets the tone and is at the centre of all activities. The change initiatives constantly pose the question whether their implementation work serves this vision, and what changes in personal patterns are required. This process is undergone by the commissioning board member to the same degree as those on the second management level or the employees at the basis. Thus a new management culture will emerge, which will lead to problems being addressed and solved where they arise, in networked cooperation, and thinking from the customer's perspective will be understood as the responsible entrepreneurial contribution to a financial service.

The crucial competence in coming years will be to understand the balance between renewal and retention and to anchor the perfectly tailored implementation in the company. For only then will it be possible to set the strategic, structural and cultural agenda within the present-day banks. Some will achieve this metamorphosis from the inside out, while others would not. A key success factor is the precise and constant observation of customer needs, and the ability to immediately introduce the changes identified into the continuous change process of one's own bank. The "industrialised workbench", with clear and agile processes, is only one necessary prerequisite in managing to contribute actively to development. It is down to the banks to develop this understanding among all stakeholders in the coming years. Although radical deconstruction and reorientation from a customer's perspective might be painful initially, it must be grasped as an opportunity, designed from the inside with in-house top performers.

References

Boston Consulting Group. (2009). *Organisation 2015—Designed to win*. Munich.

Capellmann, W., Peverelli, R., & de Feniks, R. (2012). *Wie sich die Finanzbranche neu erfindet—Was Kunden von Finanzdienstleistern wirklich erwarten*. Munich: FinanzBuch.

Disselbeck, K. (2007). *Die Industrialisierung von Banken am Beispiel des Outsourcings*. Frankfurt: Knapp Fritz.

King, B. (2010). *Bank 2.0: How customer behaviour and technology will change the future of financial services*. Brett King: Singapore.

Königswieser, R., & Hillebrand, M. (2004). *Einführung in die systemische Organisationsberatung*. Heidelberg: Carl-Auer-Systeme.

Marschall, T. (2013). Nachhaltige Geschäftsstrategie—Das andere Private Banking. *Management und Qualität, 7–8*, 21–23.

Zeb. (2013). *Market flash Switzerland*. Retrieved July 13, 2013, http://www.zeb.ch/de/aktuelles/zeb-market-flash.html

MIX
Papier aus verantwortungsvollen Quellen
Paper from responsible sources
FSC® C105338
FSC
www.fsc.org

If you have any concerns about our products,
you can contact us on
ProductSafety@springernature.com

In case Publisher is established outside the EU,
the EU authorized representative is:
Springer Nature Customer Service Center GmbH
Europaplatz 3, 69115 Heidelberg, Germany

Printed by Libri Plureos GmbH
in Hamburg, Germany